SECRETS

FROM

LORI RAPP'S KITCHEN

TALES AND RECIPES

FROM

JERUSALEM'S

POPULAR

LA CUISINE

BY

LORI RAPP

WITH

MARVIN RAPP

Published by Lori Rapp's Kitchen, 2014.

http://lorirappskitchen.com/

ISBN 978-965-555-752-7

Editors: Marian Roach Smith, Robert Brill, Lisa Baker Brill

Book Design: Michael Horton

Photographers: Michael Horton, Rebecca Kowalsky, Lori Rapp

Printed and Bound in Israel

Table of Contents

LA CUISINE CATERING RECIPES:

A WORD OR TWO ABOUT OUR CATERING pg 157

ACKNOWLEDGEMENTS

I FEEL A VERY UNUSUAL SENSATION - IF IT IS NOT INDIGESTION, I THINK IT MUST BE GRATITUDE.

Benjamin Disraeli

This book has been more than a labour of love. Much more. It has provided Marvin and myself with a much needed sense of closure to a very significant chapter in our lives. La Cuisine for us was always about people, and there were so many special people over the years who contributed to the saga. This is our chance to shout out a collective **THANK YOU** to all of you, for just about everything:

To our parents, who sacrificed so much for us and who wholeheartedly supported this daring venture from its inception.

To our wonderful boys - Yaacov, Eli, Aryeh, Yehuda, and Netanel, who stoically endured growing up in what could best be described as an unconventional household. They have encouraged and assisted us every step of the way, and now as grownups they and our two lovely daughters-in-law, Ayala and R'nana, continue to be a source of inspiration and pride.

To our brothers and sisters-in-law, Mark and Yael Slutzki and Harold and Marci Rapp and their families, who never refused an opportunity to pitch in when needed, and never, ever refused to help taste and dispose of our prodigious amounts of left-overs.

To our dear friends Elaine and Danny Shiff, who envisioned the expanded, grownup version of La Cuisine even before we did, and without whose support we could not have gotten the entire project off the ground.

To our partners: to Meir Levy for all the sweat we shared during those early, challenging years, and to Avidov Bernstein who joined us in the final years with all his energy and business savvy.

To all our staff over the years. A special hats off to Debra, Nataly, Rachel, Vera, David, Yitti, Assaf, Tair, Avinoam, Naomi, Halil, Muhammad, and Akram in the kitchen - and to Noa, Noga, Sharon, Tami, Lital, Yifat, Natan, Roni, Avivit, Esther, Michal, Elisheva, Suzanne, Yedidya, and Aurelia in the stores - for service above and beyond the call of duty. For all those who go unmentioned, there are so many of you who worked full-time and part-time in the kitchen, in the stores, and in the catering- we thank and appreciate every single one of you.

To Yohanan Graff, *pâtissier formidable*, wherever you are - I doubt that La Cuisine could have taken off the way it did without your guiding hand.

To Yitti and Josh Lawson, you are literally my lifesavers! (Check out Chapter Thirteen of the Tales…)

To Fern Reiss, self-publishing guru extraordinaire, who apart from being a loyal customer, planted the seed for this literary project and patiently endured our/*my* erratic work habits.

To Mike Horton, our book designer, studio photographer, and all round creative go-to guy, for your refreshing and inspired input and for trying ever so valiantly to keep us/*me* focused and on schedule.

To Rebecca Kowalsky, whose photographs faithfully captured the spirit and calories of La Cuisine.

To our dedicated and multi-talented editors and copy editors: to Marion Roach Smith (author of *The Memoir Project,* a truly inspiring lesson in writing), and to Rob Brill and Lisa Baker Brill - many, many thanks for your insights and patience and for humouring us on our insistence on sticking with our Canadian spelling.

To our volunteer readers and proofreaders: Ellen, Anna, and Ilan, for the many re-reads and valuable suggestions.

To our printer Meir Harush of Harush Harutzim Printers, for your timely advice and expertise, and for having your printing press walking distance from our home; we could not have asked for more on this, our first attempt at self-publishing.

To our social media mavens Dov Shore, Mordechai Rapp, and Gersh Rapp, for guiding us through the bewildering world of Facebook, Google, You Tube, Twitter, and blogs.

Lest we forget, thank you, thank you to all of our wonderful friends who over the years fed and nurtured us while we were busy feeding everybody else.

Finally, thanks to all our devoted customers and supporters from close and abroad, who over the years made La Cuisine what it was.

INTRODUCTION

LIFE IS WHAT HAPPENS WHILE YOU ARE BUSY MAKING OTHER PLANS.

John Lennon

I'm an educator at heart, but my passion has always been food. I never dreamt that my hobby would one day become my full-time occupation; but it did, twenty-one years' worth and counting…

Five years after moving to Jerusalem with my family, I was forced to interrupt my master's studies in Jewish education when the publishing company my husband Marvin worked for closed down his division. As we sat around the dining room table contemplating how long we could survive on five months' unemployment, we hardly entertained the idea of starting our own business. Until, that is, we considered exploiting our single obvious asset — our mutual love for good food.

Cooking for others had always been one of my favourite pastimes, so why not for profit? From the time I was a newlywed, my friends had encouraged me to cater their parties; well, now I had a golden opportunity to put everyone's confidence to the test. With little capital outlay and minor fanfare, Marvin and I launched our modest catering business from our four-room Jerusalem apartment, and the rest is, as the saying goes, history.

La Cuisine has been a high-octane journey from day one. Like most food establishments, ours has endured its fair share of peaks and valleys. More times than I care to remember I have found myself on the receiving end of that dreaded phone call from the bank: "So, Lori, when can we expect your next deposit?" and the only foreseeable work I have lined up is this Friday night's family dinner. Yet in spite of all the uncertainties, I can honestly say that I harbour few regrets for having taken the plunge. Marvin and I have shared a wealth of experiences that would have been impossible to duplicate in any conventional nine-to-five job. During the early home years of our business, we had the rarest of opportunities to work together almost every waking moment while watching our children grow up before our very eyes.

First and foremost, La Cuisine has been a family affair: Literally every able-bodied person in our immediate and extended family has contributed in some shape or form to its growth. Professional cooking and baking are very much a collaborative effort. Inspiration has so many sources: teachers, co-workers, relatives, even the occasional customer. People are often shocked to discover that I have borrowed from others. I'm accustomed to ordering three or four cookbooks just to find the one recipe that I can tweak or adapt to my own taste. I invite you to do the same with this book — experiment, get inspired and never be discouraged by setbacks. I still surprise myself with some of my own gaffes that I try to pawn off as dessert for my own unsuspecting family.

It should be fairly obvious to the reader that this is not your standard cookbook. Marvin says I suffer from run-on mouth, and that pretty much sums up my style of writing and talking. I'm incapable of giving over a simple recipe without some rambling digression. Ask any customer who has ventured innocently into our bakery for a muffin and coffee "to go," only to discover that they have spent the last twenty minutes schmoozing with me and their order is now very much "to stay."

Secrets From Lori Rapp's Kitchen is over twenty years in the works. Time and time again people have asked me if I can please share a particular recipe with them. "Hey, it's for my eyes only, I wouldn't dream of sharing it with anybody else," or my personal favourite, "It's not like I'm going to start my own business, so what's the worry?" Without fail, my pat answer has been, "You do realize that this is how I earn my living. Just be patient. As soon as I part ways with La Cuisine, I will gladly share my recipes with everyone." Well, it took some time to honour my word, twenty-one years to be exact. I sincerely hope it was worth the wait.

...STICATED PATRONS DOUBLE-DIP, LICK SERVING
..., SAMPLE AND RETURN PARTIALLY ~~EATEN~~ FOOD TO WHICH
...TORS, PRETEND THAT CUTLERY IS A NUISANCE AND IN GENERAL
... ~~IGNORE~~ ~~OR~~ DISREGARD ~~THE~~ VERY ~~FUNDAMENTALS~~
"GOOD TASTE." ~~WHEN~~ ~~IT~~ ~~COMES~~ ~~TO~~ ~~HUNGER~~ ~~THESE~~
~~ACTIONS~~ ~~HAVE~~ WHEN IT COMES TO THE ART OF
DINING HUNGER IS ~~THE~~ GREAT EQUALIZER.
CHANCES ARE IF YOU ~~DENY~~ ~~YOUR~~ GUESTS ACCESS
FOOD FOR A COUPLE OF HOURS, YOU CAN PRETTY
PREDICT WHAT WILL ~~TRANSPIRE~~ GO DOWN ONCE YOU ~~OPEN~~
~~IT~~ OPENS FOR BUSINESS.
BUFFET. IMAGINE IF YOU WILL, A WEDDING
~~THAT~~ ~~LASTED~~ HAVE FOUR HOURS WHILE 250
S HAD TO ~~SENSSY~~ THEMSELVES ~~ON~~
~~LATE~~ VERY GENEROUS PLATTER + VEGE
DIP. IT'S NOT A PRETTY S T ~~WAS~~
AN OUTDOOR WEDDING, WE CATERED ~~BY~~
RENT SHLOMO CARLBACH, NO
HERE WAS A LOT
ATMOSPHERE
SPIRIT AND
PHYSICAL WOULD GO ~~NEEDS~~.

...TICIPATING AN
S I DARTED F
AND TALES
...CHILD

CHAPTER ONE

TELL ME WHAT YOU EAT, I'LL TELL YOU WHO YOU ARE.

Jean Anthelme Brillat-Savarin

I was born in 1959 in Toronto, the child of Holocaust survivors Helen and David Slutzki, who had married in 1958 and settled in Canada that same year. Yiddish was the *lingua franca* in our household, and that was the only language I spoke until kindergarten. Of course, at the time this seemed perfectly acceptable to my parents since their entire circle of friends consisted of *greeners*, or newcomers, like themselves who had miraculously survived the horrors of the Second World War, and had come to Canada with the hope of re-creating their broken lives. My parents seemed to be always labouring to earn a living; it was their single greatest preoccupation. They really led an unpretentious life. They rarely entertained or travelled, they hardly ever went out, they just worked hard to ensure that my brother and I received the best private school education — and to put food on the table.

I've always loved a good piece of cake.

Not just any food, mind you. Whereas work was an unfortunate fact of life, for my folks food was their real obsession. Without any doubt, food was king in our house, secondary in importance only to health, and possibly education. Absolutely everything pertaining to food was an issue of some importance. Our family did not simply sit down to enjoy a meal together — that would have been far too easy. First came the whole ordeal of shopping — oddly enough the debate rarely concerned the price of anything. The focus of attention had more to do with the freshness or the size or the colour of what was about to be purchased. Whatever the food item happened to be, it was fussed over mercilessly before it was served, and then scrupulously analyzed after it was eaten. Every meal was either an occasion for praise or criticism, in most cases a combination of both. At the centre of this entire production loomed my father; a fastidious carpenter by trade, his seal of approval was the ultimate litmus test for any food prepared in our household.

From an early age, I remember awakening every morning, often while it was still dark outside, to the sounds of my parents scurrying about the kitchen, making breakfast, and packing lunch for my father — the daily big thermos filled with steaming hot coffee accompanied by hefty sandwiches of thickly sliced rye bread. My family sat around the Formica kitchen table, filling up on freshly cooked oatmeal, cream of wheat, or scrambled eggs — my parents firmly believed that breakfast was the most important meal of the day, at least until lunch was served, and then later supper.

My mother and father were hardly gourmands, but our house was forever filled with the smells of hearty old-world cooking. And yet something as unassuming as a traditional mushroom barley soup could spark the most animated of exchanges — either the soup was thick as porridge or too watery and without enough seasoning, invariably never hot enough for my father's liking. Even the timing of its serving was subject to heated debate as my father insisted it be served after the main course, when everyone else was too full to appreciate it, because he claimed it was good for the digestion.

A highly opinionated man under any circumstance, nothing aroused my father's passion more than the subject of his stomach's well-being. Had he had his way, every meal would have begun with a piece of herring and at least one shot of whisky — come to think of it, this was also supposed to be good for the digestion. And who could argue with his reasoning? My father remained as strong as a bull until the age of seventy-eight, indifferent to conventional medical wisdom. The man never ceased to amaze and confound me. A stickler for fresh food, he routinely planted cucumbers and tomatoes along the sides of our tiny bungalow. From May until the first frost, my brother Mark and I were expected to pick the daily haul before dinner to maximize its freshness. Everybody else's parents planned their end-of-week shopping for Thursday to avoid any last-minute crises before the Sabbath — that would have been too conventional for my father. Two hours before candle lighting, signifying the beginning of the Sabbath, he would come home laden with fresh produce and other treats. In typical fashion, he would present my bewildered mother with an equally enormous cauliflower, broccoli, and cabbage, and then insist that she prepare all three cruciferous vegetables for that night's supper. Ignoring her protests, he could be heard mumbling to himself all the way into the shower about how beautiful and crisp his choices were, and how gorgeous were the big white mushrooms that he picked? "Helen!!" he would bark between latherings. "Cook them up with lots of onions. Only ninety-nine cents a pound! Can you believe it? Only by the *Italeiner!*"

You might think that a man so fixated on freshness would avoid, like the plague, any and all commercially processed food products. Not so my dad. He had his cravings, most of which remained a mystery to the rest of the family. High on his list of indulgences were Aunt Jemima's pancake mix, Campbell's cream of mushroom soup, and Libby's deep-browned baked beans (until somebody accidentally purchased a can with pieces of pork in it — a very big no-no in a kosher kitchen!). A special place in his heart was reserved for his beloved Mallomars, the consummate expression of culinary ingenuity. With childish glee, he would savour this exquisite combination of graham cracker, raspberry jam, marshmallow, and chocolate glaze, extolling its perfection to anybody within earshot.

Only years later when I began catering did I realize that my father's food quirks were literally flowing through my veins. "You know," he smiled one day, as if to confirm my new career choice, "my mother, your Yiddish namesake, was the caterer in Mir, my home town in Lithuania." Go figure!

If my father was the general in our household kitchen, my mother was the dutiful staff sergeant. Day in and day out, she toiled in the trenches faithfully dishing out her version of comfort food. Faced with the unenviable task of pleasing everybody, she embraced her challenge with a resolute optimism that defied explanation. Unfortunately her mission was doomed from the outset; whereas my mother wanted nothing more than to nurture everyone, my father's sense of compromise required that everybody simply agree with him. He couldn't understand why the rest of us didn't appreciate our grilled meat charred beyond any acceptable degree of well-done, or our baked goods left uncovered until their outer layer was dry as Melba toast.

Then again, what could we have expected? My father grew up in Lithuania where the radish was considered an exotic vegetable. My mother, on the other hand, had a slightly worldlier upbringing. Her hometown of Slatinskiye Doli, Czechoslovakia, was nestled in the foot of the Carpathian Mountains near the borders of Romania and Hungary, and as such was influenced by the richness of Hungarian cuisine. She often spoke nostalgically about the wonderful foods she enjoyed as a young girl: *knockerlach* (dumplings), sweet noodles tossed with poppy seeds, *makosh* (yeast cake), and — her personal favourite — *mamaliga* (polenta), in all its gooey, cheesy goodness. My mother would regale us with stories of her foraging in the surrounding woods for wild mushrooms, or picking thorny gooseberries in her backyard that her mother magically transformed into jams and compote. As a special treat, she and her siblings would suck on pieces of honeycomb, courtesy of her father's beehives.

It seems now, in retrospect, that my childhood exposure to all these vivid tales and memories of old-world cooking was an essential step in my own culinary education. Even though it was the only world that I knew, I realized from an early age that it was just not going to do it for me. Bread served with pasta and potatoes — possibly a bit excessive, ya think? Yet, how was a sheltered, second-generation child supposed to satisfy her cravings for something, anything, a bit more trendy and glamorous than schmaltz herring? (Don't get me wrong, today I would kill for some honest-to-goodness schmaltz herring.)

Enter my saviour, my friend Naomi. Her parents were also Czech Holocaust survivors, but to me they seemed to have emigrated from a different continent than my parents. Naomi's father never, at least to my knowledge, lay on his living room couch in his sleeveless undershirt and garishly plaid Bermuda shorts like my father was fond of doing. I can still picture her dad relaxing in his den on a leather recliner absorbed in what for me was totally foreign — the strains of some beautiful classical composition. In their home I was introduced to the glorious tastes of French onion soup, mushroom quiche, and gazpacho. In their company I attended my first ballet and visited my first coffee shop. All of this paled in comparison to the sheer delight I experienced attending some of Naomi's family's elegant house parties. In utter amazement I would stare wide-eyed at the sight of uniformed waitresses meticulously carving a smoked turkey or elegantly serving the family's signature nut torte. I knew already back then that I longed to somehow be a part of this world. My timely exposure to high society, as it were, was all the inspiration I needed to try to jazz up my mother's kitchen.

I could not have been more than fourteen when I concocted my first original dessert: individual frosted glass bowls filled with layers of graham cracker crust, Jell-O, drained fruit cocktail, and then Jell-O with the fruit folded with non-dairy whipped cream. It was no Cordon Bleu classic, but as far as my family was concerned, it could just as well have been one. What can I say? Ecstatic, enthusiastic, they were thrilled beyond my modest expectations. One brief encounter with "modernity" and our appetites were forever changed. That was all the encouragement I needed. I hit the pavement running and haven't looked back since.

Babysitting became a valuable opportunity to study my employers' cookbooks and magazines, and hopefully to spy out some coveted family recipe. Grade twelve was my breakout year. I organized my first party, a "poor man's dinner" for a group of eight girlfriends, complete with carefully chosen take-home hostess gifts (I already had the knack for catering, I just didn't realize it back then). To this day I can cite the entire menu and recall what dish each of us contributed. Even more vividly etched in my memory is the conviviality and coziness we all experienced sitting in my parents' dining room, feeling all grown up. It was my own "Babette's Feast."

Marvin and I lived only a few blocks from each other, and we shared a lot of meals together during the two year-period of our dating and engagement. I was studying Jewish education at York University while Marvin split his time between working in an upscale bookshop and completing his master's degree in English literature at the University of Toronto. Four nights a week he sat, supposedly writing, at his library cubicle until closing time at midnight, after which he made the twenty-minute drive to my house where a full-course supper awaited him. For the better part of a year, my mother and I fattened him up with a combination of her traditional European cooking and my latest culinary experiments. This almost nightly ritual of post-midnight rendezvous raised a few eyebrows from my parents' elderly neighbours. "You should know, Mrs. Slutzki, that your daughter's boyfriend is leaving your house after three in the morning. You know, Mrs. Slutzki, that doesn't look so good." Me, I always wondered what these people spying on us were busy doing themselves up at that hour.

I suppose it should never have come as such a surprise when years later Marvin and I got into the food trade; after all, we had spent an awful lot of time together indulging our appetites. By the time we got married in 1981, I was more than anxious to begin cooking in earnest. From my years of zealous prepping, I knew that a serious cook required a well-equipped kitchen. With my modest budget in tow, I acquired all the Calphalon and Le Creuset pots, Kosta Boda serving pieces, and Evesham cookware that I could possibly eke out. The next task at hand was to stock my pantry with as many new and exotic products that came to market. After all, it was the early eighties and food was the rage. Armed with my subscriptions to Gourmet and Bon Appétit magazines, I scoured the fancy food shops in Toronto's Bayview Village, Yorkville, and Avenue Road to discover the latest arrivals. I hardly ever came home without something new like pine nuts, wild rice, or New Zealand kiwifruit.

I was totally in my element. My cookbook collection was expanding copiously in sync with our waistlines. Dozens of hours a week were spent puttering around my kitchen with my coveted Time Life series, baking and cooking up a storm. Luckily for me, I had a most eager and compliant guinea pig in my husband. Marvin's undeveloped palate was in a league of its own. Although his maternal grandparents maintained a produce stall for almost forty years in the farmers' market in Hamilton, he had no clue what a zucchini or an eggplant tasted like. His family regarded them as food fit for the *lockshen* — Yiddish for noodles, a euphemism for "Italians." Kohlrabi and fennel, forget it. The man was like putty in my hands, only too willing to indulge me in my experiments.

And experiment was what I did, with a vengeance. Quantities knew no bounds; I was incapable of cooking just for the two of us. Weekdays, weekends, it made no difference. I loved entertaining my friends and was never intimidated by a new recipe. Occasionally, in my over-eagerness I'd overreach my skills and dive into uncharted waters. Homemade gnocchi, why not? Well, for openers, they weren't quite al dente (in fact, they disintegrated when they hit the boiling water) and it took me two hours to clean up the kitchen for all my efforts. Then there was the mousseline-stuffed Dover sole (an unmitigated, expensive disaster) and a mushroom soufflé (never even stood a chance). But, more often than not, my developing repertoire of self-taught dishes elicited moans and groans of approval.

The first Tuesday of every month was the day reserved for fresh, farm-raised rainbow trout courtesy of our neighbourhood trendy food shoppe, The Nutcracker Sweet. It became something of a tradition to host dinner parties for our friends; in actuality, it was an excuse to indulge in a revelry of dishes laden with butter and cream. And chocolate. There could never be enough chocolate.

What about chicken, you ask? Most newlyweds content themselves with purchasing one whole chicken at a go. *Pas moi.* My friend Elaine's brother ran a business delivering cases of no fewer than eighteen freshly slaughtered chickens to your doorstep. As long as we were buying enough chickens to feed a football team, we figured why not squeeze an upright freezer into our starter apartment. Of course, it would take the two of us nearly an entire evening to cut, trim, and wrap this haul, not to mention the obligatory preparation of *schmaltz* (fried chicken fat) with *griebens* (cracklings) and fried onions. I kid you not. Fortunately cholesterol hadn't been discovered yet in 1981.

I was determined to discover the best of everything. Chocolate chip cookies, lemon curd, or muffins, I'd zero in on my target and then spend the better part of a month checking and testing recipes for each dish until I was satisfied. Needless to say, I gained twenty-eight pounds in my first year of marriage. Total strangers would kindly offer me a seat on the bus, and elderly women in our synagogue would knowingly smile and cluck at me, all assuming I was pregnant. What could I do? There were so many cheesecake recipes yet to be sampled…

My addiction to butter and cream had no ideological bent; I mean, I still salivated over a choice cut of rare beef. Simply put, the creative options open to dairy cooking were far too tempting for me to resist even at the expense of our traditional, religious celebrations. Amongst our peers, Sabbath eve dinner was considered the focal meal of the week. Any menu that deviated too drastically from the ubiquitous chicken soup, roast chicken, and kugel was considered taboo; offering cream of lettuce soup with fresh salmon and parmesan-baked potatoes was the culinary equivalent of serving sloppy joes at a Thanksgiving feast. But I knew better. As soon as our invited guests overcame the initial shock of what lay in store for them, they were easily converted. I cannot recall anybody refusing an invitation simply because brisket wasn't on the menu.

A dedicated schoolteacher by day, I taught second grade Hebrew and Jewish studies at a number of Toronto's private day and afternoon schools. (Although cooking wasn't on the curriculum, one of my students, Rachel, went on to become an accomplished pastry chef who has wowed restaurant-goers in some of Manhattan's most trendy eateries.) When not teaching, I spent much of my available spare time indulging my food fantasies. I wore out the bindings of my Moosewood and Silver Palate cookbooks in my quest for what was for me new, exciting and unconventional. Chicken Marbella. Need I say more? Capers, prunes, and green olives — that combination turned on its head any preconceived notion of what I had thought chicken could be. Say goodbye to onion soup mix and corn flake crumbs!

Yearning to improve my skills and broaden my horizons, I enrolled on a lark with my friend Elaine in a pastry course given by one of Canada's top cooking instructors and food gurus, Bonnie Stern. She introduced me to the joys of Swiss chocolate, buttery tart crusts, and airy cream puffs. To this day I carry with me one of her trusted maxims: It's better to indulge in one small square of exquisite chocolate or a delicious apple than to squander precious calories on an undeserving dessert. I loved every second spent in her classroom, never dreaming that the skills I acquired would serve me professionally years later.

CHAPTER TWO

ASK NOT WHAT YOU CAN DO FOR YOUR COUNTRY. ASK WHAT'S FOR LUNCH.

Orson Welles

In November of 1986, Marvin and I, together with our first two boys, left our staid, settled life in Toronto to move to the less-than-staid life of Jerusalem. Were we idealistic, naive, maybe just sick of the long cold Canadian winters? Probably a combination of all of the above. Marvin gave up a non-promising career in retail books, and I was anxious to pursue my graduate studies in Jewish education. Believe me, the furthest thought on our minds at that time was to become Israeli entrepreneurs. That was considered a very big no-no. We had been warned repeatedly by

Our first catering job.
November 8, 1991.

friends and colleagues with firsthand experience that the Israeli business scene, legendary for its Levantine bureaucracy and less-than-sportsmanlike etiquette, should be avoided at all costs. "Consider yourselves fresh meat in a pool of sharks" was one of the more memorable pieces of advice thrown our way.

So I enrolled at the Melton Centre for Jewish Education at the Hebrew University while Marvin opted for the much less lucrative but infinitely more stable world of book publishing. In his case, "infinitely" translated loosely into five years until the division he managed for a major publishing house was summarily closed down. Faced with the daunting reality that we had no savings and precious few options, we actually considered what had previously been taboo. After all, we were no longer total greenhorns. Maybe, just maybe, we could come up with some kind of winning business proposal that would prevent our having to pack up our belongings and return to the old country.

Marvin's philosophy for starting a business was pretty basic: Begin with what comes naturally. Well, in my case that was a no-brainer. Nothing came more naturally to me than eating, and preparing, food — especially good food. Our challenge was to somehow convert this talent into something profitable, preferably with little or no start-up costs. That's probably why Marvin's suggestion to begin catering from our house didn't strike me as so far-fetched. The prospect of people actually paying me for what I loved doing was too tempting to resist. Though I may have underestimated how physically taxing the cooking part would be, I sensed from the outset that there were other pressing issues to be addressed. I felt confident that I could prepare fabulous food, but I knew success would be determined by dishes that would travel well and that could withstand the rigours of reheating, often in less than ideal circumstances. And did I mention yet my decision of the previous year to become a vegetarian-lite — you know, the kind who has no problem eating fish? That alone would go a long way in determining what I'd be offering on my menus since I steadfastly refused to handle any and all offending pieces of flesh, even for capital gain. Go ahead, just ask my beef- and chicken-deprived boys.

So what was I really thinking when I made this life-altering decision to forgo mama's chicken soup? All those precious hours spent bonding with my cases of eighteen chickens were now rendered superfluous to the task at hand. Why the urge to give up succulent, pan-fried lamb chops or gingery, long-cooked Miami ribs, you may be wondering? Well, I suppose it depends upon who you ask. In my mind, it was the logical culmination of a declining enjoyment of the actual taste of meat combined with a growing aversion to the practice of killing warm-bodied creatures. In Marvin's version, the culprit was Linda McCartney's book *Home Cooking*, in particular the passage in which she eulogizes some poor lamb's unfortunate fate. Whatever the actual reason, the implications for our new business venture were obvious since no meat or poultry would be used in my kitchen, just loads of butter and cream. Truth be told, I really wasn't intimidated by the prospect of a meatless menu. At the time, there was no shortage of Jerusalem caterers proffering their versions of a quarter chicken with oriental rice and roasted potatoes. I was determined to be unique, to shake things up a bit in our provincial corner of the world.

****

It's easy enough to call yourself a caterer; I mean, who's to argue? The real challenge begins after you manage to convince a perfect stranger to entrust you with their special event. Then it's no longer just about the cooking and the menu; you have entered the planning or logistical stage of catering. And trust me, if your head isn't screwed on fairly tightly you are courting disaster. Assuming you have arrived at your destination with sufficient time to set up, the last thing you want to hear is: "I thought *you* packed the coffee and tea!" Don't expect your perfectly poached salmon to score a big hit if all your elegant serving pieces are resting safely in a basket back home on the kitchen floor. In simple language, it's all about organization.

In my case, it meant literally overnight transforming my twelve-metre kitchen into a professional workplace. Who could have predicted that within one year Marvin and I would be catering events for over two hundred people from our cramped apartment? Not me, that's for sure. At the very outset, I had no clear outline in my head as to how our business would operate. What exactly did it mean to be a home caterer? Beats me. Should we restrict our services to intimate house parties or also cater larger affairs in rented halls? What about offering a take-home menu or elegant gift baskets? Not only did we lack any semblance of a legitimate business plan, we hadn't even settled on a name for our new venture.

None of these questions really mattered because, ready or not, we were about to take the plunge. Marvin and I had only begun discussing our new career with a few select friends when we received our first call enquiring about our services. A well-intentioned colleague from Marvin's previous workplace had, unbeknownst to us, offered our number to the National Association of Psychoanalysts who were in the market for a Jerusalem caterer. To this day, I have no clue as to what this woman may have said or exaggerated to convince these people to even call us, but there I was, dexterously fielding questions about my extensive professional resume. "Absolutely, of course, I've been preparing food for years," I answered confidently. Perhaps that may have been stretching the facts a tad, but truth be told, I *had* been entertaining guests for years. So what if I neglected to mention that nobody had ever paid me for my efforts.

I'd prefer to believe it was my proposed menu of poached salmon mousse, mini quiches, tossed greens with citrus fruit, and cherry tomato and basil salad that clinched the order. In all probability it was that, combined with an absurdly low price quote that won the day for us. Either way, we had our first booking — a luncheon for forty psychoanalysts on Friday, November 8, 1991. That gave us about one and a half weeks to get our act together

— sufficient time for panic mode to kick in. Our first priorities were to officially register our business, to print invoices and business cards, and, oh yes, there remained the minor issue of what to name ourselves.

Normally, what you call yourself should be given serious consideration; after all, it's your business identity. "Normal," however, never seemed particularly relevant to any of our business decisions. From the moment we got that first booking, we estimated that we had twelve hours to come up with a catchy, memorable name. We quickly put out the word for urgent assistance. As there was no texting back then, we must have answered dozens of frantic phone calls that day. Friends excitedly blurted out their suggestions, like "rosemary," "ambrosia," "asparagus," even "sur la table" — and then summarily hung up. In the end we opted for the universal touch, a name that we believed would be accessible in all languages; hence "La Cuisine," meaning "the kitchen," "food," and "cooking." A bit exotic, intentionally vague, it seemed to us to capture the essence of the dining experience. So much for what *we* thought. In truth, we spent the next twenty years begrudgingly explaining to our perplexed customers just what La Cuisine means. "Well, it's French for 'cooking' or for 'food.'"

"Oh, I see, but what does that have to do with catering?"

"Well, since cooking food is what we do, we were under the mistaken impression that people would find it a catchy name."

Having settled on an inappropriate name, we turned our attention to the real issue at hand, namely, how do we begin? Since we had no wholesale connections to food suppliers, we opted to buy ingredients from our local supermarket — not the most cost-effective method, but at least it was one-stop shopping. As I recall, the cooking part went fairly smoothly; what threw us for a loop was the timing involved. Needless to say, we didn't get any shut-eye whatsoever the night before the luncheon. I have a vivid memory of Marvin teetering precariously at the kitchen sink at about four-thirty a.m., simultaneously spin-drying lettuce while sleeping fully upright. I had no idea until that night just how talented that man was.

By morning we were running purely on adrenalin and the nervousness of catering our first event. Somehow, we managed to revive ourselves enough to arrive on time and pull off a very respectable presentation. Nobody passed out or gagged, so all in all it was a relative success. However you rate it, somebody on their committee must have been sufficiently impressed since they booked us for the following year's luncheon as well. Few subsequent moments in our professional career could match the sheer elation of clutching that first cheque in our hands.

Money aside, Marvin and I were also relieved and happy to discover just how comfortable we were working together under such pressure. Married couples working together — I know, it's endless material for stand-up comedians. Call it chemistry or kismet; what worked for us in our personal relationship would also define us as working partners. What can I say? We truly are fortunate, or delusional.

It also helped, of course, that from the outset we both agreed upon clearly defined roles in the division of labour. Menu planning and cooking were clearly my responsibilities; Marvin's cooking skills were non-existent at best. What he did excel in was repetitious, boring, menial tasks. He could chop onions, peel potatoes, and cut *crudités* for hours on end. As long as the appropriate music was playing in the background, he could scour pots and pans until the cows came home. Shopping and *schlepping* — not very glamorous, but one of us had to keep informed of the changing prices of canola oil. Me, I preferred the personal interaction of sitting and *schmoozing* with the clients, building their personal menus, calming their frazzled nerves, then getting back to the kitchen to get my hands dirtied.

I'm not suggesting that we were the Ozzie and Harriet of the catering profession; like any normal couple we had our moments, but we agreed from the outset never to allow any personal tensions to interfere with our work. Our cardinal rule was to never, ever, ever lose our cool in front of a client; moreover, never in front of the staff. Especially the staff. Catering is an exercise in crisis management, and very little is to be gained by trying to assign blame during an emergency. Cursing each other out or yelling in front of your workers loses their respect for you and undermines your professionalism. Over the years we employed so many children of our friends as wait staff that the last thing we wanted was for their parents to hear that we were raving lunatics at work.

Everything about catering seems designed to test the limit of one's resolve. Days, even weeks, can go by without the phone ringing, and then suddenly you are inundated with calls and find yourself working for four straight days on a total of ten hours of sleep. Catering can be simultaneously terrifying and exhilarating — definitely not a career choice for the meek. It is impossible to rest on the laurels of your previous success. Our guiding motto was "You are only as good as your last event." Screw up and nobody, I mean nobody, will pat you on the back and remind you of the good times. Clients do not want, under any circumstances, to hear about your morning's emergency dental surgery (actually happened) or your aunt's untimely funeral (that too). One hundred guests are expected to show up at seven p.m. and the quiches had better be warm.

For us, reality sunk in about ten hours after the satisfaction of our first job wore off. What next? I'll let you in on "what next": a long series of less-than-profitable, sometimes irritating orders that we accepted just to get a foot into the marketplace. At the outset I was so grateful just to hear the phone ring that my initial reaction was "Yes, yes, it's no problem to prepare four portions of mushroom soup for you for tomorrow morning." Forget that I would have had to drop everything to go buy fresh mushrooms; the order itself couldn't possibly have even covered the delivery costs.

One of the most timely pieces of business advice I ever received was from a fellow caterer friend of mine. After listening patiently to one of my typical diatribes concerning difficult customers, she told me that the hardest thing to do in our profession was to learn how to say "no." Those two simple letters, she promised me, would preserve my sanity and probably contribute to my future success. Frankly, I had no idea what she was talking about. What I really needed at this point in my career were more customers, not fewer. Ask any struggling entrepreneur how "easy" it is to refuse an order, any order. You just know that once you've uttered the forbidden word "no" it's game over — you've lost that customer forever and probably the bulk of their Facebook contacts.

But a time will come when there is no option but to say "no" and when that time comes it is so, so liberating. My magical moment came when Marvin wanted to surprise me on my birthday by booking a day at a five-star hotel by the Dead Sea. While he was busy arranging our getaway tryst, I was negotiating a catered breakfast for that same morning. Surprise! How could we possibly afford to refuse an event, my birthday notwithstanding? Reluctant to disappoint a longstanding customer, I was convinced by Marvin that any normal person would understand that we are also entitled to enjoy life once in a while. Well, the world did not come to an end, and my client, though somewhat shocked by my refusal to accept the order, understood and even wished me a wonderful birthday!

Chapter Three

It's so beautifully arranged on the plate — you know someone's fingers have been all over it.

Julia Child

Turning down customers may not help pay the bills, but under the right circumstances it can be quite an ego booster. For a brief, fleeting moment, you can convince yourself that you are calling the shots, that you alone will decide when you should work. It just so happened that in my case, I felt compelled to work pretty much every opportunity that came my way, especially in the early years when almost any order seemed too valuable to turn down. I recall one winter day, at the very beginning, spending many hours preparing an elaborate gift basket

The wedding dessert reception - the lull before the storm.

brimming with fancy cookies, mini loaf cakes, homemade jams, and buttery caramels and pralines. I was expected to deliver the basket, intended for a bride and groom on their wedding day, just as a major snowfall was about to descend upon Jerusalem. Was it worth the effort exerted for this one order along with the possible risk of a fender bender? You bet! I had no way of knowing exactly who and how many guests would be tasting or even just hearing about my delicacies, but I needed people to start talking about La Cuisine. I cannot provide exact figures, but no small percentage of our larger and more profitable catering events can be attributed to some seemingly insignificant order that impressed someone along the way.

Important lesson for the budding entrepreneur: Never underestimate the value or impact of word of mouth on your business' growth. Most prospective clients will not consult the Yellow Pages directory to find a caterer. Even the Internet with all its sophisticated websites and virtual menus cannot really provide the customer with his final peace of mind. For that, he will more than likely confer with a friend or some family member who has recently employed a particular caterer. He will want to hear firsthand if the caterer was punctual, pleasant to work with, and whether he has a tendency to overdo his salmon. That kind of feedback is still garnered the old-fashioned way, by word of mouth.

In that respect we were very fortunate as home caterers. Our reputation was our most important commodity, and we were totally committed to preserving its hard-earned respect. We managed to avoid any major professional disasters by refusing to bite off more than we could chew. At least most of the time. When we occasionally veered off course, we tended to do so in splendid fashion.

Not long after we began catering, we were approached by the sister of a friend of ours to cater her upcoming wedding. She and her groom were on a very fixed budget, but they had a lot of people to entertain, around two hundred and fifty as I remember. It was by far the biggest event to date that we had even considered undertaking. It was scheduled for an early afternoon in a funky art gallery-cum-pub in the middle of town. The emphasis was on casual. Very casual. We settled on an over-the-top dessert menu featuring cheesecakes, crème caramel, mint truffle cake, bowls of mousse, butter sandwich cookies — in all, about a dozen different sweets. The groom took care of the bar leaving us to tend solely to the food. Until this point in our career we had never entertained the notion of hiring staff. Why share the wealth unnecessarily?

I have to admit that right up until the wedding itself, we actually believed that the two of us could manage to serve this ravenous horde ourselves. I even brought the cheesecakes in their springform pans, figuring I would have time to top them as the need arose. Time. What time? The buffet tables were arranged in a closed-off section of the hall, making it virtually impossible for us to get in or out. (By the way, "funky" is not short for "functional".) As soon as the ceremony ended, all eyes focused longingly on the feasting station. In one fell swoop the masses descended upon us — it was the charge of the light brigade. I lost sight of Marvin some five minutes after the first desserts were devoured, managing only to detect the occasional muffled call of distress.

It was controlled pandemonium. Fortunately nobody seemed to mind. The music was loud and jumping, the liquor was flowing, and the food was, thankfully, plentiful. We more or less gave up on the idea of actually serving the cakes and acted as referees, trying our best to minimize the carnage on the field.

Though we emerged a bit shaken from the ordeal, we still managed to claim victory. The desserts were a smash, the bride and groom were thrilled, and we gained some hard-earned kudos. Years later, people would still approach me to compliment me on that wild wedding reception that Marvin and I catered in that odd gallery in the centre of Jerusalem. Apart from surviving the party, we learned a valuable lesson that day. Call it "Business 101 for knuckleheads." Apparently, employing waiters at a catered event is not unprofitable, assuming you factor labour into your operating costs. What a revelation. It certainly was a game changer as far as La Cuisine was concerned.

An important rule to remember when employing catering staff is to demand punctuality — from yourself as well as from your workers. In my experience, most catering disasters, inedible food notwithstanding, can be traced to inefficient preparation and/or poor execution. Both are usually a factor of time mismanagement. Next time you are at a catered event, check out the caterer's facial expressions — puckered lips, furrowed brow, beads of sweat, are all usually a giveaway that his timing is in disarray. I know because I speak from personal experience. Fortunately our worst professional nightmare occurred early enough in our career for us to rebound and redeem ourselves, and to ensure that it was never to repeat itself.

Less than a year after we began working, we were hired to cater a bar mitzvah for two hundred or so guests in the Old City of Jerusalem. The ceremony would be held at the Western Wall, after which the guests would convene for breakfast in a nearby hall. Being the seasoned veterans that we were, we arranged for our hired staff to meet us at the venue two hours before breakfast was to be served. Plenty of time to arrange the tables, heat the food, and perform any last-minute kitchen preparations. Lots of time, assuming, of course, that Marvin and I arrived at the scheduled time. I don't recall if we failed to set our alarm clocks or simply slept through their ringing, but when we got around to waking up it was half past a major coronary. "What the…?" followed by "We are dog meat" followed by "What the…?" By the grace of G-d we managed to arrive at the hall approximately one hour before showtime.

When I say "arrived," I really mean touched down. Negotiating the alleyways of the Old City in a full-sized station wagon under the best of conditions requires the stamina and skill of a Hollywood stunt driver. Add to that the pressure of unloading the car and then finding a parking spot in what could best be described as an ancient labyrinth, and you'll have an idea as to my state of mind. Panic would be the sensation I felt after I began breathing again.

Success depended on the guests arriving to an orderly set dining room, without any indication of the chaos prevailing in the kitchen. All the prep work for which I had allocated two hours had to now be condensed into one half-hour. The delegation of tasks became a test of nerves, requiring split-second decisions. First order of business after arranging and setting the tables was a first course of fanned and arranged fruit individually plated with a drizzle of vanilla custard sauce. Far too labour-intensive for any shortcuts. It was now a race against the clock. There was no time to cut the cherry tomatoes in half for the green salad so, against my better judgement, I served them whole. Washed, at least, but whole. Expecting to be chastised for that *faux pas*, I was actually complimented by one of the family members for so tastefully presenting the salad with uncut cherry tomatoes. Ha! That just goes to show you that you can never underestimate the fickleness of the human aesthetic.

I figured that as long as the guests occupied themselves with their dining and steered clear of the kitchen, I might just survive long enough to laugh about this some day. Of course, there still remained the minor issue of serving the dessert. Some twenty-plus cheesecakes needed to be topped and piped with freshly whipped cream and delivered simultaneously to each table. No sweat. At this point I felt pretty much invincible. We had messed up big time by our tardiness, but I was determined to weather this storm and prove my mettle in this unforgiving profession. At the end of the day, I knew from all the compliments we received that we had pulled it off. That morning Marvin and I earned our professional aprons.

CHAPTER FOUR

A PERSON MAKES PLANS, AND G-D LAUGHS.

Yiddish proverb

Catering is mostly about organization. Well, that and a decent menu, but primarily, it's about organization. Me, I could never have survived a day without my lists — lists of menus, lists of ingredients, lists outlining my work schedule, even lists of lists. Whenever humanly possible, I tried my best to avoid any unforeseen surprises. Unless, of course, the surprises happened to be acts of divine providence, in which case even the best-laid plans are rendered useless. Granted we're not talking fire and brimstone kinds of disasters — just your random, everyday act of G-d.

A normal workday in our apartment.

Like the time we were travelling in our van to cater a bat mitzvah in Efrat, a pleasant suburban community outside of Jerusalem. The main access road was closed for repairs, so we followed an alternate back route that bypassed the Jerusalem Biblical Zoo. We were not quite five minutes into our scenic drive when, for no apparent reason, all traffic ground to a halt. It was too early for rush hour and we heard no approaching sirens, so what gives? As we inched forward, the cause of our delay became all too apparent: Smack in the middle of the road stood a rock the size of Gibraltar, blocking both lanes of the highway. The first image that raced through my mind was that of the protruding striped leggings of the Wicked Witch of the East after she was flattened by Dorothy's house. Miraculously no damage was inflicted upon body or machine when the rock had dislodged itself from an overhanging hilltop, but the interruption wreaked havoc on our schedule.

Strike one behind us, we hit the gas in a desperate attempt to make up for lost time. We were definitely close to our destination, three minutes away to be exact, when we found ourselves in yet another bumper-to-bumper jam. Nature was not at fault this time; the culprit was more of the man-made variety. Off to the side of the highway was a "suspicious object," which in this part of the world is a euphemism for a bomb threat. Nobody, not even the bat mitzvah caterer, was going anywhere too soon, at least not until the police gave the all-clear sign. That would be strike two.

Frazzled, but still in one piece, we finally pulled up in front of the banquet hall. Yet, as fate would have it, our two previous brushes with disaster were but a prelude to the evening's crowning crescendo. No sooner had we scrambled to unpack the van and begun frantically arranging the hall and heating the food then we experienced a full-blown electrical blackout. Not a one-time malfunction, mind you, but a problem that plagued us the entire evening. Dinner, for the most part, was by candlelight. The food never had a chance to heat thoroughly, and the musicians' speakers hardly functioned the entire celebration. That was definitely strike three, and we were out by a mile.

Were we in the least bit responsible for any of the day's catastrophes? Not by a long shot. Nevertheless, in these situations there has to be a fall guy, so who better than the caterer? As a parting shot, one of the guests offered us a half-hearted attempt at a compliment: "Under the circumstances you really did your best, but you should know, Lori, that the lasagna really could have been warmer."

I suppose it's unprofessional to expect a bit of human compassion now and then. No one, especially the client, really wants to hear about the caterer's personal *tzures,* especially if it comes at the expense of his own celebration. One year, when I was seven weeks pregnant, I was supposed to cater a bar mitzvah for some two hundred guests. It was early enough in my pregnancy that I was able to perform my usual workload; that is, until a few days before the party when I suddenly felt very queasy and began hemorrhaging. After a rushed visit to the doctor and an ultrasound, I was informed that I had miscarried and would require an emergency D&C. Naive trooper that I am, I figured a quick trip to the hospital on Monday evening, and then back to the kitchen to continue cooking and baking for Thursday's celebration. Right. When I got to the hospital I was told that I must rest for a few days after the procedure, no exceptions. Of course, I heard what the medical team was telling me, but my brain was not registering what was being said. "Let me get this straight — I have to rest, therefore I can't cook, therefore I can't cater. Basically I'm up the creek without a paddle."

After regaining my senses, I calmly asked the waiting doctor and nurses if I could make two quick phone calls before we tended to the business at hand. Decked out in surgical cap and gown, I made my first pay phone call (remember those?) to book a substitute caterer. The second call was the one I dreaded. Oddly enough, most of my clients were never too fond of surprises, certainly not the kind that entailed me not showing up at their event. Nobody, myself included, wants to ever consider the unthinkable — what should one do in case an emergency occurs? Is there a Plan B? Is there a reliable backup? I remember one young couple who had to scramble to find a new hall two weeks before their wedding date when it was discovered that the hall they had originally booked was unlicensed. How can the unsuspecting consumer protect himself from such a disaster? Short of prayer, probably not too much. Thankfully, in my case, when I called my client to explain my medical condition, she was understanding and sympathetic. In fact, years later, she hired me to cater another family celebration with one stipulation: "Just tell me, Lori, that you're not pregnant."

After all these years of catering, I am still at a loss to explain why family functions can be such a stressful ordeal. Much to my dismay, I have watched on the sidelines while the most rational, intelligent, mature people have come totally unglued. Too often I have witnessed a side of my clients that very few others are privy to, apart from their therapists. Caterers are like flies on the wall, silently blending into the woodwork, working our magic while some hosts are experiencing Level Five meltdowns. From my own experience, I can tell you that the customers who most enjoy their celebrations are those who are relaxed and generous hosts. They also tend to be better tippers.

The surest way to ruin your reputation as a caterer is to gossip incessantly about your clients, as tempting a prospect as that may be. Trust me, I've seen and heard just about everything, but I have always impressed upon my staff that whatever they witness or observe at an event stays with them. Stays, yes. Forgotten, no. Even back in those early years, I sensed that I was amassing enough bizarre scenarios to fill at least two volumes of memoirs should I ever decide to go public with my story. To be honest, the image of certain clients squirming uneasily in their seats as I outed their behavior was incentive enough to put pen to paper. With the passage of time, however, that kind of payback seemed less and less appealing to me, as thoughts of retribution eventually gave way to a more seasoned, cynical acceptance of people's quirkiness.

Not everybody shared my more liberal definition of quirkiness. My eldest son was about fourteen years old when he waitered with us at his first major party. He was dutifully setting a table when he overheard our host question, rather indiscreetly, his wife's intelligence. My son was traumatized; obviously, he had never witnessed such an indiscretion in his own home. He could not fathom that a grownup would scream such a terrible thing in his presence. "Try not to take it so much to heart," Marvin assured him. "You see, as far as somebody like that is concerned, we workers don't really exist."

That's no whiny exaggeration. Remember Descartes' big line — "I think therefore I am"? Well, it's a little known fact that the philosopher was referring to the plight of all caterers when he coined that phrase. Seriously, if we really existed, would normal people behave the way they so often did in front of us? I've witnessed more family brouhahas over the most insignificant issues than I care to recall. For some reason, family photo sessions tend to be the breeding ground for major crises. "You love her more than you love me" was a favourite sibling battle cry, followed by "We always have to wait for your side" and "I want to eat my dessert NOW!" Sometimes, years after catering one of these family fiascos, Marvin and I would discover that the hosts were separated or even divorced. While others who were closer to the couple would express shock at the turn of events, we would silently exchange a knowing smirk, as if we never saw that one coming.

For the most part, I spent my career as an anonymous being, expected to perform my job, collect my pay, and move on. That would have been okay, except that from time to time even collecting my pay proved to be a challenge. On more than one occasion, I was informed by my host not to expect complete payment at the end of his celebration. "My money is tied up overseas," or "I couldn't make it to the bank this month," or, my personal favourite, "I guess you'll just have to wait another month to get rich." As if I was in this racket just for the money. How insulting.

CHAPTER FIVE

THERE IS NO SUCH THING AS FUN FOR THE WHOLE FAMILY.

Jerry Seinfeld

Cooking and baking full-time for twenty years — not exactly what I had in mind when I graduated university. There has never been a master plan to my culinary career. No meticulously crafted script. No years of strenuous apprenticeship with eccentric world-class chefs while patiently biding my time, praying for my deserved break to materialize. Quite the contrary. Marvin and I have more or less winged everything from day one. Honestly, how many rational thinking couples agree willingly to convert a cramped one hundred-

"Are they for eating, or for the business?"

metre apartment, home to seven souls and the occasional pigeon, into a full-fledged workplace capable of feeding hundreds? Not a big show of hands, I would guess.

For some inexplicable reason, La Cuisine bypassed the usual preliminary phase of being a quaint little cottage industry to evolve almost overnight into an honest-to-goodness, genuine business. Try, if you can, to imagine a relatively functional three-bedroom apartment on the first floor of a nondescript seven-story building. Now picture that same modest kitchen and dining area crammed tightly with three fridges, a freezer, two regular built-in ovens plus an industrial-sized oven. Add to this combination the storage space required for all our surplus dry goods, drinks, bulky serving pieces, wicker baskets, cardboard boxes, and — oh yes — the more than occasional oversized carton or two of majestic whole Norwegian salmons. For seven years this was our home and our sweatshop.

Our five boys woke up many mornings to a table and countertop full of baked goods and other treats, asking instinctively before even thinking of touching: "Are they for eating or for the business?" Even their friends, for that matter even our friends, knew better than to touch anything in our house before getting the green light from me. Come to think of it, bedtime was often no less of a challenge for my sons. Unlike most normal households, our boys lived with the unexpected as a daily routine. Even the simplest of activities such as taking a bath could never be taken for granted. In our house it was standard procedure to always check that the bathtub was not occupied by rows of thawing salmon or by huge piles of lettuce leaves enjoying a leisurely soak (rest assured, my mother was on 24/7 alert to Lysol-clean that very same bathtub between every use).

Speaking of my mother, at a time of life when most parents are settling comfortably into their retirement years, my mother happily assumed a new career as a twenty-four-hour standby assistant caterer and bottle washer. And by no small means am I exaggerating her twenty-four-hour contribution to La Cuisine's early growth. For starters, every head of lettuce, every green herb or garnish that found its way into my kitchen was meticulously checked, washed, rinsed, dried, and when necessary, torn or chopped under her careful supervision. Legendary quantities of potatoes and onions were peeled, mashed, diced, and sautéed. Batch after batch of carrot and zucchini latkes were diligently mixed and fried. Fish fingers were cut, breaded and tossed with sesame seeds and then deep-fried. Blocks of smoked tuna were sliced ever so thinly.

But there was more, so much more, like ensuring that her own fridge and freezer were stocked with spare parsley, cilantro (which she personally cannot stand), green onions, yogurt, butter — items that I habitually ran out of around midnight. There was the washing and ironing of every pure-cotton tablecloth and runner that graced our buffet tables. Plus the running downtown on short notice to pick up three-kilo tubs of herring and somehow hauling everything home by bus. And, of course, feeding and babysitting our brood night after night to all hours of the morning while we catered and then somehow summoning up the stamina to help us unload our vehicle and *schlep* dirty serving pieces up one flight to our first-floor apartment. She did all of this willingly and enthusiastically with a smile and an cheerful "So vhat time should I be here tomorrow?"

I know that I can never do complete justice to her role in our good fortune by simply describing her sacrifices and contributions. I think what I most appreciated her for was her uncompromising support for my decision to reinvent myself even if in her heart she felt that I had lost my mind.

By no means was my father a stranger to the La Cuisine saga. He may not have been a 24/7er like my mother, but he was certainly one of our most enthusiastic fans. Not that his support was immediate, mind you, but his initial apprehension to such a risky venture eventually gave way to a real sense of parental pride in his daughter's gutsy, somewhat irrational resolve. I think he got a kick out of telling anybody willing to listen to him about my latest culinary exploits. After all, he really was a foodie at heart — someone who truly appreciated a tasty meal when it came his way. As far as testing any of my new recipes, my father was definitely available on twenty-four-hour standby. I'm sure he saw himself more as La Cuisine's quality control manager than as an extra hand in the kitchen.

Probably his greatest contribution to the group effort was the time he got to spend with his grandchildren while we were busy cooking and catering. He cherished these moments, especially if he could combine it with his other great passion, that of playing chess. For chess he had all the patience in the world, enough that he managed to teach every one of our boys to play and appreciate the game, including his most enthusiastic student, our youngest son who was only four years old at the time.

 When not helping entertain or educate our gang, my father could always be relied upon for any emergency deliveries or shopping errands. His finest moment as a team player coincided with one of our most memorable gaffes. In our haste to cater a house party on the other side of town, we left a chafing dish of cream-baked potatoes cooling on my son's top bunk bed. I know, not very professional, but things happen. We were well into our preparations at the party site when we both realized that the potatoes were nowhere to be found. Definitely not enough time to drive home and back, so we put out an urgent SOS call to our dependable backup. Like the cavalry of old, my father arrived by taxi, potatoes in hand, just in the nick of time, with our hosts not any the wiser.

Oddly enough, my greatest worries, the ones that kept me up at night muttering incoherently to myself, had little to do with cooking. After all, cooking was the fun part of catering. What really threatened my fragile state of being were the everyday, run-of-the-mill challenges that most of us take for granted. Things like electricity.

When it became obvious to Marvin and me that our built-in ovens could no longer manage our workload, we decided to invest in an industrial-sized oven that could somehow squeeze into our dining area. After careful research, we found the perfect solution, but for some strange reason, the salesperson kept asking us about three-phase electricity. "The oven I have in mind for you is a real bargain, but are you sure your apartment is wired for three-phase electricity?" Duh, what did he take us for, a couple of idiots? I was vaguely aware of the term because our electrician had increased our amperage when we purchased our apartment. I just assumed that meant we had three-phase electricity. Marvin, on the other hand, was under the mistaken assumption that the three slits found in every outlet in our house signified three-phase capacity. Savvy homeowners that we are, we were puzzled that he insisted on drilling us about our electricity.

In the off chance that anybody actually harbours the notion that those three-pronged holes in a wall outlet signify three-phase electricity, you would be sorely mistaken. For us greenhorns, enlightenment on this subject came with a hefty bill — something to the tune of ten thousand shekels, or roughly $2,500. Needless to say, our house had only standard electricity, and we required electrical rewiring and the installation of a new upgraded fuse box as well as an inspection and approval from the electric company. Suddenly that bargain of an oven seemed less and less a good buy. On the bright side, with the upgraded electricity, we were now able to operate simultaneously our water boiler, washing machine, dryer, dishwasher, and all three of our ovens without the threat of a blackout.

Not every headache can be solved with money. Words alone cannot convey how frustrating it is to pull into your parking lot at two a.m. after an exhausting catering job, dazed, edgy, and often near-ravenous, only to discover that there are no available parking spots. Let me correct myself. Actually, there are plenty of words available only none of them are appropriate for this page. We would stop in the middle of the lot and begin the exhausting ordeal of emptying the van and dragging home everything but the kitchen sink. Then we would start the frantic search for that oh-so-elusive parking space in the general vicinity of our home. Many an early morning, Marvin and I could be seen repeatedly circling our city block while alternately cursing and praying that we could finally put this day behind us.

For all of my grumbling, the real unsung heroes of this story are our five wonderful boys, Yaacov, Eli, Aryeh, Yehuda, and Netanel. Apart from sharing their living space with an excessive amount of animate and inanimate objects, they calmly accepted our chaotic lifestyle as something bordering on the normal. Each in his own unique and unselfish manner has contributed to the greater good of our cause. Resigned to the probability that I would have to wait for daughters-in-law to grace our household before benefitting from any female-type assistance, I was determined that none of my boys would be strangers in the kitchen. True to my word, every one of my sons is capable, in a pinch, of preparing an entire meal for twenty without batting an eye. And without exception, each one of them has at one time or another baked and cooked in our bakery, done deliveries, washed and scrubbed sinks full of dishes and pots, waitered, bartended, and loyally served his time behind the retail counter in our bakeshops.

In return for all their sacrifices, they have had to endure parents who missed far too many family gatherings, school meetings, and school outings. Not to mention the countless number of pizzas they begrudgingly consumed over the years as a last-minute resort for dinner — enough, in fact, to earn our entire family a private airplane tour over Jerusalem, courtesy of our favourite pilot-cum-pizza-shop owner. (If memory serves me correctly, the promotion required the purchase of fifteen family-sized pizzas per family member. Do the math.)

When friends or strangers ask Marvin what he wants to be if he ever decides to grow up, he's never at a loss for a quick reply: "That's an easy one. When I grow up, I want to be anything near as good as any of my boys."

Chapter Six

I DON'T WANT TO WORK A 9-5 JOB BECAUSE TWENTY HOURS A DAY IS JUST TOO MUCH.

Jarod Kintz

There was a time that I could not even bear the thought of holding down a nine-to-five job. Job security seemed too predictable, too stifling. I wanted to succeed on my own terms. Today, after twenty-one years of so-called freedom, I'd have to admit that the jury is still out on that call. Fact is, trading a routine nine-to-fiver for a fifteen-hour workday has somewhat dampened my enthusiasm for professional independence, especially when the reward has not always matched the sacrifice. Then again, if success could be measured by the degree of unique experiences enjoyed, then I believe my career has been none too shabby.

Perfectly blanched, slightly crisp, bright green asparagus.

It has been my distinct privilege over the years to have served clergy, politicians, government ministers, mayors, authors, journalists, and a celebrity or two in a variety of formal and informal venues. Over this same period of time, I have also witnessed my fair share of classy, sophisticated patrons double-dip, lick serving pieces, sample and return partially eaten food to their platters, pretend that cutlery is a nuisance, and in general totally disregard every known rule of good taste. When it comes to the art of fine dining, hunger is the ultimate equalizer.

You don't have to be a genius, let alone a professional caterer, to figure out what happens to a crowd of hungry guests who have gone unfed for a couple of hours. It's not a pretty sight. We once catered an outdoor wedding reception that was officiated by the legendary Rabbi Shlomo Carlebach. Gathered together on a muggy summer evening in a public park were two hundred and fifty guests who swayed and danced mystically during a four-hour ceremony with only a generous platter of veggies and dip to sustain them. Unfortunately, nobody in the wedding party deemed it necessary to warn the caterers that the nuptials would run the length of a full marathon.

With each passing hour, I juggled desperately to somehow salvage the hundreds of overheating hand-rolled mini-quiches from an untimely end. I stood by helplessly as my lush green salads gradually wilted and my whole poached salmons deteriorated into some variation of canned salmon. Once the young couple was properly joined in wedlock, I had visions of an unruly stampede of famished revelers sweeping down upon the buffet tables. I wasn't too far off the mark. Fearing for my staff's safety, I warned them to stand back and take cover — it was every man, woman, and child for him- or herself. There would be no doggie bags tonight, that's for sure.

****

"To snatch victory from the jaws of defeat" is a timely idiom for the catering trade if there ever was one. Much of what catering is about is pretty routine stuff, not particularly glamorous per se. For the most part, I would put together an appropriate menu, cook up a storm, deliver the goods, create a little magic, and collect my cheque. On those rare occasions when plans did go awry, I tended to rely upon my improvisational skills combined with a healthy dose of *chutzpah* — oh yes, and a little prayer never hurt either.

Years ago I catered a modest wedding reception in the guesthouse of St. Andrew's Church in central Jerusalem for a lovely couple. The bride was a nurse at a local hospital who thought it appropriate to arrange a kosher buffet station in a corner of the hall for her co-workers. What a considerate gesture, we thought, even if in practice a majority of her fellow workers opted for the shrimp salad that was circulating at the other stations. This unexpected boycott by her colleagues initiated a sort of cultural interchange whereby the remaining non-kosher guests were only too eager to sample the kosher food we were serving at the opposite end of the hall.

Actually, the menu was pretty straightforward. Besides quiches and pasta salad, it included a fresh green salad with bean sprouts, baby corn, toasted almonds, scallions, and a soy sauce vinaigrette. Nothing too complicated, assuming we had packed the fresh greens. Under the circumstances that would have been a fairly big assumption since there wasn't a single bit of lettuce to be found within a kilometre of the hall. In these kinds of situations, I've noticed that panic is often accompanied by a brief moment of disconnect where the brain ceases to internalize all the data it's receiving. The wedding ceremony is about to conclude, we are minus a green salad, and the only appropriate response seems to be for us to stare fixedly at each other in utter disbelief - until one of us suggested we just drop the greens and call it something original like oriental bean sprout salad. What did we have to lose, other than our reputation? Fortunately for us, most of the guests were oblivious to our inadvertent blunder, rewarding our desperate improvisation with an enthusiastic thumbs up. What could have easily been a disaster became a permanent fixture on the La Cuisine menu.

"If you can keep your head when all about you are losing theirs…" Rudyard Kipling probably never worked a day in his life in a professional kitchen, but he definitely got it right about what it takes to survive as a caterer. If this sounds a bit overly melodramatic, then you have likely never had the pleasure of feeding a group of government officials.

From my limited experience, I have noticed that most government offices are staffed by a collection of reserve minions whose primary function is to hover anxiously around the kitchen while the caterer is frantically arranging a reception for their superiors. In addition to their habitual snooping about and their constant nagging about how little time is left and "Are you sure you prepared enough food?," their primary objective is to secure enough leftovers for themselves and the rest of the lower-tier staff who did not rate an invite to that day's festivities. An intimidating force to be reckoned with, these keepers of the kitchen wield far more clout than their actual rank implies. Any caterer hoping for a return engagement to any of these offices had better be prepared to indulge their every whim, for "Hell hath no fury like a government clerk scorned."

My day of judgement caught me totally off guard. What should have been a routine dinner for the board of directors of a government bureau became a risky test of skill and endurance. Marvin and I arrived at our destination early enough to placate the most concerned of civil servants. Backing our van close to the loading dock of the underground parking lot, I remarked casually to Marvin, "This gig should be a piece of cake." A prescient observation if there ever was one. No sooner had we opened the back of our van than my precious cheesecakes performed a perfectly executed swan dive face down, onto my carefully stacked serving pieces. Under the watchful gaze of the surveillance cameras,

Marvin tried deftly to block the view behind our van as I desperately tried to scoop up the smashed remains of that evening's dessert. By now I figured that the crew behind the cameras had fallen off their chairs and were wetting their pants from laughter.

First order of business was to somehow distract the dreaded watchdogs assigned to our shift and keep them from examining those cake boxes. To make matters more difficult, Marvin and I were expected to arrange all the food in the board room prior to the arrival of the directors and then make ourselves scarce, as the ensuing discussion was obviously too sensitive for our plebian ears. Normally, I would have neatly pre-sliced the cakes and left them on their respective serving platters. That was definitely not an option this time. Plated desserts were just making their debut in the fancier venues, so now was as good a time as any for La Cuisine to unveil its own version. Waiting for an opportune time for my inquisitors to be momentarily occupied elsewhere, I performed emergency resuscitation on the surviving remnants of my cheesecakes. After a liberal *schmearing* of caramel sauce to camouflage any indentations, I strategically arranged fresh strawberries over any visible remaining cracks. All in all a pretty darn good response under very trying circumstances, even if I say so myself.

Would I rank this particular brush with disaster as my most trying moment professionally? Most trying, probably not. Most embarrassing, definitely a contender for that dubious distinction. Then again, almost any catering event is a potential catastrophe just waiting to happen. I've catered a wedding reception for two hundred and fifty guests in a national park without the benefit of electricity or running water — my poached Norwegian salmons resting comfortably on mounds of ice in the trunk of my station wagon. Then there was a wedding in Wadi Kelt (a dried-out valley outside of Jerusalem) where, remarkably, electricity or water were not an issue, but we were expected to share kitchen space with a rambunctious colony of undomesticated frogs. As if that were not enough of a challenge for one day, we had to also contend with some very unpredictable desert winds that threatened to carry off our entire menu, tables included, at any given moment.

Normally, it is pretty much a given that most fridges will perform according to script. Most, but not all. In my case, the exception was an overly enthusiastic appliance in a local catering hall that decided to freeze my cache of perfectly blanched, slightly crisp, bright green asparagus for four hundred guests into a solid block one Sabbath morning. For the record, it is possible to thaw and revive said quantity of frozen asparagus in less than two hours with the proper motivation.

As far as hernias are concerned, they are an unfortunate risk of the trade. Go ahead, ask Marvin, he's something of an expert on the subject, having suffered three of them in the line of duty. I cannot pinpoint with certainty where or when each injury occurred, but it would be a fairly safe bet to begin my search with our stints at the Israel Museum. On the occasions that we catered for the museum's board members or on behalf of some important patron, we were required to lug all food and equipment kilometres from the loading dock all the way to the reception area. This task was usually performed without benefit of any sort of trolley, as part of the journey would wind its way through some of the museum's current exhibits. As we were always accompanied by an escort of nervous armed guards, lest we damage some priceless object on their watch, we were inclined to *schlep* far more than we should have. In Marvin's case, supporting the fine arts extracted a rather hefty price tag.

Physical pain, it comes with the job description. A bruised ego, on the other hand, may never heal. I recently noticed on the Internet a book entitled *Satisfied Customers Tell Three Friends, Angry Customers Tell 3,000* by Peter Blackshaw. Without the benefit of studying the author's argument, I am inclined to heartily endorse his thesis — especially regarding the subject of food. Judging from my own experience with the eating public, complaints are far easier to come by than compliments. I have been berated rather vociferously in public by an irate wife for trying to kill her husband because said spouse could not exercise a bit of self-restraint at the dessert station. On more than one occasion, a hysterical customer has accused us of selling her a mouldy blueberry muffin or slice of blueberry-lemon pound cake, not believing that blueberries bleed a bluish-green hue when baked into pastry. Such is our lot — to "suffer the slings and arrows of outrageous fortune" while maintaining a stoic code of silence. So here is another important rule for any aspiring caterer to consider: Grow a thick skin early in your career because nasty stuff happens, and in most cases you will not earn your day in court to set the record straight. (Though sometimes you can write a book…)

CHAPTER SEVEN

STRESSED IS JUST DESSERTS SPELLED BACKWARDS.

Anonymous

Unconventional, unpredictable, nerve-wracking, exhilarating, exhausting, and occasionally even rewarding. I believe "all of the above" is the appropriate answer to the question so frequently asked of me: "So Lori, what is it like to cater from your home?" In short, it was a life changer. Without a doubt, the most challenging aspect of all was our attempt to maintain some semblance of a normal family life amidst all the confusion. Of course, normal is a relative term. What we came to accept as routine, others would probably regard as eccentric, at the very least.

Time to move the business out of the house?

Most days of the week our cramped apartment was packed with enough fresh produce and dairy goods to stock a neighbourhood mini-market. How much is so much? Enough to merit a regular stop on the delivery route of Tnuva, the country's largest dairy producer. Even our local fish wholesaler agreed to deliver cases of whole salmon to our door in recognition of the volume we were ordering. At one point, I was ordering so many eggs from my local grocer that even his supplier was pressured at times to keep up with the demand.

Funny thing, though, with all this traffic to our doorstep, not one of our neighbours ever uttered a word of complaint to us personally. I can only assume that most of our fellow tenants appreciated the aroma of freshly baked cheesecakes and quiches that wafted daily through our stairwell and as such were prepared to put up with our unorthodox lifestyle. For that matter, nobody from our building really paid much attention to the odd hours we kept. We were frequent flyers in the twilight zone, sometimes leaving our home before the crack of dawn, and too often returning after the witching hour.

Whereas I was always at my best in the early hours of the day, Marvin's stamina was a totally different story. He had this obsession with cleaning and tidying up after every catered event, regardless of how late we managed to drag ourselves home (thank goodness at least one of us was compulsive). He loathed the prospect of waking up the next morning to a disorderly workplace. Every filthy, smelly serving piece had to be scrubbed clean and put back in place before he would even consider retiring for the night.

After dispensing with the cleaning came the sacred ritual of Marvin's post-catering repast. On principle, he refused to eat on the fly at any of our catered events, insisting instead on waiting until he finished his chores at home before relaxing with his celebratory meal. On more occasions than I wish to remember, I stumbled into the kitchen at three or four in the morning, only to witness Marvin savouring the day's leftovers of salmon teriyaki with cream-baked potatoes and a couple of mini quiches on the side.

After seven years of living like this, both of us knew intuitively that something had to give. There comes a time when the novelty of sharing one's living quarters with an ever-expanding stockroom begins to wear thin, and for me that time was fast approaching. I found myself fantasizing what it would be like to entertain guests without having to explain why an oven on steroids was standing in the middle of my dining area.

For me, this turning point came shortly after I accepted a catering request to prepare two hundred-plus elegant bagged lunches for an out-of-town bat mitzvah. What at first glance seemed a fairly routine order proved to be something of a logistical ordeal. For starters, for this volume of food I obviously needed to squeeze yet another rented fridge temporarily into my humble abode. Then, of course, I had to devise a menu that was not only original and tasteful but also durable enough to withstand a lengthy bus journey to an archaeological site in the north of the country. I settled on a menu of cold soufflé roll filled with tuna mousse, pasta salad, veggies and dip, and a portion of cheesecake with a drizzle of caramel sauce. Preparing the food was challenging enough, but how on earth were we supposed to pack and store all these pretty bags in my living room for the designated six a.m. pickup?

As the case would be, the solution was staring me in my face. I simply conscripted my mother, my mother-in-law, and a senior friend of ours, Celia, for an all-night pajama party-cum-pack-a-lunch-bag party. Who said catering can't be fun? With my makeshift assembly line in full swing, we set to the task of packing each food item in its own individual container, which in turn was meticulously stacked in each lunch bag. With minutes to spare before our deadline, my crack team of indefatigable seniors completed their mission, putting the rest of us weaker mortals to shame in the process.

Such late-night fun notwithstanding, the wheels of change had been set in motion in my head. After surveying the collateral damage to my living room, it dawned on me that if I myself didn't need a move for my own sanity, then at least my sons were entitled to a more stable home environment. They were growing up and, if nothing else, they definitely deserved a bathtub of their own.

Change — real change, that is — did not happen overnight. Our metamorphosis from cottage industry to professional bakery would have to wait until the fall of '97, when Marvin travelled to Toronto for a family celebration. While dining out with my childhood friends Elaine and Danny, the subject of our business soon dominated the conversation. Elaine and I had studied together at the Bonnie Stern School of Cooking in Toronto for fun; only funnily enough I was now hoping to earn a living from those studies. Both Elaine and Danny had been enthusiastic supporters of our modest enterprise from its inception.

Danny, a successful lawyer and real estate investor, was always eager to offer his business advice whenever he deemed it helpful. "I know you guys have an excellent product," Danny said over dinner that evening, "but you will never get ahead if you continue working from your home. What you need is to open a professional kitchen and I would like to help make that happen."

Totally caught off guard by the suggestion, Marvin countered that as flattering as that may have sounded, it was far too risky a proposal to even contemplate. "Lori and I are small potatoes, Danny. What do we know about running a real grown-up business? Besides, even the most inexperienced rookie in the food trade has a pretty good idea how high the failure rate is for such ventures." Unmoved by Marvin's protests, Danny ended that evening's conversation by insisting that we would not be alone in this project, that he would become our silent partner and extend the initial investment towards La Cuisine's future expansion. Now that was far too tempting an offer, even for someone as cautious and fainthearted as Marvin, to dismiss outright.

By the time Marvin arrived home from his trip, he was all pumped up and eager to begin a new chapter in our career. The only remaining obstacle to our salvation was yours truly. Forgive me for ruining the party. I for one did not share my husband's enthusiasm for reinventing ourselves. I was far too skeptical, hesitant, and nervous to even entertain such a risky undertaking. Of course, I understood that it was in our best interest to expand, but who, pray tell, would be responsible for all this increased cooking, baking, and producing? I did not have to be a clairvoyant to answer that brainteaser. The onus would land squarely on my shoulders, and forgive me if I wasn't eager to jump on this bandwagon. Who were they kidding? I had no formal training to speak of. I had never set foot in a professional kitchen, had never seen, let alone operated, a forty-litre mixer, and had certainly never supervised a kitchen staff. It all seemed presumptuous for me to even contemplate.

To Marvin's credit, he decided not to press me for a quick decision — "No problem, Lori, you take your time and weigh all the options before you reject the opportunity of our lifetime." Right, no guilt intended at all. Timely offer notwithstanding, I demanded more concrete assurances than a whimsical promise of potential success. Something that would bolster my confidence — something, say, like a baking course overseas at the Lenôtre School of Baking in France. Not only would that add to my credentials, it would also go a long way towards diminishing my skepticism of our proposed venture. That would be my trump card. If La Cuisine believed I was up to the task, then part of the initial budget had to include a stint for me at a proper chef school. And that, in a nutshell, was how I came to fulfill a longstanding dream that previously had seemed so unthinkable.

As nervous as I was about uprooting our business from the security of our home, I admit that the thought of someday opening my own bakery had been bouncing around inside my head for some time now. Over the years, I noticed that few things elicited moans and groans of ecstasy more than an amazing dessert. No matter how weight-conscious people professed to be, they were always eager to at least sample some of my baking. I once catered a home reception where the hostess reminded me at least half a dozen times about one particular guest who fanatically observed a strictly fat-free diet. I was expected to arrange a specially prepared plate for her, on which every item was to be meticulously scrutinized for her approval. Said guest was so proud of her willpower after forgoing all the fat-laden dishes, that when dessert was served she rewarded herself with not one, but two healthy portions of caramel cheesecake. I was so relieved to learn that evening that butter, cream, and thirty percent cream cheese qualified as fat-free foods!

Dessert was the lingering memory on their tongues that guests took home with them from a La Cuisine event. I suppose it was no coincidence that a significant percentage of our catering was at that time devoted to elegant dessert entertaining. Clients appreciated that the simplest of menus could be dramatically upgraded by supplementing them with a luxurious dessert buffet. And growing numbers of those satisfied customers were now calling me at home simply to order cakes. It was no secret that baking was my true passion, so I usually accommodated these requests even though they were so time-consuming. Perhaps that hysterical lady who accused me of killing her husband with my desserts was on to something. If somebody was actually willing to risk bodily injury just to indulge in another slice of my cake, then maybe we really should bet the farm on a product that the public really seemed to crave.

CHAPTER EIGHT

AS FOR BUTTER VERSUS MARGARINE, I TRUST COWS MORE THAN CHEMISTS.

Joan Gussow

L 'Ecole Lenôtre, the Lenôtre School of Baking. The very name says it all. Without parallel it is the Mecca of culinary training for any amateur or professional who has ever harboured a fantasy of studying with some of the world's best teachers. Founded in 1971 by Gaston Lenôtre, the granddaddy of French *pâtissiers*, the school continues to churn out hosts of culinary masters. Located in the Paris suburb of Plaisir, it is a sprawling edifice, which at the time I was enrolled in May of 1998 employed a staff of approximately six hundred in its production facility alone.

Full circle- March, 2012. Me and Phillipe Gobet, director of L'Ecole Lenôtre.

Not surprisingly, my first thoughts upon approaching these hallowed halls were: "What the heck am I doing here?" Suddenly I was reliving the trauma of my first day in grade one — complete with queasy stomach and major palpitations. Walking apprehensively towards the school's entrance, I couldn't help but notice a formidable fleet of purple-coloured Lenôtre delivery vans parked nearby. No doubt about it, this was definitely the big leagues and I was the unpolished rube from the sticks. Here I was surrounded by the *crème de la crème* and my only assets were my rudimentary understanding of French and my untested, spanking new chef's jacket. It didn't help my confidence to discover that I was the only non-professional baker enrolled in the two courses I had chosen to study. L'Ecole Lenôtre, on the other hand, had absolutely no reservations about overlooking my lack of credentials after I forwarded them my hefty enrollment fees.

Fortunately, most of my insecurities were unwarranted. Because these courses were designed primarily for professionals, the size of each class was limited to nine participants. This, in turn, made for a more intimate, informal atmosphere for learning — this was hands-on instruction at its very best. Both of my instructors, Jean-Louis Clément and Philippe Gobet, bore the honourable title *ouvrier de France* — which, by the way, is a very big deal for the French. Amongst other entitlements, it allows the holder to wear the three-coloured ribbon around his neck and that gravity-defying sky-high toque on his head. In spite of their pedigree, neither teacher ever came across as aloof or snobbish. Both were patient and affable, but above all else they were excellent teachers. In my case, they went out of their way to try to accommodate what to them must have seemed rather quaint — my demanding kosher restrictions. I can only imagine how foreign the very idea of eating only certified kosher foods or of separating dairy and meat products must have struck these veritable giants of French cuisine. In France, butter is not simply regarded as an ingredient, it's a way of life, and all breathing creatures are considered fair game for consumption.

Even though the language of instruction was French, that proved to be less of a handicap than my dietary constraints. It seems that all those boring hours I suffered during French class were not in vain. Truth be told, I was miles ahead of some of my other peers who were totally clueless in the *français* department. Lord knows how they navigated their way around the recipes, let alone how they even weighed or measured their ingredients. But I wasn't there to compete with anybody. My goal was very simple: I wanted nothing more than to leave that institution confident in the knowledge that I could call myself a bona fide baker. Though my classmates may have benefitted from some previous formal education, I had to rely on all my years of determined self-education. And for the most part, I was more than able to keep up with the demanding pace of instruction.

Just by virtue of being in that incredible setting one could not avoid being inspired and motivated to excel. On my first tour of the production line, I remember being overwhelmed by the sheer opulence of the kitchens. These were state-of-the-art facilities lined with computerized proofers (for raising yeast doughs) and banks of walk-in ovens and walk-in freezers. Everywhere one turned one could see some original piece of equipment specifically designed to perform a particular function.

There was an entire wing devoted to the national treasure, the noble *macaron*. Row upon row of sinks with adjoining stainless steel counters that were specially slanted to allow water to flow gently underneath the sheets of baking paper without coming in direct contact with the *macarons*. This ingenious procedure allowed for the safe and easy removal of each almond cookie from the paper without damaging or disfiguring the precious little gems. And those ovens, *comments magnifiques!* An entire wall of them, operating continuously twenty-four hours a day. Tray upon tray of perfectly shaped *macarons* were arranged on trolleys that were wheeled directly into these ovens that slowly turned them to their uniform finish. Talk about attention to detail.

And the baking ingredients — Oh my gosh! Daily shipments of stunning fresh raspberries, endless sheets of edible twenty-four-carat gold leaf, bottles upon bottles of expensive brandies, cassis, and *framboises*. Flour — every variety imaginable. Under each worktable in every classroom rested sleek metal bins filled to the brim with five different grades of flour. And butter — Oh the butter. The freshest, creamiest, butteriest butter in quantities I had previously thought unfathomable. All of this bountiful goodness was not merely for show. Students were encouraged to sample everything we worked with — before, during, and after each lesson, including a gorging frenzy at the conclusion of each course. For most of us these tastings were deemed well-deserved perks of our hard labour in the classroom. By most of us, I mean everyone but myself. Alas, the strict laws of *kashrut* limited my indulgences to sniffing, touching, drooling, and fantasizing while allowing for prolonged nibbling on chocolate, fresh berries, and whipped cream.

I must confess, there was one moment of weakness when I felt I could no longer resist the hypnotic allure of those freshly baked croissants and brioches. After all, I rationalized; they were made from the purest of ingredients: flour, water, butter, and sugar. Surely there must be some religious allowance for academic research? Then again, maybe not. Just as I began my dogmatic exchange with myself, my instructor produced an extremely pink-looking non-kosher sausage and summarily stuck it into the communal bin of flour in order to dust it. In one fell swoop he managed to quell any further discussion by rendering anything that would come out of that kitchen off-limits to me.

Temptations notwithstanding, my time at Lenôtre was, hands down, one of the highlights of my culinary career. If I harbour any regrets, besides not being able to sample all those goodies, it is that I was unable to spend more time studying there. I had a bakery back home to open, so I chose the two courses that I felt would most benefit our business. My first course concentrated on perfecting the technique of making doughs — in particular puff pastry, brioche, croissant, and Danish. The tips I learned would sustain me throughout my baking days at La Cuisine. In time, our Danishes would become the talk of the town. Loyal customers would jockey for position in our stores on Friday mornings to secure their favourite flavours before the supply ran out. Those less inclined to run that risk pre-ordered, such as one particularly dedicated fan from New York who routinely phoned in his order of cinnamon Danishes before his visits to Jerusalem — eight rolls with extra raisins, extra paper lining in the box, and no icing sugar glaze.

My second course was probably more important for the skills I learned but chose not to adapt to my style of baking. Entitled "Cake Decorating and Dessert Building," it symbolized everything for which French pastries were famous: elaborate displays of multi-coloured marzipan decorations complemented by lavish garnishes of gold flakes and marbleized architectural structures in every shape and flavour conceivable. We learned to temper chocolate, to work extensively with stencils, and to master the techniques of glazing. I recall being somewhat shocked by the extensive use of gelatin and food colours in the baking; even the sacred *macaron* was not spared this obsession for decorating with the boldest and brightest of shades.

This celebration of excess and ornateness never really worked for me. I preferred the more natural and understated look which eventually became the trademark for my own bakery. One fact is for certain: Had I not insisted on attending Lenôtre, I would never have had the confidence to contemplate opening my own business. I had studied with the best, and I had the certificates to prove it. When we finally opened the doors to our shop, Marvin insisted that I hang my diplomas right out front for everyone to see. "Why not," he reasoned, "you earned the bragging rights, so go ahead and flaunt it." Eventually I relented, and there they hung until I called it quits in 2012, a silent testament to my membership in a pretty exclusive club.

I suppose it was only fitting that shortly before Marvin and I left La Cuisine for good, we travelled to Paris to attend our very first Europain Pastry Exhibition — one of the more prestigious trade shows of its kind in Europe. For me, in particular, I felt that our trip to Paris brought my journey full circle. As we wound our way through the fairgrounds, we eventually came upon the formidable area occupied by Lenôtre. Suddenly I felt a nostalgic urge to share my experiences at the old alma mater with some of the young, preppy staff manning the booth. I guess Marvin and I came across as a pair of *schlumps*, because none of those nattily attired reps seemed remotely impressed by my account of studying with Monsieur Gobet, now the director of the venerable institution, some fifteen years earlier in Plaisir. "Veeery nice story, but would Madame care to sign up for any new courses?" So much for nostalgia.

Feeling somewhat dejected, I turned to make my exit when out of the shadows of the booth emerged, as if on cue, the master himself. Standing face to face, I began to blurt out my introduction when suddenly he flashed me a huge smile and extended a warm embrace. "But of course I remember you" — sure, how many suckers spent so much money on tuition without ever sampling their own work? Pointing to Marvin, he instructed him to take a picture of the two of us and then insisted that I enlarge it and hang it proudly on my bakery wall next to the certificates. To my regret, I neglected to record the wide-eyed, gawking expressions of all those snooty staffers who now watched my hearty exchange with their revered director in disbelief. What a sweet moment. And what a fitting way to say *au revoir*.

Chapter Nine

When you come to a fork in the road, take it.

Yogi Berra

I don't recall all that much about my return flight back to Jerusalem from my studies in Paris, but one thing is for certain; I was flying a lot higher than that airplane. For starters, I was so excited to be reunited with my family. Until this trip, I had never been separated from my crew for such an extended period. At the same time, I was busting at the seams, anxious to begin experimenting with all the new recipes and techniques I had just learned. After all, I was now a Lenôtre graduate, which empowered me to be daring and innovative enough to try to break new ground. So much of what appealed to me about opening my own bakery was the opportunity to leave my mark on the food scene.

Humble beginnings- our first retail shop, July 1998.

Not that the bar for creativity was set all that high back then in the spring of '98. By no means am I such a food snob that I can't appreciate a soft, mushy rugelah or a classic black-and-white cake with sticky fondant icing. But in those days, there weren't even a handful of Jerusalem bakeries that recognized butter as a legitimate ingredient. Unbaked cheesecake and overdone cheese buns pretty much summed up the status of dairy baking. The prevailing business attitude in Jerusalem was that the local consumer was too conservative and too price-conscious to go for anything too fancy or too expensive. Me, I wasn't buying into that old-school malarkey. True, Jerusalem was a far cry from the trendiness of cosmopolitan Tel Aviv, but Israelis in general were travelling to every conceivable vacation spot on this planet, and in the process they were experiencing world-class cuisine at every opportunity. It only made sense to me that these very same vacationers would be more than willing to indulge in some *nouvelle cuisine* at La Cuisine. It was high time that my fellow citizens began each morning with a fresh, buttery Lenôtre-inspired Danish or a moist Canadian muffin alongside their coffee. I guess you could say I felt a civic duty to introduce these simple pleasures to the greater public.

So I had a social cause, a foreign diploma in hand, and plenty of ambition, but that's about it. It was pretty much the same script from seven years earlier when Marvin and I plunged blindly into our catering business, except this time the stakes were considerably higher. Who do I turn to, to help open a bakery from scratch? Ask that same question today and the answer would be fairly obvious: Just Google "How does one go about opening a bakery from scratch?" and roll the dice.

Back then, our options were a bit more limited. Without the benefit of a local business mentor we ended up relying on our gut instincts. At least we were seasoned enough to know the sacred mantra of retail doctrine — namely, the three L's of location, location, and location. In fact, even before I left for my studies abroad, Marvin and I had begun our search to secure that perfect place.

Personally, my definition of perfection was based largely on proximity to our home. Part of what appealed to me about opening a bakery in the first place was the belief that it would lead to a more stable home life. A bakery meant fixed hours and a regular work week. The closer we would be to home, the more free time we would have with our children. Well, that at least was the game plan.

Our search for the perfect location ended practically before it began. We settled on pretty much the first property we saw, a storefront in Jerusalem's industrial zone of Talpiot, about one hundred and ten square metres in size. Its biggest plus was that it was a mere twenty-minute walk from our house. Come to think of it, that was really its only plus, but at the time we signed for it, we were thrilled just to have in our possession a rental lease on our very own place. Like so many other thrills, this one was short-lived and overrated. Only after we signed the lease did we discover how many rules and regulations there were for opening a bakery, pesky details that we had managed to ignore while working from our home. Suffice it to say, there were many. Definitely way too many. I know this firsthand because our dream location had a very hard time conforming to a whole bunch of them.

In Jerusalem, the blessed guardians of our health department oversee a draconian system of regulations that probably rivals the safety code of NASA. Bakeries are required to have a separate room to store fresh eggs, a separate room to whip fresh cream, and, I think, a separate room to store one's anxieties. Until recently, I was convinced that the entire department of health had no other priorities besides keeping La Cuisine on the straight and narrow. And then I came across a little gem of a book entitled *My Life From Scratch,* the memoir of Gesine Bullock-Prado, which helped me realize that I'm not alone in my struggles. As I made my way through her book, it dawned on me that this woman, a total stranger to me, could easily be describing a good chunk of my own story. Granted, she left a successful career in glamorous Hollywood to open a bakery together with her husband in rural Vermont, whereas I abandoned the glitz of Jewish education to follow my calling halfway around the globe. All the same, I was intrigued by the fact that so many of her trials and travails, her doubts and triumphs, mirrored my own experiences. "Ah, the glamour of small business ownership," she writes. "It's filled with so much more than fifteen hours of baking. … You add to these small annoyances lack of sleep, taxes, vendors' bills, health inspector visits, and wild card employees, and my dream bakery turns into a shop of horrors. … Now it's three years later and we've survived. Just barely."

Wow! That in a nutshell pretty much sums up the grueling challenges that every small-time bakery endures in an industry that is dominated by mega-chains and franchises. Unfortunately, the mom-and-pop business model that we practiced is rapidly becoming an endangered species. In our case, I always felt that our business suffered extra obstacles by virtue of just being in our neighbourhood — you know, the whole Middle Eastern "souk"/bazaar way of conducting commerce. Crushing bureaucracy, endless red tape, and indifferent and unsympathetic civil servants. Marvin and I were fond of lamenting the fact that had we opened La Cuisine back in the "old country," our business would have really taken off. And then I read about somebody else who has battled the same frustrations I've experienced, only her bakery is in Vermont, one of the hippest states in the union! What a small world. What a bummer.

Tell me, who isn't a business maven with the benefit of hindsight? It's only natural to see everything as very rosy when one starts out in business and not to dwell on the possible pitfalls. When Marvin and I laid eyes on Number 4 Yad Harutzim, we were hooked. Situated off a main thoroughfare, our future address occupied part of the ground floor of an unassuming six-story kind of strip mall. I am sure that other more astute, experienced entrepreneurs would have likely vetoed this location because it was too small for any expansion and too far-removed from the exposure of the main street. We, on the other hand, saw an affordable, modest workspace that was ideal for our immediate needs. Fashionable it wasn't, but what it lacked in style it made up for in character. We loved that we were surrounded by a bevy of artsy, off-beat, bohemian neighbours: sculptors, artists, a marble and glass engraver, two dance studios, an acting school, a photography school, a school of visual theatre, and lastly, Israel's renowned Sam Spiegel Film and Television School. Who wouldn't be attracted to such an eclectic collection? Even if we were set back from the street, we were confident that our customers would make the effort if our product was worth a few extra steps.

Our business plan was pretty straightforward: Bang out a product that was consistently a cut above the competition. If I had learned anything at Lenôtre, it was to never, ever compromise on the three Q's of baking — quality, quality, and quality. Only, Talpiot was a far cry from Paris, and I had no clue where to begin ordering all of those necessary quality ingredients. As luck would have it, a former co-worker of Marvin's put me in touch with a veteran baker who was willing to share with me the secrets of our trade. That was one conversation that I wish I had recorded for posterity. To his credit, my newfound advisor was very patient and helpful in answering my basic questions. Our conversation became slightly more animated when I began enquiring about the more expensive ingredients I planned on using: Belgian chocolate, higher quality nuts such as pecan, hazelnut, and macadamia, and, of course, butter and thirty percent cream cheese. I think it must have been the mention of butter that hit a sensitive nerve. "Butter? Who uses butter when there is butter-flavoured margarine that is just as good? Macadamia nuts? Are you nuts? Every baker knows that you add at least ten percent ground peanuts to one's recipes and there isn't a customer alive who can tell the difference. If you even think of using butter, I give you and your husband two weeks, maximum four, before you close shop!"

Clearly we were not kindred spirits. As far as his prediction, fortunately we managed to stick around for fifteen years before we called it quits on our own terms. But I must admit, the man definitely knew a thing or two about profit margins. Then again, I was never a stickler for profit margins. Call me naïve or stubborn, or a combination of both, all I really wanted was to bake the best desserts possible with the best available ingredients I could lay my hands on. Easier said than done. Over the years, I have probably spent more of my time pursuing, tracking, and fighting for all those essential ingredients than any other task, save for baking itself.

From day one, I learned that nothing should ever be taken for granted, especially when it comes to your supplies. Shortages of butter and fresh cream could always be expected as the holiday seasons approached. Imported goods were known to drop from sight for weeks on end, held up in customs or the port authority because of some union dispute or other bureaucratic nonsense. And then, of course, there was my personal favourite pastime of negotiating with our local rabbinical council. Entrusted with the serious task of assuring the consumer public that establishments registered as kosher are indeed using only kosher ingredients and conforming to kosher production requirements, their sensibilities were somehow consistently upset by one Lori Rapp from La Cuisine. And I mention all of this as someone who personally is very committed to observing the strict laws of *kashrut*.

Nothing seemed to test the patience of my supervisors more than my insistence on using certain imported ingredients: quality chocolate from Belgium, high-fat, dark, fragrant De Zaan Dutch cocoa powder, fabulous fruit purées and glazes from France, and even corn syrup from the good old U.S. of A. Even though each of these items was certified kosher to the highest degree in its country of origin, I was forced to fight tooth and nail to be allowed to bake with them in my kitchen. Maybe the rabbis felt some patriotic obligation to protect our local manufacturers from foreign competition, or maybe they harboured some aversion to deciphering labels in a foreign language. Whatever their reasoning, I was much too obstinate to surrender unconditionally to their demands. On more than one occasion I insisted that my supervisors contact their counterparts overseas to resolve any outstanding issues about a particular product's *kashrut* status. Hey, Callebaut chocolate is definitely worth the fight.

Quarrelling over chocolate sounds a bit over the top but it's all in a day's work. It's no less demeaning, I suppose, than pleading with a bank manager for more credit. Such are the joys of running your own bakery. Glitzy it wasn't. Who had the time or the energy to even fantasize about photo-ops for an issue of Bon Appétit? I was more preoccupied with trying to figure out how to function in a country that was capable of launching a satellite into space but could not produce a decent bottle of pure vanilla extract.

This was by no means a laughing matter. Vanilla — that is, good vanilla — is the lifeline of any respectable bakery. For the better part of fourteen years I relied exclusively on the goodwill of a whole network of couriers to smuggle in from abroad my elixirs of choice — either McCormick's or Eurovanille pure vanilla extracts. I believe Marvin himself set the indoor record back in 2001 when he successfully transported twenty-four half-litre bottles in his luggage on a return flight from Toronto.

For the longest time, I couldn't imagine that anybody else could possibly be as obsessive as I was about securing their favourite ingredients; that is, until very recently, when by chance I caught a 2012 interview with French-born chef Albert Roux on the CNN program "Talk Asia." Albert, together with his brother Michel, opened Le Gavroche restaurant in London in 1967. Famous for its classic French cuisine, it became the first restaurant in the UK to be awarded a Michelin star, the first to win two stars, and then the first to win three stars. Reminiscing about the restaurant's early years, Albert remarked how difficult it was back then to procure certain first-class ingredients, quality olive oil, in particular. For approximately fifteen years, he admitted, they smuggled their precious cargo into the country once or twice a week, courtesy of the rural French farms across the channel. Brilliant. Who could ever imagine that I share a common shady past with the legendary Albert Roux?

My guess is that by now Le Gavroche's smuggling days are a chapter from the past. For me, I retired my illicit trading about eight years ago when it became acutely apparent that my unpredictable supply of contraband vanilla could not keep pace with my production demands. The solution materialized miraculously when a fellow caterer, who was aware of my predicament, asked me somewhat incredulously, why I wasn't making my own vanilla extract. "I guess that would be because I had no idea that you could do that." The recipe, I'm happy to share, is embarrassingly simple and incredibly wonderful. It's on page 156. Solving the vanilla dilemma definitely changed my life as a professional baker. Other problems? Let's just say, they were a bit more challenging.

CHAPTER TEN

BUREAUCRACY IS THE ART OF MAKING THE POSSIBLE IMPOSSIBLE.

Javier Pascual Salcedo

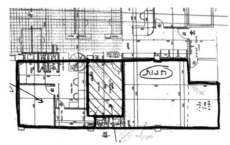

Our "innocent" floor plan...

Don't even think of opening your own bakery or restaurant if you have any hang-ups about spending time away from your beloved ovens. If you expect, and I'm sure you do, your kitchen to run smoothly, then you had better get used to the idea of dealing with a host of mundane, irritating tasks that have very little to do with cooking. Chances are you will have work schedules to write up, payroll lists to oversee, suppliers to argue with, and probably the occasional friendly chat to have with your bank manager. Management skills are often more important than cooking prowess. Just like I had to scramble to find my source for imported Belgian chocolate, you can be sure that some poor restaurateur in Fargo, North Dakota, is banging his head, trying desperately to pin down a local supplier for fresh hummus and tehina.

As much as I dreaded tending to these duties I never considered it a waste of my time. Wasting time was reserved for a whole other kettle of fish. There is little doubt in my mind that when I applied for my license to open my bakery, somebody tipped off the authorities at City Hall and the Ministry of Health that I was a live one, ripe for the picking. From day one, I have squandered countless hours sparring with a minor army of civil servants, specially trained to make my life miserable. In most instances they succeeded. Up and down the corridors of power I have wandered futilely, in a Kafkaesque pursuit for a simple answer to the question, "Why me?" Was I the only sap in this entire city whose application for a building/business permit necessitated the personal attention of so many vindictive, ill-tempered, unsympathetic, petty-minded hacks?

Sure, I had been forewarned by anyone I consulted not to expect an easy time at the hands of the city's licensing bureau. That's why I committed myself to studying and memorizing every relevant bylaw and ordinance in the city's handbook for opening and operating a food establishment in Jerusalem. If I ever plan on opening a bar, I can quote how many urinals are required in order to obtain a license. Even so, I preferred not to run the risk of misinterpretation. Therefore I secured, at no small expense, the services of an "architectural facilitator" to expedite my licensing process. A "facilitator" is just a fancy title for an architect who has made a career of tweaking and modifying building plans like mine to comply with municipal requirements, preferably with the addition of having the right connections in city hall, wink-wink, nod-nod, say no more. It seemed to work. The man eventually fulfilled the task he was paid to do, and I was free to begin my renovations at 4 Yad Harutzim Street. Armed with City Hall's blessings, I instructed our contractor to go ahead and build us a legal bakery and storefront. If you are expecting horror stories about my contractor, there isn't a whole lot to report. I remember there being lots of empty beer bottles and cigarette butts, and that was about it for excitement. Work began in May of '98, and we were ready to open as scheduled in the beginning of July that same year.

Not long after the renovations were completed, the lackeys down at the Ministry of Health suddenly woke up and decided to take an active interest in our little enterprise. Prior to their initial visit, I was pretty satisfied that together with my architect we had designed a very efficient and functional workplace, considering the limited space at our disposal. At least that's what I felt until my first inspection. For openers, I was immediately informed that fresh vegetables have no place being in my kitchen alongside raw doughs. Considering that quiches were expected to be one of my bakery's mainstays, I was not at all amused by this ruling. "Do you have any idea, Lori, how many germs are camped out on your veggies, waiting to contaminate everything within their reach?" Apparently not. This was the first I had heard of the serious health threat that fresh vegetables posed to the unsuspecting consumer. We compromised on a separate sink with a heavy-duty Lucite divider tucked far away in our egg room, where I promised repeatedly to scrupulously wash, prep, and sterilize said vegetables before they made their way into the baking area.

For some inexplicable reason, my inspectors had a thing or two against doughs. It bothered them to no end that our bain-marie, used for heating chocolate very gently and gradually, stood right next to one of our mixers. Call me eccentric, but I always considered chocolate and dough to be a winning combination. I quickly learned that there was little to be gained by questioning their decisions. A silent nod of the head, followed by a heartfelt promise to mend my ways usually did the trick — at least until the next visit, when the same inspectors could be counted on to uncover some new global hazard fermenting in my kitchen.

During one of these routine inspections, I noticed my ever-vigilant inspector gazing intently upon a very small strip of ceiling outside my kitchen entrance. "Why is this piece of ceiling in your hallway painted blue?" she demanded. I was so caught off guard that my initial reaction was that this had to be some kind of a trick question. Then again, what do I know? Maybe raw doughs react adversely to the colour blue. Give me a break, it was such an inconspicuous strip that I doubt I had even noticed it before she brought it to my attention. "I think it's sort of a *feng shui* thing — blue is supposed to remind us of the sky above." I should have known better. No sense of humour.

The offending piece of ceiling was four metres high, which is thirteen big feet off the ground. Why on earth would I even care what colour the previous tenant decided to paint that particular corner of his warehouse? "Well, maybe you should pay a bit more attention to these kinds of details, Lori. The law is very clear on these matters — all tiles and ceilings in a bakery kitchen must be the colour white. Now fix it pronto, or I'll have no choice but to fine you and maybe even close you down." So fix it we did. Very pronto. I borrowed a professional ladder from one of my neighbours, my baker constructed a super-long roller, then we halted all production for a morning so we could dutifully remove every last trace of the menacing colour. Am I a coward? Absolutely. Some battles are just not worth the fight.

Don't think for one minute that my buddies at the Health Ministry cornered the market on narrow-mindedness. Consider this Solomonic ruling issued by some of the brain surgeons down at City Hall. After the bakery was up and running for about two years, we decided to open a small retail outlet in the middle of town, which eventually became Marvin's principal domain for the next five years. The entire storefront could not have been more than eighteen square metres — room enough for a display fridge, a cash register, a few bar stools, and a couple of customers. Apart from selling our baked goods, we had this novel idea of also selling coffee, together with a Danish or maybe a slice of cake. Who knew, maybe such a radical concept would catch on with the public. Not if City Hall had any say in the matter. Upon discovering the espresso machine on our counter, the city inspector flew into a tirade, threatening Marvin with removal of his license if he did not remove the offending piece of equipment from the premises within twenty-four hours. "What makes you think you can sell coffee in your pastry shop? You aren't licensed for such an operation, so who are you to make up your own rules as you see fit?" Indeed, what were we thinking? Coffee and pastry, what a volatile mix. Here's the real kicker. Apparently, it was okay for Marvin to prepare a cup of coffee for himself from said machine; he was just not allowed to sell it. I guess that City Hall was less concerned about Marvin's own well-being than with that of the general public, even though he was the guy paying all of those taxes to the municipality.

I wish I could say that this had been a one-off isolated incident of what seemed, at best, an arbitrary ruling. The reality is that time and again I found myself sitting across from some unsympathetic figure of authority at City Hall, listening in disbelief while it was explained to me in painstaking detail how other entrepreneurs were permitted certain leniencies that were explicitly forbidden to me (like the right to make oodles of money…). "Don't *you* look at what other people are doing? *You* behave like a good girl and do what *you* are told." Their emphasis was always on the word "you" — as if to suggest that the entire code of city bylaws was written specifically with only me in mind. How flattering.

Bureaucratic woes notwithstanding, life really got interesting when the time came to finalize the purchase of our major appliances — ovens, fridges, freezers, heavy-duty mixers, etc. A walk-in fridge and freezer were definitely not in the plans as we were severely limited by space and budget. Instead, we were strongly advised to invest in new upright fridges and freezers because used models were more inclined to break down, and the last thing any baker wants is to be greeted in the morning with a packed fridge or freezer that had gone off in the middle of the night. I have experienced this agony on more than one occasion, and it is truly heart-rending.

Budgetary restraints dictated that our ovens, mixers, dough-rolling machines, and stainless steel counters and sinks be purchased secondhand. For major acquisitions such as these, all roads in Israel lead to one central location, the flea market in the old city of Jaffa, next to Tel Aviv. Combining a certain old-world charm with a heavy dose of underworldly sinisterness, the market is regarded by everyone in the trade as a paradise for all food-related equipment. Store after store, packed to the rafters with every make and model of appliances imaginable, some new, most used. Real bargains are to be had if one is up for the bargaining process. After all, this is the Middle East.

I knew the first time I set foot in the famed market that I was no longer in Kansas. There was a distinct Scorsese-like feel to the whole scene. Running down the entire length of the street was a motley collection of unmatching chairs and stools, occupied by the elder statesmen of the neighbourhood — shady-looking guys with their shirts open to their navels, sporting enormous pinky rings. Who they were, or what exactly they did all day, was anybody's guess. Most likely, they were the early warning system against any approaching tax authority official. I didn't even rate a once-over; I had "patsy" written all over my face.

I'm not a big fan of bargaining, but it comes with the territory. It's supposed to make you feel good about *schlepping* halfway across the country just to purchase a secondhand oven or fridge. Most of the time both parties come out winners. On some occasions, however, the purchaser does not fare so well.

In 2005, we moved our retail location up the street to more spacious premises. Shavuot (also known as Pentecost, a major Jewish festival that pays homage to that icon of Jewish cuisine — the humble cheesecake) was fast upon us, and we urgently needed another cake-display fridge to accommodate the mounting orders of cheesecakes. In order to save time and a bit of gas, we decided to chuck the usual trek down to the Jaffa market in favour of ordering the fridge directly from a catalogue. We settled on a new supplier from the market who sounded like an honest, upright merchant from our phone conversation. We agreed on the model, the price, and the delivery date — what more could we expect? A fridge in proper working order would probably be a good start. The fridge that we received — on time, mind you — would have been perfect had we wanted to sell salads and cold cuts. Cakes, not even close. After a few frantic phone calls, it was agreed that we should return the inappropriate model, at our expense, of course, and we should expect delivery, at our expense, of course, of a more suitable cake model posthaste.

Eight years later and we are still waiting for that replacement fridge. This should be the part where superior management skills are supposed to kick in. Supposedly, in the name of efficiency we prepaid for the defective piece of merchandise on our credit card, rendering it impossible for us to cancel the transaction without the approval of our new-found friend. That unfortunate gaffe on our part would cost us dearly. It seems our supplier was something of a literalist. He reasoned that possession being nine-tenths of the law entitled him to keep both our money and the fridge in question. "Listen, honey, you ordered a fridge and that's what I delivered. Unless you agree to take it back, at your expense, of course, then you can go chase me for the money!"

I had no intention of chasing anybody, that's why G-d created lawyers. "Lori, this is pretty much an open-and-shut case of customer fraud," I was assured by my legal counsel, and fortunately the judge who heard the case in small claims court was of this same opinion. The only party who seemed to disagree with the court's ruling was the man holding our fridge and our money. Apparently, he interpreted the court's decision to award us compensatory damages as a verdict that required his voluntary agreement. To this date, we have exhausted every legal means at our disposal — including liens on his bank accounts and his credit cards — but all to no avail.

The moral of the story: Sometimes you are better off staying put in Kansas and buying retail.

CHAPTER ELEVEN

By working faithfully eight hours a day you may eventually get to be boss and work twelve hours a day.

Robert Frost

July 8, 1998: the date La Cuisine was scheduled to open its door to the public. As the big day loomed ever closer on the calendar, I began to have second thoughts about my plan to fly solo in the kitchen. Who was I kidding? Two diplomas from Lenôtre and Marvin as backup just might not be enough to get things started. I needed help and I needed it fast. Wolfgang Puck would be nice, but I'm afraid I would have to lower my sights just a tad. A well-seasoned, veteran baker was next in line on my wish list — someone who

Yohanan working his magic on Debra's wedding cake.

would patiently guide me through the birth pangs of running my bakery.

No sooner had I put out some feelers than my cousin Ilan from New York called me with a hot lead about an immigrant Swiss baker who was residing incognito somewhere in the religious neighbourhood of Har Nof in Jerusalem. My cousin had it from a very reliable source that this chap was the genuine article — Swiss-trained and apprenticed, and fully certified. There was only one catch. Apparently my saviour had hung up his apron shortly after arriving in his adopted homeland. It seems that my mystery chef was presently content on splitting his time between religious studies and delivering chickens for a local butcher. Not the most promising of prospects, but I was intrigued enough to try to hunt him down.

Without the benefit of Facebook or Google, I managed after some diligent sleuthing to contact Yohanan and arrange a meeting with him at his apartment. I don't know which one of us was more surprised when we first laid eyes on each other. I'm certain I did not strike him as a professional baker and he, well, let's just say I was not exactly prepared for the image of the man who stood before me in his doorway. A towering figure with graying beard, traditional sidelocks (*peyot*) and piercing blue eyes, Yohanan struck me more as a Talmudic scholar than a celebrated master chef.

After exchanging a few pleasantries, I launched into my well-rehearsed sales pitch: "Here's the thing, Yohanan, my husband and I want to open a new kind of bakery in Jerusalem, one that will combine classic European recipes with a liberal dose of "new world" trendiness. There will be butter and fresh cream, lots of butter and fresh cream. And chocolate. Lots of great Belgian chocolate. I've heard such great things about your work that I would love for you to help us get our project off the ground."

Silence. Yohanan sat across from me, poker-faced, slowly digesting the whole *shpiel* that I just dropped on him. "I'll be honest, Lori, I'm flattered that you think so highly of my skills, but I think I'm pretty happy where I am at for the time being. It has not been particularly pleasant for me baking in this country. Maybe I'm just not cut out for the Middle Eastern way of doing business."

Fair enough. Time to switch to plan B. "Okay, Yohanan, let's cut to the chase. How much will it take for you to reconsider coming out of your early retirement?"

Bingo. It's all in the phrasing. Without batting an eye, he threw out a rather substantial figure that was significantly beyond anything we had budgeted for a chef. Trying to maintain a certain air of professionalism, Marvin and I excused ourselves to quietly crunch over our nonexistent numbers to decide if we could really afford such an outlay. We figured if our family could subsist on peanut butter and jam sandwiches for the next six months, we just might be able to swing a deal. Sensing our apprehension, Yohanan had his own ace to pull out of his sleeve. Without any fanfare, he laid open a catalogue featuring a mouthwatering collection of his culinary handiwork. Well, that's all she wrote for me. "Stock up on peanut butter," I whispered to Marvin, "come July 8th I want that man by my side!"

From the very first day that Yohanan donned his apron in my kitchen, he proved to be worth his weight in gold. For me, he was the personification of a Swiss watch — precise, reliable, and not too flashy. The man was a workhorse. He was capable of producing more in a single morning shift than any of my subsequent bakers could accomplish in a day and a half. A somewhat brooding figure, he could work for long stretches in total silence, but when he offered a compliment or a word of encouragement, you could be certain it was carefully weighed and completely sincere.

When Yohanan first walked through our doors, I was expecting some kind of cynical remark about our rather eclectic collection of second-hand equipment. Instead, his eyes zeroed in on my wall-mounted collection of gleaming new Henkel, Wüsthoff, and Victorinox knives. I could almost hear the wheels turning in his head. "Maybe this lady actually understands a thing or two about baking. Maybe she really isn't some bored housewife living out her fantasy of opening her own bakery." Without uttering a single word, Yohanan silently acknowledged that maybe I was somebody he might eventually come to respect.

There you have it, the starting lineup for opening day at La Cuisine: Yohanan, Marvin, and myself. No sous chef, no office manager, no dishwasher, no retail staff, no delivery person, not even a janitor. We were lean and mean. Of course, what choice do you have when you are operating with a shoestring budget? Yohanan and I shared all the baking and cooking duties while Marvin divided his time between running the storefront, washing the pots and pans, running deliveries, shopping, and tending to all the cleaning chores. Marvin and I did not share a fancy office; we spent the better part of most days getting our hands good and dirty. When the opportunity finally availed itself for us to hire additional staff, I believe we were both better bosses for having experienced firsthand the daily grind of running a kitchen. None of our future workers, assuming we could ever afford any, would ever be able to pull a fast one on us because we had been there and done it all.

My father would have approved of our work ethic. There was nothing fancy about the way he approached the subject of work: You just roll up your sleeves and do the job. He loved to quote the classic line, "When you have to shoot, shoot, don't talk," from his favourite spaghetti western, "The Good, the Bad, and the Ugly" — a straight shooter, that was definitely my father. I regret that he did not live to see me open our bakery. He would have been proud. By the time Marvin returned from Toronto armed with the idea of expanding our business, my father was already admitted to a local hospice suffering from a fatal brain tumour. I shared our plans with him, but he was no longer able to focus on details. I know he would have loved having a place to go to where he could enjoy a cup of hot coffee, a cup of *very hot* coffee. I also know if he had been around to keep an eye on our contractor during the renovations, he would never have allowed him to get away with installing such narrow drainage pipes — a nuisance that regrettably plagued us until the day we closed the bakery.

Staff, or the lack thereof, was not our main concern at the very beginning. How to attract a few customers, now that was definitely on our minds. Our children had enthusiastically distributed flyers around town announcing our grand opening, and we were holding our breath, dreading the prospect that nobody would show up. Our lawyer's cautionary advice was constantly ringing in my ears: "Lori, when you start a new business you must always assume the worst case scenario, that perhaps not a single breathing soul will enter your establishment for the first two months. If you can't handle that kind of pressure and frustration, don't even consider going into business for yourself." Not exactly the kind of pep talk I was expecting from a man whose advice did not come cheaply. I kept praying silently to myself that his words would not become a self-fulfilling prophecy.

The best thing I can say about opening a business is that it is a wonderful opportunity to lose a load of weight real fast. As opening day approached, it occurred to me that pretty much everything we possessed short of our children was now tied up in a couple of second-hand ovens and one reticent Swiss baker. I was nervous, anxious, and strangely enough without appetite. Honestly. As far as diets go, and I'm something of an expert on that subject, this one ranked up there with the best. But it was short-lived. As soon as Yohanan showed up attired in his spanking white baker's jacket, a certain calm descended upon the kitchen. By the time that first tray of chewy, buttery chocolate chip cookies emerged from our oven, my appetite was working on all cylinders. Those cookies were the first goodies to be baked at La Cuisine, and hardly a day passed after that morning that the entrancing aroma of freshly baked chocolate chip cookies did not waft through our bakeshop.

Our first day went without fanfare. There were no lines out the front door, but on the upside we didn't have to wait two months to serve our first customer. My opening day jitters subsided. Now I could look forward to the run-of-the-mill everyday jitters that would accompany me for the next fifteen years. Of course, those very first months were uniquely challenging. Sometimes the simplest of tasks took on epic proportions. I have such a clear image in my mind of the three of us spending hours in the kitchen unwrapping one hundred gram bars of butter and opening little two hundred and fifty gram containers of cream cheese. Back then there was such limited demand for dairy baking in Jerusalem that the dairy producers saw no need to package their products for wholesale baking. It just so happened that our biggest sellers were our New York-style cheesecakes and our quiches, both of which required copious amounts of butter, thirty percent cream cheese, and fresh cream. Eventually the market caught up to what we were trying to introduce, and we were able to order butter in twenty-five kilo blocks, and cream cheese in two kilo tubs. I don't claim to be solely responsible for this revolution in taste, but I'm pretty darned proud to say I had a part in it.

I figured we were doing something right because not long before we concluded our first year in the bakery, Yohanan approached me to complain that he could no longer keep pace with all of our orders. Finally, I had a complaint that I could savour. He was right. After all, we were straining not only from the demands of stocking the bakery but also from the pressures of servicing the catering part of our business. For a while there, the three of us managed, just barely, to juggle it all without any of us suffering a major breakdown.

A typical day at La Cuisine during that first year would begin by five-thirty a.m. with the preparation of the morning's Danishes and muffins. If there happened to be a catering event that day, we would juggle the preparation of the event with our regular schedule of preparing doughs, quiches, tea breads, cookies, cake bases, ganaches, toppings, and whatever special baking orders we had for that day. As most of our catered events were in the evening, Marvin and I would rush to close the bakery, assemble our catering staff and equipment, and drive off to perform the day's second act. With any luck whatsoever we might make it home before one a.m. in order to catch a few winks before the next day's festivities began all over again. Morning catering jobs? Don't even ask.

We kept up this frantic work schedule for almost a year before Yohanan raised the white flag. "I must have some help in the kitchen, an extra pair of hands, otherwise I cannot continue." Okay, this is a good sign, I kept telling myself. But how could I afford another baker when we still weren't making enough to support the three of us? "Simple, just don't hire another baker," was Yohanan's advice. "I don't need somebody with a fancy degree who thinks he knows everything, somebody I have to unteach and train all over again. Better you find me an assistant who has two right hands and really wants to work hard. The rest I'll take care of."

If anybody knew anything about hands, it was Yohanan. On those rare occasions that he shared a glimpse of his past with me, he often spoke of his apprenticeship years at the Chef Training School in Lausanne. "Back then, if you made a mistake, you could expect a rap across the knuckles from whatever instrument was in arm's reach of your instructor."

That reminded me so much of my father's standard response to somebody's sloppy handiwork. *Mir dafen zey opphacken de hendt,* which loosely translated from the Yiddish means, The offending party should have their hands cut off. Literally. Those old-world types may have had a preoccupation with hands, but they sure knew a thing or two about the quality of workmanship.

Yohanan soon got his chance to test his own advice when the daughter of a good customer called me looking for work. Debra had just completed her National Service and was hoping to earn some money before she began art studies. Soft-spoken and polite almost to an extreme, she made a wonderful first impression save for one minor drawback. I had serious doubts as to whether she even knew how to boil an egg. Yohanan was undeterred. "Let her work with me for the morning and I'll know if she is worth training." No sooner had the morning passed when Yohanan came up to me and announced in his usual loquacious manner, "You keep her." And that was that.

I have no idea what transpired that morning between the two of them. Yohanan recognized some inherent, hidden talent because Debra became a fixture in our kitchen for the next year. She took to baking like a duck takes to water. Not only was she able to keep pace with Yohanan's demanding schedule, she was a fast learner capable of performing baking tasks one would expect from a more experienced baker. And dedicated — that's one work trait that is virtually unteachable; either a worker has it or she doesn't. In Debra's case, she had plenty to spare — I don't think she missed a day of work the entire year.

Like I said, Yohanan was right about that extra pair of hands. Debra's pair sure came in handy that Shavuot holiday, when we had just opened our new location in the centre of town and we were working around the clock to keep up with the unexpected volume of orders for quiches and cheesecakes. Which brings me to the subject of cheesecakes. Most people like them, some a lot more than others. Either way, never, ever stand between a customer and his precious cheesecake. No joking. While Yohanan, Debra and I were trying to hold down the fort, Marvin was tending to an ever-growing mob of anxious customers assembled outside our new shop. They wanted their cheesecakes and they wanted them now. After what must have felt like an eternity to Marvin, I pulled up with our van fully laden with freshly topped cheesecakes. Nothing I had studied at Lenôtre prepared me for what was about to go down. Mature, grown adults, some even grandparents, for goodness sake, began jostling very aggressively for position alongside the curb. I barely managed to swing open the rear door when in a flash, several eager customers climbed into my truck hoping to extricate their orders from the neatly stacked piles of boxes. As soon as I managed to regain my composure, I went into grade school teacher mode. Civilly but firmly I ordered everybody to behave themselves, stand back, form an orderly line and patiently await their turn or there would be no recess.

I left Marvin to fend for himself so I could race back to the minor calamity going on in my own store. One of the advantages of having only one store, previously, was that I didn't have to worry too much about the details of running it — that was Marvin's problem. I never gave two thoughts about replacing the tape inside the cash register. That roll is supposed to last forever, at least while I'm on duty. As good ol' Murphy would have it, cash registers are programmed to run out of tape only when there's a lineup of impatient customers. Help, could this day be any more stressful? Oh yeah…

The day's *coup de grace* was reserved for the end, when a couple of customers' orders went missing in action. One was for a beautifully arranged fresh fruit tart and the other was for a set of thirty-five chocolate kisses — almond macaroons with a chocolate ganache filling and a shiny chocolate-and-butter glaze. I believe this was the one and only instance in my career that I practically cried to a customer while explaining how there was no time left in the day for me to fill her special order. I've discovered that most customers in such situations are quite understanding, especially if you are up front and honest, and are prepared to offer them an alternate dessert free of charge.

Somehow, mercifully, we survived the rest of that day's trials. In spite of its number of anxious moments, we actually managed to glean a few valuable lessons from all of the chaos. Indeed, the customer should always come first, even at the expense of your own family's needs. Since I seriously miscalculated how long I would be stuck in the bakery that holiday eve, our own festive meal that I had been planning to cook when I got home went the way of those missing chocolate kisses. Even the last caramel cheesecake in existence that I had earmarked for home ended up being delivered by taxi to some desperate customer who claimed to have missed out on his order. Though my own family's holiday dinner that night consisted of matzah (I had oh so naively planned to bake my own challah) and a piece of cheese kugel from my mother's freezer (sad but true), I was only too happy to ensure that others would celebrate their holiday in a truly festive manner. Right.

With time, we became adept at organizing and handling the frenzied workload of all the holiday periods. We got the selling part pretty much down to a science. All the orders were scrupulously alphabetized by name to minimize any foul-ups. Customers who bothered to pre-order were given time slots for their pickups, and for those who didn't order we made sure to keep enough reserve stock on hand. Our system was customer-friendly and very efficient. The only thing that it was lacking, though, was drama. That first Shavuot in our new store was so intense and so completely unnerving that anything thereafter seemed somewhat, well … boring.

CHAPTER TWELVE

RULE 1: THE CUSTOMER IS ALWAYS RIGHT.
RULE 2: IF THE CUSTOMER IS EVER WRONG, RE-READ RULE 1.

Stew Leonard

I wish I had a dollar for every time somebody told me how lucky I am to own my own bakery. Apparently owning or running some kind of food establishment is on the minds of lots of people these days, or so I've read. Approximately half of those dreamers have felt the urge, at one time or another, to share in detail with me their culinary fantasies. The sad truth is that something like sixty percent of all restaurants close shop within five years of their opening. That's not a very promising statistic for financial security. So what gives? My guess is that many

Busting at the seams - a day in the life of our walk-in freezer.

prospective entrepreneurs romanticize about leisurely days enjoying the best of foods and wines while hobnobbing with all the beautiful people.

Well, I hate to be the killjoy who bursts that bubble. I've been dishing out food professionally for over twenty years and glamorous is not the first word that comes to mind. My workday was so hectic and followed such a demanding regimen that I had neither the stamina nor the inclination to become glamorous. I discovered very early on that my bakery would function smoothly only when order and routine held the upper hand — *mis en place* at all times. Posted prominently on the walls of my kitchen were lists upon lists that meticulously outlined every single task that my staff, myself included, was expected to complete every day the bakery was open for business.

Every morning, that is, very early every morning, we began our day with the sifting of the flour (a lot of interesting surprises can be found inside those huge sacks of flour — some inanimate, like strings or bits of cloth and paper, and some very animate...). Our celebrated muffins and buttery Danishes and croissants were mixed, rolled, filled, decorated, baked, and glazed for the day's wholesale orders and for the morning crowds in both our shops. All of the previous day's baked products that had set overnight were now wrapped, packaged, weighed, and labeled. Doughs for our twenty-something varieties of cookies and for our sweet and savoury tarts had to be mixed and rolled out. Ganaches and cake bases (vanilla and chocolate sponges) were prepared, apples were peeled, cored, and chopped, fresh lemons scrubbed, grated, and juiced, and kilos upon kilos of fresh veggies (onions, green onions, red peppers, Swiss chard, sweet potatoes, zucchini, eggplants, and mushrooms) peeled, sliced, diced, roasted, and sautéed for our quiches.

The storeroom, the fridges and freezers, and the storefront all were carefully checked for restocking. And then, of course, there were all the day's special orders that required tending to — birthday cakes with personalized writing were always a popular item and one that under no circumstances should ever, ever be forgotten or botched. From midweek on we began gearing up for the weekend rush. Special attention was given to the preparation of dark and white chocolate mousses, apricot and chocolate glazes, cheesecakes with caramel, blueberry, and fresh lemon curd toppings, chocolate-marble cheesecakes, tofu cheesecakes, fresh fruit tarts, and finally, the tending to of all the finishing touches for all the fancier cakes.

Fridays were by far the busiest day of the week for retail sales. The bakers stumbled into work much earlier than usual to churn out the extra quantities of Danishes, croissants, muffins, and yeast cakes for the end-of-week crowd. As soon as the last special order was delivered or picked up, we began a military drill-like cleaning of the entire kitchen followed by a thorough end-of-week stock check. With a bit of luck we closed the kitchen around 1:30 p.m. ready to begin the entire process all over again from scratch early Sunday morning. Being a kosher establishment had its perks. At least we had the Sabbath to rest and lick our wounds.

To keep us on our toes we could always count on some catering orders to break up the monotony of our daily routine. Say, a cocktail party for a couple of hundred, or maybe a formal luncheon for one hundred. Besides our catering, the staff could always look forward to the holiday seasons for some real excitement. Holidays were the special times of the year when La Cuisine got to showcase its seasonal treats: moist, pure honey cakes for the New Year, traditional apple/poppy seed hamantaschen for Purim, and, of course, our classic cheesecakes for Shavuot.

Fortunately for us, the holidays were also the time of year when our customers loved to entertain family and friends alike. In general, Jewish festivals are not for the fainthearted or the weak-of-appetite. Meals, very big meals, are the order of the day, and our customers responded enthusiastically. Orders for two or more of the more decorative cakes, assorted cookies, tea breads, and a couple of quiches were standard fare.

And the orders — they just kept piling up until the last possible opportunity, which was loosely defined as the moment when it was physically impossible to cram one more cake box anywhere inside the bakery. Fortunately for me, I've always had neighbours who were also in some branch of food production who were kind enough to lend me storage space in their walk-in fridges and freezers. During these hectic periods, I also had the good fortune to know I could depend on the helping hands of my five strapping young sons. Holidays were considered special family time, when everyone pitched in, everyone complained, and everyone dutifully served his time. Many an all-nighter was spent in the bakery baking brownies for Passover or preparing fillings for the Purim hamantaschen. Cookies needed to be packaged and weighed and tea breads wrapped and labeled, orders had to be boxed and delivered, and lest I forget everyone's favourite tour of duty, help was needed with sales in the retail shops. After the last holiday sale was rung up and the kitchen passed its final inspection, I could finally put my feet up and marvel at the whirlwind of activity that had just passed through our little fiefdom.

Of course, the baking part is only half of the fun. A bakery is not a museum. All those delicious creations are on display for one reason and one reason only. You can plaster your walls with endless, glowing food reviews, but all the accolades in the world won't amount to much if you aren't moving your product. Personally, I never had much patience for the retail part of our business. That's why I designated Marvin to be the chief marketing executive of La Cuisine. At its height, he supervised a staff that included himself, two part-time workers, and any one of our reluctant sons whom he could manage to conscript.

Retail. My take on the subject is either you are born with the right temperament, or you aren't. Marvin is a natural. He was totally in his element when the store was empty of customers, absorbed in his expansive jazz collection and his shelf of books. He was equally at ease when there was a lineup of customers and the phone was ringing and a couple of tables were waiting for their coffees and Danishes. Well, maybe not perfectly at ease, but he was still pretty good at what he did. He was particularly popular with the retirement crowd. I'm not quite sure what went on over there in his store, but there was a legion of mature women who insisted on leaving their bakery orders only with our chief officer. "You needn't be so concerned, Lori," I was assured by one of Marvin's most faithful patronesses. "Your husband has enough energy for both of us."

The first two years we were open, the retail shop was attached to the bakery. The storefront was Marvin's territory and I loved coming out of the kitchen periodically to share a coffee and chit-chat with the people. When sales got hectic we worked side by side, but mostly I left him alone to do his own thing.

For somebody who didn't know the first thing about baking, Marvin seemed to know exactly what each customer wanted, even if they themselves weren't so sure. He had the patience to answer over and over again the same tiresome questions: "Is it fresh from today?" "What's a torte?" "What's a ganache?" "Are the Danishes smaller now?" "Can I freeze the leftovers?" And lest I forget, "Why is everything so expensive?" He knew which customers to coddle and which ones to back away from, who favoured an off-colour joke and who preferred to discuss eighteenth century English literature. The atmosphere in the store always seemed so relaxed. Maybe too relaxed. I rarely ever saw Marvin lose his cool with his staff or with his customers, which probably explains why, when we moved to our second store on Aza Street, Marvin had nourished such an eclectic assortment of devoted fans.

Or maybe it was just the music. I swear there were times I was convinced that people were more interested in the daily offerings of jazz than in admiring the fruits of my hard labour. I think Marvin was moonlighting as some kind of a DJ. Regulars popped into the store to make their requests or to drop off samples of music they wanted him to play. He even played cassettes. That's right, cassettes, some of them over thirty years old. His shop was probably the last known establishment in Jerusalem, maybe in the whole of Israel, that featured a working cassette player.

But that was part of what endeared our little corner to all walks of life. We offered a quiet, cozy alternative for those holdovers who still enjoyed the art of conversation without competition from loud, inappropriate music. Sure we're fans of Hendrix and the Stones; we just preferred not to serve them with our croissants and cappuccino at nine-thirty on a rainy morning. We may not have been hip or chic, but we were home to a diverse collection of writers, journalists, politicians, artists, thinkers, rabbis, and sinners. Maybe they liked the wood — it's part of being Canadian, I guess. In front of our main store we built an elevated pine-wood deck to surround an absurdly tall palm tree. Our round wooden tables were slightly wobbly and the accompanying chairs did not all match. Casual. I would have said the look we were after was early casual.

And for some reason it worked. La Cuisine was a sanctuary for so many people from our neighbourhood, people who frequented us daily, weekly, or somewhere in between. They would drop by for a drink and a bite or to pick up something on the way home from work. Often it was only to share some personal news or to complain, but always, always, our regulars came by to check out the daily free samples for tasting. It could be something new we were trying to push or something less than new that we were also trying to push. Whatever the reasons, these treats developed into a permanent tradition. When things got hectic, cookies were often passed around to put everyone at ease, grownups and children alike. Some of our patrons regarded these impromptu tastings as an obligation on our part rather than a treat. Like the woman who upon discovering that the day's muffins were finished, helped herself to a very generous portion of that day's cheesecake sample and contently announced, "That will have to do for now," and then turned to make a prompt beeline for the exit. How should you respond to such a gesture? You don't. You smile to yourself and take it in stride, happy in the knowledge that your customers feel perfectly at ease to enjoy an occasional nosh on the house. Today's taste tester could easily stop by tomorrow to pick up a couple of cakes unannounced.

In a word, it's about comfort. There are still plenty of us relics out there who prefer to sip our coffee in a familiar, slightly rumpled shop than in some faceless, sterile clone of a mega-café chain. Tell me it's not a great feeling to be greeted by your name when you step into your local watering hole. We had staff who stayed with us for two years or longer, an anomaly in our profession where veterans are usually measured by the amount of months, if not weeks. Noa, Noga, Sharon, Tami, Lital, Yifat, Natan, Roni, Avivit, Esther, Michal, Elisheva, Suzanne, Yedidya, and Aurelia were all beloved by our regulars not only because they made the effort to learn their names, but more importantly, they remembered how each customer enjoyed his or her drink of choice — a double shot of espresso with a touch of hot water and cold milk on the side, or very weak but very, very hot with extra foam. It was that extra effort that forged a unique bond between our customers and La Cuisine. La Cuisine, we were up there with the U.S. Postal Service. "Neither rain, nor snow, nor sleet, nor hail" prevented our customers from keeping their appointed rounds.

In Jerusalem it doesn't snow all that often, but when it does, practically every moving thing comes to a standstill. Regardless of the actual amount that has fallen, people are mesmerized, traffic is paralyzed, and business, let's just say it's a lost cause. The other constant is that it only snows on a Thursday or Friday after we had painstakingly filled our display fridges with the usual end-of-the-week's goodies. The very first time this happened was just after we opened our bakery and had no idea what a havoc one snowfall could cause. Here it was, Friday morning, the key to our week's success, and the only thought on every Jerusalemite's mind was how to build the largest snowman. Resigned to the hopelessness of the situation, I suggested that we enjoy the day off with our children in the park with all the other revelers. Marvin agreed that I should do just that because, snow or no snow, he was walking to open up our shop. "There is no bloody way an entire city can grind to a halt because of a little snow." What an optimist. What a *neb*. After trekking all the way there, he spent the next four hours staring out the window until the phone finally rang enquiring if we were open for business. Praise the Lord; Marvin's faith in mankind had been reaffirmed. The day's sole patron somehow negotiated her car into our parking lot and made off with the day's only haul — one carrot cake plus an apple torte with a toasted almond topping. For years afterwards whenever she entered our store, we would remind her that she was La Cuisine's most dedicated and loyal supporter.

Of course, I would be lying if I said that everyone who walked in through our doors was a happy camper. The customer may always be right, but the more accurate line according to Marvin should be "the customer is always the customer." Like family, you have to take the good with the less than good. Just when you think you have seen or heard everything, somebody manages to come up with something new to shock your sensibilities. Infuriating at times, but on the odd occasion, very original.

One particular Friday when the store was pleasantly packed, an audaciously opinionated customer piped up for all to hear that she was a skilled baker who knew exactly what ingredients went into our chocolate pecan torte and how much it cost us; therefore she felt she was entitled to a discount. Without missing a beat, Marvin calmly replied that if indeed she was so plugged into our business, then surely she knew how expensive Belgian chocolate and imported pecans were, how much our labour costs were, as well as our utilities and packaging costs, municipal taxes, and value added tax. All things considered, we were actually undercharging for that particular torte and therefore, the answer is no, nothing off the price for you today.

Pricing will always be an issue, especially when the product you are selling is a high-end item. Good ingredients are expensive, and a skilled, dedicated staff does not come cheaply. When tested, Marvin would delicately remind our customers that La Cuisine was not a hobby of ours. To those who persisted in questioning our prices, Marvin would often quip, "We are pricey so that Lori and I can retire early to some Caribbean island." Not everybody appreciated Marvin's humour.

For me personally, shopping for pastry is one of life's simplest pleasures. The thrill of discovering and tasting something completely new and different, does it get any better than that? Not so for everyone. Judging by the strained looks on some of our customers' faces, purchasing a cake is anything but a pleasant experience. Especially when it involves couples. Couples together in a bakery can be a highly combustible mixture. Far too often, one of the spouses is in a generous, spending mood while the other is pleading bankruptcy. "What is the matter with you? Why on earth do we need so much dessert?" "I don't see why one cake isn't enough for twenty-five people." "It's okay, it's only your family, and if they're still hungry they can eat fruit." "I'll tell you what would really be okay, is if you go and wait this one out in the car."

Standing behind the counter, serving people over the years, you can learn quite a bit about human nature. It's a lot like an ongoing Psychology 101 course, only in real time. There are the indecisive customers, the ones who will deliberate longer over which cake to order than I probably spent on purchasing our apartment. The extravagant of heart, G-d bless them, they are the ones who will order three large cakes for eight guests because "You know, people like choices." And then there are my personal favourites, the counters, as in "My three grandchildren are coming for a visit, so I will need four cookies." I could never figure out how they decided which of those lucky youngsters deserved a second cookie.

I knew when I opened the bakery that the workload would be anything but easy, but I always envisioned the selling part to be a fun experience for my customers. At least for most of them. So how do you respond to a customer who accuses you of "ruining her life" because the cheesecake she ordered without whipped cream rosettes arrived unintentionally with the offending decoration? Oops! The cat was out of the bag. Now all the guests would know that the cake was not baked by their gifted hostess. When Marvin's suggestion that he remove the unwanted cream and replace it with fresh cut fruit fell on deaf ears, he sympathetically pointed out to the grieving customer that she still possessed her health, and she should remember that in the bigger scheme of things "it's only a *farkakte* (you can look that one up) cheesecake, and, oh yeah, get a grip…" The funniest thing about the entire incident is that the next day, when calmer heads prevailed, the same customer called Marvin to thank him for the delicious cake and to apologize for her behavior.

The truth is it's never a good policy to bungle a customer's order. If you are going to forget something you better make certain it's not somebody's inscription on his or her cake. There are no sins of omission or commission that remotely approach the anguish of a botched or forgotten written dedication. It's as if the cake itself is merely a decorative pedestal to accommodate that all-important and ever so original "Happy birthday, we love you" message that we used to pipe with melted chocolate onto a piece of rolled-out marzipan. Customers have actually refused to purchase their specially ordered cake because of a foul-up regarding their inscription. This in spite of Marvin's offer to sing "Happy Birthday" over the phone.

I've yet to meet any food entrepreneur who can claim infallibility. Order slips have been known to stick to each other or to inadvertently fall behind some fridge, only to surface two weeks after the order was scheduled for pickup. I've had mousse cakes that were improperly wrapped for the freezer that went out to customers with mould on the bottom. I've had customers crack their teeth on the tiniest pieces of nut shell (these misdeeds usually hurt me more than the injured party). I've even had bakers who have seen fit to alter my recipes without informing me, much to the regret of my unsuspecting customers.

I managed once to make a mess of things when my intentions were to help a longstanding customer in his hour of need. After scrambling frantically to deliver a last minute order of quiches for a family in mourning right after the funeral, I belatedly discovered that some of those well-intentioned quiches belonged to a previously arranged order. Suffice it to say, it was not one of my finer moments when I later showed up, cap in hand, at the grieving household to plead for some of those quiches back. Ouch.

Chapter Thirteen

I cannot afford to waste my time making money.

Louis Agassiz

Counting other people's money — who hasn't indulged in this pastime just a bit? I for one am guilty as charged. I also know how unnerving it feels to be the subject of other people's counting. For years I've had to tolerate numerous rumours about how Marvin and I are supposedly raking in the big bucks. "Let's see, you guys own two shops, a bakery, and, oh yeah, let's not forget all that expensive catering you do. Wow! You guys must be loaded." Loaded I might be, but not with money. For the record, we never owned any of our business locations. They were

Caramel sauce - the way it is meant to be enjoyed.

all rentals, and rent does not come cheaply in our holy city. More to the point, if you've never experienced the pleasure of operating your own bakery or café, you probably haven't the foggiest notion of how much capital and sweat it requires to keep such enterprises afloat, let alone for them to be profitable. If by some fluke you do know the answer, than feel free to share it with me.

What I do know is that every time we thought we were turning a corner in our struggles, something unexpected turned up to derail our good fortune. The "La Cuisine Tango", as we affectionately called it, was a very easy dance step to master. First, we took one step forward, then two steps backwards, and just kept repeating until the bank called. And call they did.

Loans became another fact of life, a form of lifeline so to speak. Sure, it can be discouraging, but we just kept plugging away because so many people seemed to love what we were doing. Virtually every year we were in business we succeeded in increasing our sales. Unfortunately, our running costs never kept pace with our revenues. As soon as we could see some daylight, a fridge motor (or two) would blow, or the engine would give out in our van. Bylaws would change overnight and suddenly we would be required to replace our electrical board or redo our entire sprinkler system. Even on the rare occasion that I caught a break from the income tax authorities, I have suffered the humiliation of having to return my tax rebate because of their own miscalculations.

So why even bother? Because baking and cooking can be so intoxicating. How can you walk away from something you are so passionate about and to which others respond so appreciatively? What better feeling can there be than to show up at work each day knowing that what you do brings so much joy, pleasure, and meaningful calories to so many friends and complete strangers alike? When the feedback is positive, you never tire of the compliments, even if they don't necessarily pay the bills. And they don't.

Over the years we were fortunate enough to count the various banks we dealt with as our steady customers. Whenever a cake or quiche was needed for one of their board meetings or for an employee's birthday, La Cuisine could be counted on to deliver the goods. Being chummy with the bank employees had its advantages. Unfortunately, getting a break in my credit line was not one of them. Satisfying their sweet tooth did little to quell their appetite for more deposits. Nor did it help much to prevent those dreaded phone calls that were uncannily timed to unnerve you when your store was full of restless customers, as if you couldn't wait to argue about your overdrawn account in earshot of all those strangers. Did these harbingers of "good news" really think they were fooling any of us by withholding their identity on caller ID? For years I avoided answering any "withheld" phone calls. I figured if somebody was not polite enough to identify himself, then he would have to find an alternate way to get in touch with me.

Needless to say this was not a foolproof strategy. You can only avoid the bank for so long before it gets a bit testy. I didn't require any outside help to remind me of the precarious status of my account. Believe me, it was never far from my thoughts. What I really needed was a serious time-out from anything to do with my bank and its well-being. All the same, I probably should have been more "careful about what I wished for" because my very wish came true on Tuesday, June 3, 2003. That particular day was my wake-up call, the day that I learned firsthand that there are far more important values in life than a balanced account, values like staying in one piece.

That Tuesday was two days before the Shavuot holiday, unquestionably the busiest time of the year in our kitchen. I remember that morning as being particularly hectic. We had cheesecake orders coming out the wazoo. We were all falling off our feet from two late nights in the bakery and I still had four huge pots (twelve litres each, to be exact) of caramel sauce to prepare for decorating the cheesecakes. My first three batches came out letter perfect — just the right hue of amber and that unmistakable heavenly aroma. The fourth pot didn't fare so well. For some reason or another I was distracted, and in an instant, heavy billows of smoke began to fill up the kitchen. Empathetic boss that I am, I saw no reason that the staff should suffer the pungent smell that accompanies badly burnt caramel. Reacting instinctively, not necessarily intelligently, I immediately transferred the smoking pot to the nearest deep industrial sink without the recommended protection of oven mitts (a feat never, ever to be done again in the kitchens of La Cuisine). It was pretty much downhill from there on in. As I bent over the sink, face down, I gave little thought as to how that angry pot of caramel might react when we parted ways. For the record, burnt caramel reaches temperatures of over 200°C (in Fahrenheit, that's over 400°, which sounds a lot more impressive) and takes on the texture of boiling black tar. When it is agitated it can be very fickle and extremely mobile as evidenced by the huge glob of sauce that splashed up directly onto my scarf-covered head and not-so-covered face as well as onto my entire bare right arm and hand. A smaller amount plopped onto my left hand, but by this point I stopped keeping score. In that split second that my mind registered disaster striking, I watched incredulously as patches of skin on my right arm began to bubble and split open.

By now my right eye was glued shut from the caramel and my left eye, well, it had seen enough. Everything happened so quickly, but the pain was so incredibly intense that it felt like forever. My partner at the time, Meir, a trained firefighter volunteer and an ex-combat soldier, took charge. With no time to call an ambulance he ordered Josh, an off-duty medic and ambulance driver, to rush me ASAP to the trauma unit at Hadassah Hospital in Ein Kerem, Jerusalem. By some act of providence Josh, who was married to my baker Yitti, had dropped by to grab lunch with his wife. Instead of sharing a few leisurely moments together, the two of them piled me into their compact car and sped off with Josh's portable red light flashing on his roof. Driving like a man possessed, Josh ignored stoplights while driving over islands and sidewalks. Yitti tried valiantly to prevent me from lapsing into shock by pressing a cold bottle of water on my neck and ensuring me every few seconds that "We're almost there." True to her word, we made it in fifteen minutes flat — an amazing feat considering that it should normally have taken at least thirty minutes in lunchtime traffic. (Only much later would Josh admit to me that he had damaged his car's axle during that record-setting stunt.)

The hospital's emergency department had been forewarned and the staff was waiting outside to receive us with a wheelchair and moral support. That poor doctor who first stepped forward to examine me. I can still picture his horrified expression as he bent close to my face to assess the damage. "What on earth is this mess and can somebody tell me how to get it off?" Not exactly the most reassuring of words to put my mind at ease. Normally, I consider myself to be a very cooperative patient, but this day was anything but normal. By the time the morphine had kicked in I was calling the shots in the trauma room. The nurses tried desperately to keep me from repeatedly trying to get off the examining table while they did their best to wash the hardened caramel off my skin without peeling me alive. "Doesn't anybody here get it?" I kept shouting in frustration. "It's Shavuot and I have to get back to my bakery right now!"

"Sweetie, I don't think *you* get it. You've suffered second and third-degree burns and the only place you are going now is upstairs to the burn ward."

Clearly they had no idea who they were up against. "I demand that you release me immediately." I tell you, pain and drugs, they can wreak havoc with one's mental faculties. Crazy or not, my persistence paid off as someone with authority decided that she had seen and heard enough and agreed to discharge me to the home care of one of my closest friends and neighbours, Anna, who just happens to be a senior nurse and lecturer in the school of nursing and on the faculty of medicine at the same Hadassah hospital. (To tell you the truth, neither of us had any idea of how serious a commitment this would be on her part. For a solid month, this angel of mercy made her way to my house morning and night to scrub and dress my burns.)

My guess is that the nurses were pretty relieved to hand me over to somebody else's care. They had enough on their plates aside from dealing with the ravings of a drugged-out basket case. I think I secured my exit pass when I requested, actually more like demanded, that I be driven to my polling station so I could vote in that day's municipal elections. To me it seemed like a perfectly legitimate request. Hey, I'm Canadian, and we take our civic duties very seriously. This being a very important election, I was determined to cast my ballot for first-time mayoral candidate Nir Barkat.

After I was formally released from the hospital, Yitti and Josh, who had stayed by my side throughout the entire ordeal, carefully escorted me to their car for the ride home, which included one pit stop along the way. After witnessing my mini tirade in the trauma ward, Josh knew better than to try and dissuade me from voting. Fortunately for me, there was a specially designated station for handicapped voters in the caravan of our neighbourhood elementary school, not so fortunately for all those unsuspecting children who were innocently playing in the schoolyard when I stepped out of Josh's car. Reminiscent of Boris Karloff in the 1932 classic "The Mummy," I was still decked out in surgical cap and hospital shift (my street clothes and kerchief had all been cut away in the hospital) with both arms heavily bandaged and my face heavily greased to protect and soothe my unsightly blisters and dangling pieces of skin. One by one, those poor, traumatized youngsters dropped their soccer balls and basketballs in disbelief, eyes transfixed on this ghastly figure lumbering unsteadily in their direction. For the record, Nir Barkat lost the election, but not because of me.

So where was my husband, you ask, during this crisis? He was alone minding the shop, pretty much in the dark as to the day's unfolding drama. Marvin was only told that I had suffered a minor accident and that everything would be fine and there was no need to panic. Boy was he in for a shock when he finally got home. It was probably a good thing that neither of us had a clue as to what lay in store for me that next month. I have given birth naturally five times, but nothing, I mean nothing, could have prepared me for the sheer agony of having my wounds scrubbed and sterilized twice daily for 45 grueling minutes. I needed only to hear the approach of Anna's footsteps outside my front door to trigger a Pavlovian response of spontaneous uncontrollable whimpering. Anna was my own personal Florence Nightingale served up with a liberal dose of Julie Andrews. In an inspired effort to divert my attention from the painful treatments, she insisted we sing out loud every Beatles song, every Broadway show tune, and every TV theme song from our childhood that we could remember. To this day I can still recite at the drop of a hat, word for word, the lyrics to "The Beverly Hillbillies" and "The Brady Bunch."

Musical duets were not necessary for the next phase of my recovery. From home care I found myself back in the hospital, this time for a five-day stay to undergo a skin graft to try to repair my disfigured right arm. Apart from missing valuable time in my bakery, about the only thing I got to show for the latest ordeal were some real attention-grabbing scars. And show them I did. After the surgery I was required to leave my arm exposed to enable the skin to heal. What I did discover was, as a rule, most people prefer that you don't parade your disfigurations too blatantly in public. My business demands did not afford me the luxury of staying at home to recuperate like most burn patients. I returned to the bakery at the first opportunity, throwing myself right back into the thick of things. Fortunately for me, I've always been pretty thick-skinned, no pun intended, when it comes to my looks, so I was actually slightly amused by some of the near-hysterical reactions of some of my customers on my return. Like the memorable "I don't understand how you can walk out your front door looking like that" to the ever more subtle "That is really quite disgusting. Why can't you just cover it up?"

And all this time I was under the impression that "beauty is only skin deep" — once again, no pun intended. If anything, physical beauty is pretty darn fleeting — anyone can lose it in the blink of an eye. I know that I could have suffered a lot worse than I did. Thank G-d, my face was left with only a bit of scarring and a few discoloured splotches. I found my work to be totally therapeutic. As soon as I was back in the saddle, the first thing I did was to demonstrate to my sons how to make a batch, albeit a small batch, of caramel sauce without igniting my body in the process (I believe in confronting my demons head-on). I knew that I had screwed up big time, but I did learn some valuable lessons from my painful experience. I learned that I am blessed with a wonderfully supportive family and group of friends and co-workers — friends who prepared meals for us and chauffeured me around until I was able to drive again, and co-workers who unselfishly picked up the slack during my absence. My partner Meir slept on the bakery floor two nights in a row to ensure that all the Shavuot orders went out without a hitch. The store was bedlam, but Marvin managed to make it home in time to properly usher in the holiday. Demons or no demons, that year we opted for a fruit-topped cheesecake instead of our usual caramel.

CHAPTER FOURTEEN

IF I WERE IN THIS BUSINESS ONLY FOR THE BUSINESS, I WOULDN'T BE IN THIS BUSINESS.

Samuel Goldwyn

I've never been one to dwell for long on any of my personal setbacks. I guess I inherited this trait from my mother. She's a very pragmatic individual — not an optimist, per se, but a pragmatist. I grew up in a household where stories about my mother's experiences in Auschwitz were retold in a matter-of-fact manner. Melodrama was not her style. She was far too preoccupied with restarting her life and raising a family to linger over the tragedies of the past. I don't recall her ever questioning why "this or that had to happen to me?"

Me in the blue shirt - a night out enjoying meat between treatments.

Somewhere along the way, her take on life and fate must have rubbed off on me. After a year spent going to physiotherapy and wearing a full-length pressure bandage, it was fairly apparent to me that my damaged arm was not about to be featured any time soon in some glamour photo shoot. Any lingering hopes for a miraculous recovery that I may have entertained were formally put to rest by a pair of examining doctors from the National Insurance Institute's medical review board. These two middle-aged experts were assigned by the institute to determine how much percentage of disability I was entitled to as a result of my burn accident. They took their work very seriously. They probed, massaged, and scrutinized every mark and scar on my face and arm until they concurred in unison, "This is definitely one ugly piece of work."

Cry? Laugh? Me, I prefer to laugh. Laugh and bake. I figure if you can't change the hand you are dealt, you might as well enjoy a fresh Danish and call it a day. I had gotten so used to the awkward side-glances, the disbelieving gawks, and the outright stares that I made no special effort to hide my scars. Who can blame people for their stunned reactions? What I had no way of knowing back then was that my entire burn ordeal was really just a warm-up act for the real show-stopper that awaited me down the road.

For the next three years, it was pretty much business as usual at La Cuisine, whatever "usual" meant in our peculiar world. In November of 2005, around my forty-sixth birthday, I treated myself to my first mammogram through our local health fund. Informed by the examining doctor that the small markings that showed up on my X-ray were *not* suspicious, I was sent packing home with a recommendation to book a follow-up appointment in six months' time. I never made it to that second scheduled examination. Early sometime in April, I woke up one Saturday morning to discover bloodstains on the front of my nightgown. From that shocking discovery it was only a matter of days before my worst fear was confirmed: Yes, I indeed had breast cancer. Needless to say, those cloudy spots on my mammogram were anything but innocent, and by the time I met with my surgeon, it was affirmed that some of my lymph nodes were also infected. I was hastily booked for a mastectomy plus additional surgery to remove twenty-six of my lymph glands.

As if the news wasn't bad enough, this entire drama was played out a week and a bit before Passover, arguably the most family-oriented holiday in the Jewish calendar. I generally loathe keeping secrets, but I was reluctant to share this new revelation with anyone other than Marvin for fear of upsetting everybody's holiday. My compromise was to wait until after the first night Seder to inform our boys, and then to wait another couple of days to break the news to my mother. My guys passed with flying colours — so positive and supportive. With that hurdle out of the way, how do you tell your Holocaust-surviving mother that her only daughter has breast cancer? Basically, Marvin and I, together with my brother Mark and his wife Yael, just sat her down at the dining room table and told her straight out everything that we knew from the doctors up to that point. True to her character, my mother did not lose it, as I had feared she might. After silently mulling over the facts, she got up from the table and announced: "So we'll do what we have to do." Good enough for me.

Those initial two weeks were a whirlwind of activity. Sunday, the day after I woke to the bloodstains, I underwent a six-hour thorough examination at Halá, Jerusalem's top private breast clinic at the time. By Tuesday, I was sitting across the desk from Dr. Strano, waiting for him to confirm what I already suspected was the diagnosis. Visibly surprised that I had shown up for our consultation alone, he insisted that I should reconsider my decision: "Mrs. Rapp, I think you might appreciate having your husband by your side for what I'm about to tell you."

"Quite frankly, Doctor, I don't think my husband's presence is necessary to our discussion. He's far too emotional at this stage to be all that helpful." At which point I rolled up the right sleeve of my shirt to show him my scarred arm. "You see, Dr. Strano, I'm already damaged goods, so just tell me how we are going to get this poison out of my body as soon as possible." That sort of took the oomph out of the counseling part of his speech. He understood from my little demonstration that I wanted him to deliver me the straight goods without any sugarcoating.

When I called Marvin to update him on my appointment, I sensed a quiver in his voice as well as a half-hearted attempt to hold back a sob. I believe that was the one and only time I had to read him the riot act. "Listen, you better cut it out and get on board real fast. If you want to be any help to me, you'd better start thinking and acting positively." That was it, short and to the point. From that moment on, Marvin and I were a team — same focus, same determination, and same offbeat, almost morbid sense of humour.

The very next morning, Marvin and I were sitting in the office of Dr. Olsha, one of the top surgeons at Jerusalem's Shaare Zedek Hospital. He had that pensive look on his face, as he seemed to be weighing carefully his choice of words. Here we go again, I thought to myself. Another sensitive doctor trying to pussyfoot around before giving me his verdict. "Look, Dr. Olsha, if this will make things easier for you, I have nursed five healthy, strapping young men. My work is done in that department. Now it's your turn to do your job and leave me to worry about mine. I want this cancer, all of it, out of my body, as in yesterday." I think he actually appreciated my candor, and it seemed to me that he may even have gotten a kick out of my personal brand of tactfulness.

I'm pretty sure he was expecting me to drill him about all the gory details and side effects that are associated with a mastectomy and follow-up treatments. You know, "How will I look?" "Will I be lopsided, bloated, etc.?" and, of course, "What's going to be with my hair?" All perfectly legitimate questions. After all, nobody ever volunteers for this gig. For better or for worse, I was just not that concerned with all the aesthetic issues. I suppose I had suffered so much physical trauma as a result of my burn that my focus was on getting this nightmare behind me as soon as humanly possible. I had absolutely no interest in getting a second opinion. I left Dr. Olsha's office with my surgery date booked for the 23rd of that month. As I left his office, I told both him and Marvin not to mention to me anything at all about statistics. I was determined to read up and do everything needed from my end to ensure that I would be dancing at my grandchildren's weddings.

So, here I am, only four days after receiving my life-altering diagnosis and I don't have even a moment to spare to contemplate my future. That's because on top of everything else, I am still a caterer and in two days' time I have to prepare a logistically challenging, off-site Sabbath bat mitzvah celebration. There is no time for self-pity, no time to pawn this event onto somebody else; if I am lucky I just might have enough time to pull off some sort of miracle. Already I can see that mine would not be your standard, textbook recovery program. Whether it would be due to surgery, chemotherapy, or radiation treatments, my crazy business demands would ensure that I would be far too busy to attend to every little *kvetch* or side effect. Work, as it turned out, was far from an annoying distraction. It was yet again my saviour, together with an incredible medical, family and friend support system.

I knew right from the outset that I was in good hands with Dr. Olsha as he was no stranger to our family. He had performed two of Marvin's three hernia operations and he was also a customer of La Cuisine (at least I knew he had good taste). Alone with my thoughts the night before my surgery, I actually caught myself thinking how fortunate I was to have suffered my burn accident three years earlier. How absurd a thought is that! I knew that no matter how disfiguring this new surgery could be, at least the pain could never come close to what I had already suffered. Some consolation.

On the day of my surgery, Dr. Olsha dropped by my bedside for a last-minute checkup and brief chat. Marvin, who was also present, slipped him a La Cuisine bag with a couple of Danishes inside. "Just in case you didn't have a chance to grab some lunch, I don't want you operating on Lori on an empty stomach." That image of my surgeon in his surgical greens, happily munching on one of my pastries was the last vivid memory I carried with me as I was wheeled into the operating theatre.

Parting from my family, however, was a whole different story. As we exchanged our "See you later's," everyone — my mother, Marvin, the boys, and myself included — put on our bravest faces. I didn't envy their having to wait out the next couple of hours in one of those solemn, no-nonsense operating waiting rooms. Much to their surprise, the wait was far from a somber affair. Somehow word leaked out about the scheduled time of my surgery and no sooner had I vacated the scene than a troupe of very enthusiastic and upbeat family and friends descended upon the waiting room. "It was like one continuous pep rally," Marvin recounted later. "There was no time for anybody to dwell on any morbid thoughts." Well, good for them, I thought, I am happy to bring people together for a good time.

Sometime later that evening, I was admitted to my ward room and for the next two nights I hosted my own private slumber party. The first night Anna stayed by my side to help with the initial discomfort and nausea that usually accompanies surgery. The following day I was tended to by a rotating group of dedicated friends, anxious to keep my spirits up. Thursday night's vigil belonged to Aviva, who curled up on the floor next to my bed and proceeded to keep me in stitches (the other kind) for most of her watch. Friday morning was the moment of truth. I showered myself, the decisive test for being released, and by the afternoon I was home with my family in time to celebrate the Sabbath. Unbelievable, not even two full days after my surgery and I was out of the hospital. I was never released so quickly after any of my natural childbirths. At least this time around I had no problems sitting without the aid of a cushion.

My chemo was scheduled to begin in a month's time — every other Sunday for sixteen consecutive weeks. A week after my operation I was back in the bakery, without any visible scars to impress anybody this time. Instead, I was sporting two odd and bulky drainpipes from my incision that were sort of camouflaged by a heavy sweatshirt vest. That's me — always ready to spring a new look on my customers.

Here's what I have to say about chemo. First off, I'm no stoic and chemo is definitely not my idea of a good time, but it sure beats the alternative. My oncologist offered me this timely bit of advice before my first session that I have since shared with numerous cancer patients to bolster their spirits. It goes something like this: "Before the chemo, you looked great and healthy but you were actually very, very sick. Now the chemo will make you look and feel very, very sick, but actually, now you're fine." Dozens of times a day during my treatments I repeated my own mantra over and over again: "Chemo is my friend, chemo is my friend…"

Quite the friend — very helpful, but not so hospitable. In addition to experiencing general nausea and frequent stomach upheavals, I proceeded to lose every single hair on my body, eyelashes included, and a couple of finger and toenails. Gross. Thankfully, the one thing I didn't lose was my sense of humour. Believe it or not, laughter truly is the best medicine, or so a number of studies claim. Truthfully, I can't verify how conclusive the scientific evidence is regarding the treatment of cancer. Laughter helps the brain release endorphins, which are a natural painkiller, and they also act against certain stress-related hormones. Imagine that, the Marx Brothers receiving an endorsement from the American Cancer Society! Medical studies notwithstanding, our household quickly amassed a growing collection of classic comedies and films from friends who were only too eager to help make me laugh. As I remember it, Marvin and I spent an awful lot of time that year doubled over from laughter.

Work. More specifically, work in combination with laughter was my preferred method of coping with my latest challenge. And meds, let's not forget all those wonderful meds. I've never been a big fan of needles, but I certainly got over that aversion in a hurry after I was instructed to give myself shots in my thigh every other day to strengthen my immune system. Fortunately, my morale was never in need of strengthening — nothing that a colourful head scarf couldn't handle. That, and meat — lots and lots of meat to build up my supply of vitamin B and protein. Oh yeah, seventeen years of loyal vegetarianism out the window in one fell swoop. Like the saying goes, "One man's joy is another man's sorrow." Ask any of my boys and they will happily confirm that "Every cloud truly has a silver lining."

I don't purport to be some kind of inspirational guru. I don't have the answer to any of the big questions in life. I have a hard enough time just trying to balance my chequebook. People often ask me what my secret is to maintaining an upbeat attitude in the face of such trying setbacks. For starters, it's a good thing I'm not a superstitious person by nature; otherwise, I'd be very hard-pressed to explain why my burn accident happened two months before my son Yehudah's bar mitzvah and my breast cancer was diagnosed two months before my youngest son Netanel's bar mitzvah. But I am not a superstitious person. I am the daughter of Holocaust survivors. I was taught not to waste time wondering about the "whys" in life. What's the point? You can't change them. What I managed to derive from my two serious ordeals was a whole lot of perspective, perspective with a capital P.

Businesses come and businesses go, but health, family, friends, they are for keeps. Such an unexpected outpouring of help and concern from so many different sources — from the closest of friends to the most casual of acquaintances. People phoned or dropped by to share their own experiences or simply to offer some encouragement. There was lots of cooking. At times it seemed as if everyone I ever bumped into was cooking or baking something for my family. If they weren't dropping off food, then they were offering to feed us in their own homes. Apart from sampling a lot of different recipes that year, our family also managed to mark some important milestones. Besides Netanel's bar mitzvah (a very spirited and emotional celebration under the circumstances), we also celebrated our twenty-fifth wedding anniversary and Marvin's fiftieth birthday. In both instances, mind you, we made do without the obligatory surprise parties; Marvin and I were more than content to quietly celebrate my road to recovery minus any fireworks.

Chapter Fifteen

I DID TOY WITH THE IDEA OF DOING A COOKBOOK … MY IDEA WAS TO PUT A FRIED EGG ON THE COVER. I THINK A LOT OF PEOPLE WHO HATE LITERATURE BUT LOVE FRIED EGGS WOULD BUY IT IF THE PRICE WAS RIGHT.

Groucho Marx

Twenty-one years. That's an awful lot of cheesecakes. Actually, it's an awful lot of anything. So many — probably too many — long days and even longer nights, slaving away in the kitchen. The early years of the business were the most tiring, especially Thursdays. Marvin usually worked in the store, alone, until ten p.m. getting everything ready for the Friday morning rush. Me, I would often work by myself in the bakery until late in the evening, finalizing orders and tending to any last-minute baking. I spent a good chunk of that time assuring myself that it was okay to be alone in such a deserted part of town. Not totally alone, mind you. A few dozen metres from our bakery there operated a twenty-four-hour men's "social club," that everyone in the neighbourhood assumed was a front for a gambling casino of questionable legal status. Most of the membership looked like the type of fellas whose wives didn't ask them too many questions. I for one never asked them anything, preferring to be just a good neighbour.

The end of an era.

On those nights that I worked late, I was quite relieved to know that they were there, 24/6, protecting my backside. Not that anything of note ever really happened.

Except for one particular evening, Thursday the 24th of May of 2001. That was the night of the Versailles wedding hall disaster in Jerusalem. The dance floor on the third level of a four-story building collapsed in the midst of a large wedding celebration, causing the worst civilian disaster in Israel's history: twenty-three dead and some three hundred and eighty injured. At the time of the accident I was preparing quiches by myself in the bakery, for yet another upcoming Shavuot holiday (there can never be too many Shavuot stories…). I recall being more on edge than usual about working alone. It was the height of the second intifada, and everyone in Jerusalem was wary of further terrorist attacks.

Shortly after ten-thirty p.m., the evening's silence was shattered by the wailing of sirens. For a brief moment, I felt that my bakery had been plunged into the middle of a war zone. Adding to the confusion was the deafening racket of a number of very low-hovering helicopters with their searchlights trained on the immediate vicinity surrounding my kitchen. My initial reaction was that a bombing had taken place nearby and a fugitive terrorist was on the loose somewhere close at hand. "Close at hand" was far too close for comfort — baking quiches should not be a life-threatening proposition. Panic soon gave way to disbelief and then shock when I discovered the real cause of the night's commotion. The Versailles wedding hall stood a few short blocks from my front door, and as the extent of the tragedy unfolded, I could think of nothing more irrelevant for me to do than to hang around and bake some more quiches.

Fortunately, most days at La Cuisine passed by rather uneventfully — hectic, for sure, but nothing headline-grabbing, and that was just fine with me. I'm sure if I hadn't decided to call it quits in the fall of 2012, I'd still be doing the same old same old — churning out the same quiches and the same cheesecakes that I began preparing back in my own home twenty-odd years ago.

Evidently that was not in the cards. I knew in my heart (and in my shoulder, and especially in my feet) that the time had come for me to hang up my apron. There was no gas left in the tank, and I so dreaded the prospect of dealing with another cycle of holiday baking. That's not a good place to be. You should never try to pull a fast one on your loyal customers. They can recognize immediately when you are simply going through the motions because the food never lies. If I am proud of any of my accomplishments as a baker, it would probably come down to my obsession with consistency. Few things gave me greater professional satisfaction than hearing from a customer that the cake they had just purchased still tasted as great as it did the first time they had sampled it years ago.

My recipes may have stood the test of time, but I personally underwent a few serious transformations along the way. The naïve, innocent novice who began it all in her home eventually gave way to the seasoned, slightly jaded entrepreneur in the twilight of her career. When I decided to put some of my memories to paper, it occurred me that I would be hard pressed to acknowledge the contributions of so many players who have accompanied me on my journey. Some undoubtedly will question my tendency to ramble on about certain details (because that's what I do best) while others will criticize me for leaving out so many important people and events ("So why am I not mentioned?"). In all fairness, I never set out to write my autobiography — hopefully there are a lot more unfinished chapters ahead of me to fill. Apart from being a cheap form of therapy, I hoped, more than anything else, to draw a few insights into this significant period in my life that I could never have predicted would unfold as it did.

Of course, I could never have accomplished a fraction of what I managed to do by myself. As any business maven will attest, "You are only as good as the people you surround yourself with," and I have been surrounded by a whole slew of first-rate supporters. When I hired my first baker, Yohanan, way back when, I asked myself, "Do I know what the heck I'm doing?" because I had no idea how I could afford to keep him on staff. Years later when he left us I asked myself again, "Do I know what the heck I'm doing?" only then I couldn't imagine how we would manage without him in the kitchen. But we did. I discovered, somewhat late in the game, that one way to preserve one's sanity in business is to share one's headaches with another willing player — in my case, I decided to bring in a partner.

Why a partner when I already had Marvin? The short answer is that both of us were so caught up in the daily grind that neither of us gave the necessary attention that is required to run a growing business. Truth be told, the business part of the business was never our strong suit. Marvin and I were pretty good at writing and cashing cheques, but understanding spreadsheets and the concept of diminishing marginal returns was a whole other ballgame.

I decided my new replacement for Yohanan would have to be as equally adept with his head as he was with his hands. Moreover, he would have to be willing to share the risks that Marvin and I had been shouldering alone until this point. Fortuitously, our search began and ended in our own kitchen. Our new Yohanan's name was Meir, who was working part-time in the bakery and was only too eager to fill the void left with the departure of his mentor. Only Meir was not interested in coming on board as a full-time employee. He was young and ambitious and wanted to be on equal footing with Marvin and myself. What the heck, I figured, there's plenty of responsibilities and debt to be shared all around. I was only too willing to relieve myself of much of the bureaucratic burden so I could concentrate on what I did best. Bottom line, Meir was an experienced combat officer and, at the very least, he'd whip everybody into shape. And he did, for close to five years.

One thing for sure, the time spent together with Meir was anything but dull. Without question our business expanded during his tenure. Our kitchen space doubled in size, our storefront and office moved next door to much more spacious quarters, and our main retail outlet in the centre of town moved up the street to a site almost double in size. Meir also had the dubious honour of being around when I suffered my two major medical setbacks. At the end of the day, however, the bottom line never matched everyone's expectations. We parted ways as dear friends and continue to share recipes with each other to this day.

I've never been one to shy away from a good challenge. Meir's departure meant either bringing in a new partner or trying once again to go it alone. Marvin and I opted to give it the old college try, and for the next four years we did what we do best — work ourselves ragged while managing to tread water. Our accountant kept assuring us we were on the verge of turning things around; to what, I have no idea. Whatever it was, it was one long and elusive verge. I was definitely not in the market for a new partner until my accountant suggested Avidov, a longtime acquaintance who also ran his own catering operation. This was a promising opportunity for all of us to move up to the big leagues. I'm not quite sure in what league we ended up, but we had ourselves some real good times working with Avidov, and as a bonus he brought La Cuisine into the computer age. Young, energetic, creative, Avidov is the consummate entrepreneur, zipping about town on his trademark scooter. If only Marvin and I had been twenty years younger when we hooked up with him, then maybe we would have been able to keep up with his high energy level. As things were, we were in no shape to go another round. Better to "leave 'em laughing" I say, than to hang on like a star athlete past his prime. Bittersweet though it was to say goodbye, a major consolation for me was knowing that when I handed over the reins of La Cuisine to Avidov I was leaving my "baby" in very capable hands.

Did I really write "baby" to describe my business? You're darn right I did. I have no qualms about using a clichéd metaphor to drive home an important point. Like any good parent, I nurtured that baby all through its conception and cradled it through its infancy while trying valiantly to tame it during its rebellious teens only to have the good common sense to leave it to fend for itself when it reached maturity. I harbour no regrets whatsoever. I took a chance on a long shot, and it was what it was. Would I have preferred an easier way to make a living? Yes. Seeing that I didn't marry into or inherit a bundle, I at least tried to make my odyssey as interesting as possible. I offer no neat, tidy summary because this is still a work in progress. So, if you must know if "Is it really fresh?" I can only promise you that it's about as fresh as it's going to be … for now.

pastry is called theused a
little bit differently than
do it's better for use

DANISH
4x recipe   (for

Gazpacho
½ English cucumber - sliced thick
about ½ big green pepper - sliced
1 small onion - sliced
1 clove of garlic
1 tablespoon oil
2 (maybe 3) table
salt

3 c. fresh lemn
½ onion
3/4 tsp. curry   - pan
½ tsp. salt   add ¼
¼ tsp. pepper   - crea
1½ tbsp. flour   - hot
½ c. stock
2 tbsp. butter

Cheese Stratta
12-14 slices of white ready sliced bread cut
Tossiinto : 3 TABLE   marg.   Arrange ½
greased pan. 1 cup   ese.
Arrange anoth   put on top
cheder cheese 350 ml.
Beat to   1½ c 600 ml.
           water   Rice
2 tsp.

Curried

Before You Bake or Cook

La Cuisine meant different things to so many different people. For some, we were their preferred address to satisfy their sweet tooth; for others, we tended to their catering needs for family celebrations or special events. There were even those who depended upon us for all of the above and more…

Hopefully, this book conveys the very essence of what made La Cuisine so special. With that purpose in mind, I designed this cookbook to reflect the two faces of our enterprise - our bakery and our catering company. These are the recipes that we produced day in and day out both to stock our bakeshops and to fill our catering orders. I've done my best to adapt what were essentially commercial recipes to a format that is manageable for home use.

Please bear in mind that this is not a general, all-purpose cookbook, nor is it a collection of my *greatest hits* - some of my personal favourites did not make the final cut because they were not a part of the La Cuisine repertoire. This book is also not a training manual for the kitchen novice, although many of the recipes are quite easy to follow. Where more skill is demanded, I have tried to simplify the techniques as much as possible.

What this book is, however, is a kosher cookbook. Granted, kosher baking has its limitations, but that should not prevent anyone who enjoys a decent croissant from giving these recipes a whirl. Non-dairy baking (a kashrut requirement for desserts eaten after a meat meal) can be particularly challenging for the baker who prefers to limit the use of margarine. At La Cuisine we expended a lot of time and energy in trying to upgrade our non-dairy baking. The secret can be summed up in one word: ingredients. We relied, as I suggest you do in your own kitchen, on the best, most natural products that we could hunt down: premium imported chocolate and cocoa, the most fragrant, intense vanilla and flavourings, fresh nuts, freshly grated and juiced lemons, and the ripest, seasonal fruits.

Many cookbooks go to great lengths listing and explaining all kinds of equipment and ingredients. I've kept mine simple and to the point - I'm going to assume that most of you know what butter is and what is meant by mixing bowls and a microwave. What I have outlined are a few essential pointers that you should keep in mind when tackling these recipes.

MEASUREMENTS:

Here in Israel, as in much of the world, the system of measurement is the metric system. We use grams for weight, litres for volume, and metres for length. My American readers, on the other hand, still use measurements based on cups and quarts, ounces and pounds, and inches and yards. It wasn't easy, but I wrote all my recipes for this book in dual measurements, in what, I hope, is a clear and understandable format. The U.S. measures do not always equate exactly to standard metric measures; therefore, sometimes I had to round off amounts, and some of the conversions may sound a bit odd to the reader.

EQUIPMENT:

Mixer:

I am aware that not everyone has a stand mixer in their home, but for some of these bakery recipes you simply won't be able to manage without one. For example, a hand-held mixer just does not have enough power to get the proper volume and stiffness out of beaten egg whites. Without properly beaten egg whites, you will be unable to make a foolproof meringue, nor will you be able to fold them into any stiff batter.

Pastry Brushes:

Always keep a few of these on hand, especially ones made of the new silicone material. Gone are the days when an unsuspecting guest might discover a dislodged hair from a pastry brush resting comfortably in the glaze of his fruit tart.

Rubber Spatulas:

The more the merrier - they will make your cooking and baking life infinitely easier. Store up on all sizes - from the smallest and narrowest to the very largest you can get your hands on. The smaller sizes are great for scraping just about everything from little spaces, while the bigger ones are indispensible for folding large amounts of egg whites and creams. The ones made of the new silicone material have the added bonus of being heatproof.

Scales:

I'm a strong believer in weighing ingredients, especially when it comes to baking. Not only is it easy, but it is by far the most accurate form of measurement in the kitchen. Need convincing? Try measuring a "cup" of flour without the benefit of a scale. A cup of flour should weigh about 140 g (5 ounces). Did you dip and sweep? Did you even the top of the cup with your finger? Or maybe with a knife? Was the flour sifted? Did you possibly bang the container a few times on the table before measuring? Weigh your "cup" after each of the methods just mentioned, and you will discover a significant difference in the weight measurements of your "cup" of flour. Such discrepancies are unacceptable in baking, and could possibly make a big difference in your finished product.

There are all sorts of digital, small, relatively inexpensive kitchen scales available these days. Make sure you buy one that balances to zero (tare) in between every weight. That way you can conveniently put your mixing bowl on the scale and add your ingredients one at a time, balancing out to zero after each item is added.

Whisks:

They come in various sizes and I recommend you stock up on them. I have tiny ones to whisk one egg yolk in a small cup, and large ones for whipping big bowls of meringue that are heating over a large pot, and pretty much every size in between.

INGREDIENTS:

Brown Sugar:

In my recipes I do not specify dark or light brown sugar because both kinds are equally suitable. Personally, I prefer the darker sugar because I love the strong aroma and flavour of molasses, so that's what we used in all La Cuisine recipes.

Chocolate:

In our kitchens we used bittersweet Belgian chocolate, 54-56% cocoa solids, either Callebaut or Fruibel. In these recipes there is no need to use chocolate with a higher percentage of cocoa solids; in fact, doing so may adversely affect the outcome of your baking. We also used Belgian white and milk chocolate, but my rule of thumb is to use any quality chocolate that you like to eat.

Cocoa:

Our brand of choice was De Zaan with 20-22% fat content, a dark, rich, intensely chocolaty-smelling cocoa.

Cream:

In the recipes I use the term "heavy cream" to signify dairy heavy whipping cream of at least 38% fat. For the non-dairy substitute, I refer to it as "non-dairy heavy whipping cream."

Eggs:

All eggs in the recipes are size large (unless indicated otherwise). Large means that the whole egg out of the shell weighs about 55 g (2 ounces), the white alone weighs 32 g (1.1 ounces), and the yolk alone weighs 22 g (.8 ounces).

About the use of raw eggs: in the bakery the health department would not allow us to use raw eggs in any food which was not going to be heated enough to kill any possible salmonella bacteria. We used industrial containers of pasteurized whole eggs, egg yolks, and egg whites in all our mousses or uncooked creams and fillings. If salmonella is a concern where you live, check with your local Egg Board for information and direction about food safety and proper usage. If you're in doubt, better safe than sorry, and just skip the recipes that contain raw eggs if you can't get your hands on the pasteurized kind.

Flour:

When I studied at pastry school in France, we used no less than five different grades of flour in various combinations for different baked goods. At La Cuisine we used only one basic, standard type of white flour, which was a combination of soft pastry and all-purpose flours. It works fine with all the recipes in this book.

Lemons:

The tinny flavour of bottled lemon juice just doesn't cut it for your carefully, lovingly prepared baked goods and salads. When you can afford the time, grate fresh lemon rind in bulk and then store it in the freezer in a closed container, ready to use whenever you need some. Trust me, there is no substitute for freshly squeezed lemon juice.

Oil:

My oil of preference for all baking or cooking that does not call for olive oil is canola oil. It has a light flavour and it has a higher smoking point than most other commonly used oils.

Vanilla:

Vanilla extract, although usually added to baked goods in tiny amounts, is very important for the aroma it imbues in your recipe. The quality of vanilla greatly influences your finished product; therefore, it is crucial to invest wisely in the kind of vanilla you use. We went to great lengths at La Cuisine to acquire good quality vanilla (see Chapter Nine of the Tales) until we learned to make it ourselves. Please check out my easy and economical recipe for homemade vanilla extract (pg 156). Otherwise, just buy the best you can find.

Mis En Place – The prep work is in place.
Now you can roll up your sleeves
and start cooking and baking.

CLASSIC CHEESECAKE

dairy

Although I'm Canadian by birth, I've been told countless times by my American customers that this cake is a classic New York-style cheesecake. Whatever its nationality, it was the all-time best-selling dessert on our menu - La Cuisine's signature creation. Rich, dense, creamy, this cake has been frozen and packed in many a customer's suitcase for an overseas flight. I lost count a long time ago as to how many I've baked – rare was the catered event at which it was not featured.

The caramel topping was by far and away the most popular flavour, but I strongly advise trying all of them. You won't regret the calories.

Makes one 24 cm (9 inch) cake
■ 24 cm (9 inch) spring form pan, lined with baking paper for easy removal of the cake later, and aluminum foil wrapped around the bottom of the pan so the butter doesn't leak out into your oven

PREHEAT THE OVEN TO 180°C (350°F).

CRUST:

Mix all the ingredients together in a small bowl and then press the crumbs into the bottom and a little bit up the sides of the pan.

CRUST:

165 g (1½ cups) Petit-Beurre or Marie biscuit crumbs

50 g (¼ cup) brown sugar

80 g (2½ ounces) butter, melted

FILLING:

900 g (32 ounces) 30% cream cheese

300 g (1½ cups) sugar

5 eggs

10 g (2½ teaspoons) vanilla

8 g (2 teaspoons) freshly squeezed lemon juice

TOPPING:

2/3 cup of any one of these toppings:

caramel sauce (pg 153)

lemon curd (pg 150)

forest fruit sauce (pg 152)

DECORATION:

120 ml (½ cup) heavy cream

1 tablespoon sugar

non-dairy

FILLING:

Beat the cream cheese in a mixer with the paddle until it's smooth. Add the sugar and beat the mixture until it's smooth and you don't see any granules of sugar. Slowly beat in the eggs, scraping down the sides of the bowl with a rubber spatula once or twice. Beat in the vanilla and the lemon juice. Scrape the bowl once more with the rubber spatula, making sure no plain cream cheese gets left unmixed on the bottom or the sides of the bowl. The mixture should be smooth with no lumps.

Gently pour the mixture into the crust that's in the pan - make sure you don't disturb the crumb crust.

Bake the cake for about 60 minutes, until the top is golden and puffy and just barely jiggling.

Let it cool. After about half an hour, the cake will have fallen back down and become nice and flat. At this point, cut the cake around the sides with a regular kitchen knife, loosening it from the outside ring. Do not take it out of the pan. Let it cool completely and then refrigerate it overnight while still in the pan.

TOPPING:

Spread the topping on the top of the cake.

DECORATION:

Remove cake from the pan.

Whip the cream and sugar in a mixer until stiff peaks form. Scrape the cream into a piping bag with a star tip.

Decorate the top outer edge of the cake with rosettes of whipped cream. This masks the uneven parts of the cake.

TOFU CHEESECAKE

One of our bakery's most original cakes. It was the flip side to our other flagship dessert, the classic dairy cheesecake (pg 75). I spent months trying to get this recipe just right. I tried every single type of tofu on the market, as well as every brand of processed tofu spread I could lay my hands on, but the only one that worked for me was the registered trademark Tofutti® spread. Nine out of ten of our customers were convinced they were eating the real thing when they sampled this cake for the first time.

Here in Israel, Tofutti® is an imported product which pretty much insures that its supply is erratic at the best of times. Often before a major holiday when we could expect an increase in orders of this cake, our importer would be out of stock, or his shipment would be held up in the port awaiting its release from the customs authority. Suffice it to say, on these occasions I would have a lot of very upset customers.

Over the years, I tried all different kinds of flavours for a tofu-based cheesecake, from chocolate to coffee to halva, but only lemon or mixed berry worked - the others were too heavy and dense and I could always taste the tofu.

Makes one 24 cm (9 inch) cheesecake

■ One 24 cm (9 inch) spring form pan, lined with baking paper for easy removal of the cake later.

PREHEAT THE OVEN TO 180°C (350°F).

CRUST:

Mix all the ingredients together, and then press the crumbs into the bottom and a little bit up the sides of the pan.

FILLING:

Beat the Tofutti® cream cheese and sugar in a mixer with the paddle until smooth. Slowly add the eggs, vanilla, and lemon juice. Scrape down the sides once with a rubber spatula and mix again until it's smooth.

Pour and lightly spread about 240 ml (1 cup) lemon curd onto the bottom of the prepared crust. Gently and carefully pour in the cheese mixture.

Bake the cake for about 50-55 minutes, until it's puffy, lightly golden, and a little bit wobbly.

When the cake cools and sinks back down, loosen it from the pan by cutting around the inside of the ring with a sharp knife, but leave the ring on. Refrigerate it overnight, and then remove the outer ring. Lift the cheesecake off of the bottom by pulling on the baking paper. Carefully pull off the paper.

LEMON CURD:
One batch non-dairy lemon curd (pg 150)

CRUST:
180 g (1½ cups) Petit-Beurre or Marie biscuit crumbs

50g (¼ cup) brown sugar

85 g (3 ounces) butter-flavoured margarine, melted

FILLING:
900 g (32 ounces) Tofutti® spread, in plain cream cheese flavour

300 g (1½ cups) sugar

5 eggs

10 g (2½ teaspoons) vanilla

8 g (2 teaspoons) fresh squeezed lemon juice

About 240 ml lemon curd (1 cup)

120 g (4 ounces) lemon curd

1 tablespoon warm water

1-2 tablespoons non-dairy heavy whipping cream, unwhipped

DECORATION (OPTIONAL):
Mix the lemon curd with a tablespoon or two of warm water and pour it on top of the cooled cake, letting it run evenly almost to the outer edges.

Pour the unwhipped cream into a pastry bag, cut off a bit of the tip with scissors, and zigzag a design onto the lemon curd, pulling in to various designs with a toothpick or tip of a sharp knife.

Variation: Instead of 240 ml (1 cup) lemon curd in the filling part of the recipe, pour and lightly spread 240 ml (1 cup) of forest fruit sauce (recipe pg 152) onto the bottom of the prepared crust, and gently and carefully pour in the cheese mixture. After the cheesecake has baked and chilled in the fridge, you can decorate the top with about 240 ml (1 cup) mixed berry sauce instead of the 120 g (4 ounces) lemon curd.

dairy

One 24 cm (9 inch) La Cuisine tart crust recipe (pg 142), but made according to the following directions:

CRUMB CHEESECAKE

Cheesecake made with gelatin - are you kidding me? That was my first reaction when I moved to Israel and discovered that this was the country's most popular way to make cheesecake. Light, fluffy, unbaked - I couldn't even bring myself to sample some. When I finally gave in, I had to admit that I had wasted a lot of time being so stubborn. There is definitely room for this lovely, delicate creation next to a cup of tea.

Makes one 24 cm (9 inch) cake
■ 24 cm (9 inch) spring form pan lined with baking paper for easier removal later.

PREHEAT THE OVEN TO 180°C (350°F).

TART CRUST DIRECTIONS: Roll out the La Cuisine tart crust according to the directions in the basic recipe. However, here you are going to use the bottom of a closed 24 cm (9 inch) spring form pan as the guideline. Cut out a circle the size of the pan from the rolled out dough. Pick up the circle of dough with a large flat spatula or roll it up carefully over the rolling pin and lay it down into the closed pan. Lay down the remaining rolled out scraps of tart dough on a baking sheet lined with baking paper and also put the pan on the sheet.

Bake for about 15-20 minutes or until the pastry is fully baked and golden brown. Set aside the spring form pan with the baked pastry bottom in it to cool.

Grind the baked pastry scraps into crumbs in a food processor. Set them aside.

FILLING:

Have ready two stainless steel mixing bowls, one large and one even larger. Fill the largest mixing bowl with a handful of ice cubes and 2-3 cups of tap water. Set it aside.

Pour 100 ml (⅓ cup plus 2 tablespoons) water into a small heatproof glass bowl. Sprinkle the gelatin into the water and let it soften for 5 minutes.

Heat the mixture for 30 seconds at a time in the microwave, whisking it after each time until the gelatin is completely dissolved. Check with your fingers to make sure no grains are left. Whisk in the milk.

Transfer the mixture to the large, empty stainless steel mixing bowl and whisk in the cream cheese, egg yolks, lemon rind, and lemon juice. Place the bowl into the ice-filled larger bowl to chill it quickly. Whisk it every few minutes until the mixture begins to thicken.

Beat the heavy cream with the powdered sugar in a mixer until stiff peaks form. Fold it into the gelatin mixture.

Pour the entire mixture into the cooled spring form pan and freeze it for at least 2 hours.

Take the cake out of the freezer.

Sprinkle the top of the cake with the ground tart pastry crumbs to generously cover the cheese filling.

Store the cake in the fridge until serving time.

Variation: You can also cover this unbaked cheesecake with forest fruit sauce (pg 152) instead of crumbs.

*Note: There is a kashrut issue with gelatin. Many people do not wish to use gelatin that comes from the stomach lining of a cow. Fish gelatin is a relatively new product and is what we used in La Cuisine's two products that used gelatin. It works a bit differently than regular gelatin - it's more granular, and you really have to make sure the grains totally melt in your mixture.

FILLING:

100 ml (⅓ cup plus 2 tablespoons) water

20 g (2 tablespoons) fish gelatin*

240 ml (1 cup) milk

500 g (18 ounces) 9% cream cheese

2 egg yolks

3 grams (2 heaping tablespoons) lemon rind

8 g (2 teaspoons) freshly squeezed lemon juice

500 g (18 ounces) heavy cream

210 grams (1¾ cups) powdered sugar

CHOCOLATE ESPRESSO CHEESECAKE

dairy

Not every cheesecake that came out of my bakery had caramel topping, it just seemed that way. Cheesecake, chocolate, and espresso - what more could one ask for in a dessert?

Makes one 24 cm (9 inch) cake

▪ 24 cm (9 inch) spring form pan, lined with parchment paper for easy removal of the cake later, and aluminum foil wrapped around the bottom of the pan so the butter doesn't leak out into your oven.

CRUST:

Mix all the ingredients together, and then press the crumbs into the bottom and a little bit up the sides of the prepared pan.

PREHEAT THE OVEN TO 180°C (350°F).

CRUST:

130 g (1¼ cups) Petit-Beurre or Marie biscuit crumbs

15 g (2 tablespoons) cocoa

3 g (2 teaspoons) instant espresso granules

85 g (3 ounces) butter, melted

FILLING:

900 g (32 ounces) 30% cream cheese

250 g (1¼ cups) sugar

60 ml (¼ cup) coffee liqueur

15 g (3 tablespoons) instant espresso coffee granules

12 g (1 tablespoon) vanilla

4 eggs

170 g (6 ounces) chocolate, chopped

CHOCOLATE GLAZE:

160 g (5½ ounces) chocolate, chopped

180 ml (¾ cup) heavy cream

14 g (1 tablespoon) sugar

7 g (1 teaspoon) corn syrup or glucose (adds elasticity to the glaze and prevents it from cracking; may be omitted)

DECORATION:

120 ml (½ cup) heavy cream

15 g (1 tablespoon) sugar

FILLING:

Beat the cream cheese in a mixer with the paddle until it's smooth.

Heat the coffee liqueur and espresso coffee granules in a small glass heatproof measuring cup in the microwave for 30-40 seconds and then stir it until it's smooth. Add the vanilla. Add it to the cream cheese mixture while you're beating it. Add the sugar and beat the mixture until it's smooth and you don't see any granules of sugar. Beat in the eggs slowly, scraping down the sides of the bowl with a rubber spatula once or twice. Make sure no plain cream cheese gets left unmixed on the bottom or the sides of the bowl. The mixture should be smooth with no lumps.

Gently pour *ONLY HALF* the mixture into the crust that's in the pan - make sure you don't disturb the crumb crust.

Bake the cake (it is only half full at this point) for 25 minutes.

While it's baking, melt the chocolate in a small glass heatproof bowl in the microwave for 2 minutes at half power. Stir it with a heatproof spatula or a whisk until it's smooth. If it's still lumpy, return it for 20-second increments to the microwave at half power, and stir it every time until it's smooth.

Stir the chocolate mixture into the remaining half of the cheesecake batter.

Take the pan out of the oven, and carefully pour the remaining half of the batter over the half-baked cake. Return it to the oven.

Continue to bake it for about 20-30 more minutes, until the top is golden and puffy and just barely jiggling.

Let it cool. After about a half hour, the cake will have fallen back down and become nice and flat. At this point, cut the cake around the sides with a regular kitchen knife, loosening it from the outside ring but leaving the ring on. Let it cool completely, and then refrigerate it for 6-8 hours or overnight.

CHOCOLATE GLAZE:

Heat all the ingredients together in a glass heatproof bowl in the microwave for 5 minutes at half power. Mix it until it's smooth.

Let it cool at room temperature for about 20 minutes, and then pour it over the top of the cheesecake. Refrigerate it until the glaze is set, at least half an hour, and then carefully remove the ring.

DECORATION:

Whip the cream with the sugar to form stiff peaks.

Scrape the whipped cream into a piping bag fitted with a star tip and decorate the top outer edge of the cake with rosettes of whipped cream. This masks the uneven parts of the cake.

If you really want to go over the top with your decoration, melt 50g (2 ounces) of chocolate in a very small glass heatproof bowl in the microwave at half power, and drizzle it decoratively with a fork all over the top of the cheesecake, both over the glaze and over the whipped cream rosettes.

LEMON AND WHITE CHOCOLATE CAKE

dairy

This eye-catching, best-selling cake was one that we served at just about every catering event that had desserts, right behind the caramel cheesecake in popularity. I've included some step-by-step photographs below, just to show you how easy it really is to put together. The bottom edges come out a bit uneven so that's why I decorate it with chopped nuts - you can use any kind of nut, we usually used chopped pistachios because I liked the colour contrast of the yellow with the green. Read through all the directions first so you'll know how to proceed with enough time for all the parts to chill.

Makes one 24 cm (9 inch) diameter, bowl-shaped cake
- 30 cm x 40 cm (12 inch x 17 inch) pan lined with baking paper.

LEMON FILLING:

Bring the sugar, lemon juice, butter, and lemon rind to a boil in a small saucepan.

Whisk the 2 eggs with the 3 egg yolks in a medium-size bowl.

When the butter is entirely melted in the saucepan, pour the mixture into the eggs while whisking (get someone to help you if you feel you're not coordinated enough) and then pour the mixture back into the saucepan.

Bring the mixture back to a simmer while whisking. When bubbles start to break the surface and the filling thickens slightly, pour it out through a sieve into a clean bowl.

Chill the filling. This can be prepared the day before you put the cake together.

CAKE:

PREHEAT THE OVEN TO 200°C (400°F).

Whisk the sugar, eggs, and egg yolks in a mixer on high, until it is very thick and creamy.

LEMON FILLING:

115 g (generous ½ cup) sugar

120 ml (½ cup) freshly squeezed lemon juice

113 g (4 ounces) butter

1 tablespoon lemon rind

2 eggs

3 egg yolks

CAKE:

160 g (¾ cup) sugar

3 eggs

4 egg yolks

140 g (1 cup) flour

4 g (1 teaspoon) baking powder

50 ml (¼ cup) milk

28 g (1 ounce) butter

White Chocolate Filling:

255 g (9 ounces) white chocolate

60 ml (¼ cup) freshly squeezed lemon juice

20 ml (1 tablespoon) water

360 ml (1½ cups) heavy cream

Decoration:

About 120 ml (½ cup) of best quality apricot jam

About 25 g (1 ounce) chopped nuts

Sift the flour and baking powder, half at a time, into the egg mixture, folding very gently but thoroughly.

Heat the milk and butter in a heatproof glass measuring cup in the microwave until the butter is melted. Pour it into the mixture. Fold it all together gently but thoroughly. Pour it into the baking pan. Smooth it gently, preferably with a long metal spatula.

Bake the cake for about 10 minutes until it's golden.

When the cake is cool, turn it over onto another sheet of baking paper. Carefully peel off the paper that is now on top, and turn the cake back over onto the first sheet of paper. It should now be right side up again.

Spread the cooled lemon filling on the cake.

Using the baking paper as a guide, roll the cake up tightly. Wrap it tightly closed with the baking paper that it's on, and freeze it for a few hours or overnight so it's easier to slice.

Remove the cake from the freezer.

Line a metal or plastic mixing bowl that can hold 1½ litres of liquid (6 cups) with a generous piece of plastic wrap so that a lot of the wrap hangs out over the edge (you'll use that extra bit later on to cover the cake).

Slice the roll of lemon-filled cake into about 1 cm (scant ½ inch) slices. Use the nicest slices to line the plastic-lined bowl tightly, leaving aside 8 slices. They will later go on the very top of the cake (which really will end up being its bottom). Chop up any remaining cake into cubes and set them aside. Now make the white chocolate filling.

White Chocolate Filling:

Only make this filling once your bowl is lined with cake and ready to fill - this filling waits for no one!

Melt the white chocolate, lemon juice, and water in a glass heatproof bowl in the microwave at half power for 4 minutes. Stir it until all the chocolate is smooth and melted, returning it to the microwave for 10 seconds at a time if needed. Let it cool until it's just barely warm but still runny.

Whip the heavy cream in a mixer until soft peaks form, and then fold it together with the chocolate mixture. Pour it straight into the cake-lined bowl.

Sprinkle on any remaining cubed chunks of cake, and then arrange the last 8 slices of cake on the top (which will later become the bottom). Fold the rest of the extra plastic wrap over the cake and press down tightly to even out the filled cake.

Freeze the cake until it's firm enough to take it out of the bowl, at least 4 hours.

Decoration:

Take the cake out of the freezer. Gently take the cake out of the bowl by pulling on the plastic wrap. Lay the cake right side up, the flat side on the bottom, on a serving platter and remove the plastic wrap.

Heat the jam in a glass heatproof bowl in a microwave for about 40 seconds, until it's melted.

Brush the melted jam all over the surface of the cake with a pastry brush, paying special attention to the uneven bottom edge of the cake.

This will keep the cake moist as well as give it a warm glow. Make sure to get some jam into all the crevices so the chopped nuts will be able to stick.

Press the nuts into the very bottom edge of the cake all the way around to decorate the uneven edges.

> Note: Make sure you don't serve this cake while the inside is still frozen; take it out of the freezer to thaw in the fridge the day before serving (the best option), or else take it out to stand at room temperature for an hour or two.

CHOCOLATE SYMPHONY CAKE

dairy

This easy, dense chocolate cake was introduced to La Cuisine by our part-time baker, Rachel, who loved to serve it ungarnished for her children when they were young. In the bakery, we decided to make it adult-friendly by adding the two ganaches, a sprinkling of crushed raspberries to cut the sweetness of the white chocolate filling, and a wonderful glaze. This was the "go to" chocolate cake for many of our customers who were looking for a chocolaty celebration cake that would appeal to kids and adults alike.

> Note: Start this cake at least two days before you plan to serve it - three days is even better!

Make the ganaches and bake the cake on day 1. Plan the assembly of the cake for day 2, and serve it on day 3. It tastes best if you can wait that extra day.

Makes one 24 cm (9 inch) cake

■ 24 cm (9 inch) spring form pan, lined with parchment paper for easy removal of the cake later.

CAKE:

240 g (8½ ounces) sugar

190 ml (¾ cup) milk

85 g (3 ounces) chocolate

28 g (1 ounce, or 4 tablespoons) cocoa

160 g (5½ ounces) butter

4 eggs, separated

4 g (1 teaspoon) vanilla

170 g (6 ounces) flour

8 g (2 teaspoons) baking powder

MILK CHOCOLATE GANACHE:

200 g (7 ounces) heavy cream

200 g (7 ounces) milk chocolate

WHITE CHOCOLATE GANACHE:

200 g (7 ounces) heavy cream

200 g (7 ounces) white chocolate

ASSEMBLY: (DAY 2)

190 ml (¾ cup) soaking syrup (pg 151)

120 g (1¼ cups) crushed raspberries

CAKE:

PREHEAT THE OVEN TO 180°C (350°F).

Heat half the sugar, and all of the milk, chocolate, and cocoa in a small saucepan until the chocolate is melted. Whisk the mixture, add the butter, and whisk it again until it's smooth.

Let the mixture cool.

Add the egg yolks and the vanilla to the cooled mixture and stir it well.

Whip the egg whites with a mixer until soft peaks form and then add the other half of the sugar. Continue beating until the peaks are stiff but not dry.

Fold half of the beaten egg whites into the chocolate mixture to lighten it, then add the flour and the rest of the egg whites and fold it all together gently but thoroughly.

Pour it into the pan and bake for 35-40 minutes. Allow the cake to cool on a rack, then refrigerate it for 6-8 hours or overnight.

MILK CHOCOLATE GANACHE:

Put the cream and the chocolate in a heatproof glass bowl or measuring cup and microwave it for five minutes at half power. Take it out and whisk it until it's smooth. If it's still lumpy, return it to the microwave for 20 more seconds at a time at half power and then whisk it until it's smooth.

Refrigerate the ganache for 6-8 hours or overnight.

WHITE CHOCOLATE GANACHE:

Put the cream and the chocolate in a heatproof glass bowl or measuring cup and microwave it for five minutes at half power. Take it out and whisk it until it's smooth. If it's still lumpy, return it to the microwave for 20 more seconds at a time at half power and then whisk it until it's smooth.

Refrigerate the ganache for 6-8 hours or overnight.

ASSEMBLY: (DAY 2)

Cut the cake around the outer edge with a knife to loosen it from the spring form ring, and remove the ring. Turn the cake out onto a cutting board and put the spring form pan back together with the baking paper again lining the bottom. Cut the cake crosswise into 3 even layers.

Place what was the top layer of the cake upside down into the bottom of the pan. Brush the layer with one third of the syrup, making sure to moisten the cake all the way to the edges.

Beat the white chocolate ganache with an electric mixer and the paddle until it's thick and stiff. Spread it on top of the first layer of cake and then sprinkle it with the crushed raspberries.

Now add the next layer of the cake. Brush it with half of the remaining syrup, again making sure to go all the way to the edges.

Beat the milk chocolate ganache in the same mixer bowl you used before, until it's thick and stiff.

Set aside 4 tablespoons of the beaten milk chocolate ganache for decorating the outside of the finished cake. Spread the remaining milk chocolate ganache on the second layer in the cake ring.

Place the last layer bottom side up on top of the milk chocolate layer. Brush it with the remaining one third of the syrup, all the way to the edges.

GLAZE:

Heat all the ingredients - the cream, chocolate, and glucose - together in a glass heatproof bowl in the microwave for 5 minutes at half power. Mix it until it's smooth. Pour it on top of the cake.

Freeze the cake for at least 3 hours - it makes it easier to pick up and decorate.

The following can be done either at the end of day 2 prior to serving or on day 3:

Remove the cake from the freezer and cut around the outer edge with a knife to loosen it from the spring form ring; remove the ring. Lift the cake off with the parchment paper, and set it down on a plate.

Take the remaining 4 tablespoons of the beaten milk chocolate ganache and spread it with a knife around the outside of the finished cake.

DECORATION:

Press the chocolate sprinkles into the entire outside of the cake with your hands.

If you like, you can also sprinkle the top of the glaze with some cocoa.

Let the cake rest at room temperature for at least a half hour before serving it.

GLAZE:
90 g (3 ounces) heavy cream
60 g (2 ounces) chocolate
25 g (1 ounce) glucose

DECORATION:
90 g (½ cup) chocolate sprinkles
Cocoa (optional)

CHOCOLATE MOUSSE CAKE

non-dairy

Hands down our most popular, best-selling non-dairy cake. The base is a baked chocolate mousse topped with a rich, creamy chocolate mousse. In the bakery we wrapped the cake in a thin layer of marzipan and then coated it with a shiny chocolate glaze.

There is no flour in this recipe, so it can be easily adapted for Passover enjoyment.

Makes one 24 cm (9 inch) cake

■ 24 cm (9 inch) spring form pan, lined with parchment paper for easy removal of the cake later. You can also bake it directly into a foil pan to make it less fancy or more portable.

BAKED CAKE BASE:

PREHEAT THE OVEN TO 180°C (350°F).

Heat the chocolate, vanilla, instant coffee, and boiling water together in a heatproof glass bowl in the microwave for 3 minutes at half power. Stir until it's smooth and the chocolate is fully melted. If you need to, you can microwave it a bit more, 30 seconds at a time at half power.

BAKED CAKE BASE:
150 g (5½ ounces) chocolate, chopped
2 g (½ teaspoon) vanilla
2 g (4 teaspoons) instant coffee
38 ml (2½ tablespoons) boiling water
5 eggs, separated
100 g (½ cup) sugar

CHOCOLATE MOUSSE:

300 ml (1¼ cups) non-dairy heavy whipping cream

540 g (19 ounces) chocolate, chopped

5 g (3 tablespoons) instant coffee

7 egg whites

100 g (½ cup) sugar

240 ml (1 cup) non-dairy heavy whipping cream

Easy Dessert: You can use this mousse also as a separate dessert - prepare it and pour it into a bowl, or into small plastic or glass cups. Serve it with some fresh fruit or cookies.

MARZIPAN WRAPPING:
300 g (11 ounces) marzipan

Whip the 5 egg whites in a mixer, with a pinch of salt until the peaks are stiff but not dry.

Whip the 5 egg yolks in a separate (or a thoroughly cleaned) mixer bowl, with the sugar, until the mixture is thick and fluffy.

Gently but thoroughly fold together the melted chocolate mixture, the yolks, and the egg whites in a large bowl.

Scrape the mixture into the pan.

Bake the cake base for 20 minutes; cool it on a rack.

Press down the cake base with your fingers gently to even it.

When it's cool, pour on the chocolate mousse.

CHOCOLATE MOUSSE:

Heat the 300 ml (1¼ cups) cream, instant coffee, and chocolate together for 5 minutes in a large heatproof glass bowl in the microwave at half power. Then stir it until it's completely melted. Let it cool until it's just slightly warm. (If you don't have a large enough heatproof glass for everything to fit in it, use a small one and then transfer the melted chocolate to a large mixing bowl.)

Whip the egg whites until soft peaks form. Then add the 100 grams (½ cup) of sugar and beat until the mixture is stiff but not dry. Set it aside.

Whip the 240 ml (1 cup) cream until stiff peaks form.

Fold a bit of the beaten egg whites into the melted chocolate mixture to lighten it. Add the rest of the egg whites and all of the whipped cream and gently but thoroughly fold the mousse all together. It will be slightly runny. If you're going to glaze the cake, save about 2 tablespoons of mousse on the side.

Pour the mousse onto the baked and cooled cake base.

Refrigerate or freeze it until it's set, or until you need it.

If you're going to leave it in the freezer for more than a few hours, wrap it well.

The cake is good enough to serve like this if you don't feel like bothering too much with decorations or adding too much to the expense. At La Cuisine we always wrapped it in marzipan and glazed the finished product.

MARZIPAN WRAPPING:

Take the cake out of the freezer and out of the ring. Lift it off the bottom of the pan and peel off the baking paper. You can place it now on a rack or straight onto your work surface or onto a decorative cake carton.

Pick up some of the extra 2 tablespoons of chocolate mousse with a flexible metal spatula, and spread it around the bottom half of the cake - the baked base that is not made of mousse, so that the marzipan will stick to all of the cake.

Roll out the marzipan as thinly as you can to a circle bigger than the cake diameter including its height, about 40 cm (15 inches) in diameter. Sprinkle it with powdered sugar as needed so it doesn't stick to the rolling pin or to your surface.

Pick the marzipan up on the rolling pin and strategically place it centrally over the cake, letting it fall down naturally. Now with your hands, gently straighten out the sheet of marzipan, pressing out the folds and making it adhere to the top and sides of the cake. With a sharp knife, trim the excess marzipan by cutting it off in small movements while pressing the knife against the base of the cake. Try to create a perfect finish of the marzipan by smoothing it all over with the flats of your hands, or with a special fondant smoother available in cake decorating stores. (We actually always just used our hands.)

Return the cake to the freezer while you prepare the glaze.

Glaze:

Glaze:

180 g (6½ ounces) chocolate, chopped

75 ml (4½ tablespoons) canola oil

Melt the chocolate and the oil together in the microwave in a small heatproof bowl for 4 minutes at half power. Stir until smooth. Let it then get back down to a temperature where it will feel just warm if you dab a bit on your upper lip - this is a quick-temper that will allow the glaze to stay shiny on the cake.

When you glaze the cake, first place the cake on a rack and put the rack over a baking sheet that is lined with either a piece of baking paper or a piece of plastic wrap. Then you can collect all the extra glaze that runs off the cake, sieve out any loose crumbs that may have fallen in, and freeze it to use another time.

Pour the glaze carefully over the top and sides of the cake, smoothing it with a long spatula.

Refrigerate the cake to set the glaze.

Two-Layered Mousse Cake

dairy

Dubbed "Mousse B" by my first partner, I think the "B" was short for "double." Whatever you prefer to call it, it was one of our bakery's most requested dairy birthday cakes. Two delicate layers of mousse, white chocolate and dark chocolate, resting on a base of moist chocolate cake. Either of these mousses alone, of course, can also be used to fill bowls, little cups, or a trifle.

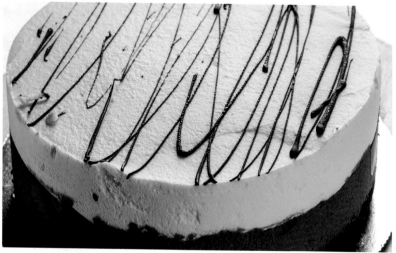

Slice of 24 cm cocoa sponge layer for base (pg 149)

About 60 ml (about ¼ cup) basic soaking syrup (pg 151), flavoured with coffee, chocolate, or triple-sec liqueur (optional)

DARK CHOCOLATE MOUSSE:

270 g (9½ ounces) dark chocolate, chopped

35 ml (2½ tablespoons) espresso or strong coffee

6 g (1½ teaspoons) brandy

2 egg yolks

270 ml (1 cup plus 2 tablespoons) heavy cream

40 g (scant ¼ cup) sugar

2 egg whites

50 g (¼ cup) sugar

WHITE CHOCOLATE MOUSSE:

270 g (9½ ounces) white chocolate

90 ml (1/3 cup) water

420 ml (scant 1¾ cup) heavy cream

Note: Make sure you don't serve the cake frozen. Keep it in the fridge until serving, or leave it at room temperature for a half hour or so.

Makes one 24 cm (9 inch) cake

■ 24 cm (9 inch) spring form pan, lined with baking paper for easy removal of the cake later.

Place the cocoa sponge layer into the bottom of the spring form pan. Brush the cake layer liberally with the soaking syrup. Make sure to brush the outer edges of the cake also, so that the outside won't taste dry, but don't overdo it or else syrup might ooze out of the finished cake.

DARK CHOCOLATE MOUSSE:

(make this before you make the white chocolate mousse)

Melt the chocolate and the espresso coffee in a heatproof glass bowl in the microwave for 5 minutes at half power. Stir until it's smooth.

Whisk in the brandy and 2 egg yolks. Let it cool slightly.

Whisk the 2 egg whites in a mixer until soft peaks form. Add the 50 g (¼ cup) sugar and continue whisking until the peaks are stiff but not dry. Scrape out about half the egg whites with a rubber spatula onto the chocolate mixture and fold it in gently to lighten the mixture. Add the rest of the whites and fold them in only partially.

Whisk the heavy cream in the same mixer bowl, with the 40 g (scant ¼ cup) sugar, until the peaks are almost stiff. Don't overbeat! Scrape the cream onto the chocolate mixture with the rubber spatula, and fold it all together gently but thoroughly. Scrape it all into the cake-lined spring form pan.

Freeze the cake for at least half an hour, until the chocolate mousse is set.

WHITE CHOCOLATE MOUSSE:

Melt the white chocolate and the water in a heatproof glass bowl in the microwave for 4 minutes at half power. Stir it with a heatproof spatula. If it's still lumpy, return it for 30-second increments at 20% power and stir it every time until it's smooth. *Be very careful melting white chocolate as it burns easily* - trust me, I speak from experience.

Let it cool to just barely warm, about 20 minutes or so.

Whisk the heavy cream in a mixer until the peaks are almost stiff. Don't overbeat! Scrape the cream onto the white chocolate mixture with a rubber spatula, and fold it all together gently but thoroughly. Scrape it all into the spring form pan, on top of the dark chocolate mousse. Smooth the top with a long flexible metal spatula, or with a drop spatula.

Freeze for a few hours until it is solid.

We used to decorate the top with some squiggly designs made with drizzled melted chocolate. You can also leave it undecorated, or decorate it with some sweetened whipped cream or chocolate mousse rosettes.

Take the pan out of the freezer, cut around the edge of the mousse with a knife to loosen it from the ring, remove the outer spring form ring, and lift the cake off the base by the baking paper. Peel off the paper and place the cake on a serving platter.

Concorde Cake

L a Cuisine's version of a French classic. Layers of light cocoa meringue thinly sandwiched with chocolate mousse and covered with more meringue. As there is no flour, this cake can easily be adapted for Passover use (using potato starch instead of corn flour if necessary).

Makes one 24 cm (9 inch) cake

■ 24 cm (9 inch) spring form pan, lined with baking paper for easy removal of the cake later.

MERINGUE:

This amount will make 3 cocoa meringue discs and a lot of strips. Use what you need to make the concorde cake, and any remaining meringues are great to nibble on, or can be stored indefinitely in a dry place that has absolutely no humidity.

Draw 3 circles with a pencil or marker on the wrong side of parchment paper on two baking sheets, using your 24 cm (9 inch) spring form pan ring as the stencil. Draw the lines inside the ring, making the circles slightly smaller than the pan. Then measure the height of your pan and with a ruler draw a rectangle down the length of your pan that is as wide as your pan is high. Make sure you then

MERINGUE:
6 egg whites
160 g (generous ¾ cup) sugar
160 g (1⅓ cups) powdered sugar
28 g (4 tablespoons) cocoa
2 teaspoons corn flour

MOUSSE:

300 ml (1¼ cup) non-dairy
heavy whipping cream

540 g (19 ounces) chocolate

5 g (3 tablespoons) instant
espresso granules

7 egg whites

100 g (½ cup) sugar

240 ml (1 cup) non-dairy heavy
whipping cream

turn the paper over, ink-side down, so you don't get ink on the meringues.

PREHEAT THE OVEN TO **140°C (285°F).**

Beat the egg whites in a mixer until they're almost stiff. Add the 160 g (generous ¾ cup) regular white sugar slowly, and beat until they're stiff and shiny.

Mix the powdered sugar, cocoa, and corn flour together, and fold it gently but thoroughly into the beaten egg whites.

Spoon the mixture into a piping bag with a small round tip and pipe in a circular motion to fill the 3 circles on your baking paper. Make sure to keep the meringue piped within the circles as they swell during baking.

Pipe skinny short lines of meringue crosswise to fill the rectangle. These short lines will become the strips of meringue that go around the circumference of the finished cake, the height of the cake.

Bake for 80 minutes. If you have the time, it's good to leave the meringues for as long as possible in the turned-off oven, so that they dry out really well.

MOUSSE:

Heat the 300 ml (1¼ cup) cream, chocolate, and instant espresso together for 5 minutes in a large heatproof glass bowl in the microwave at half power. Then stir until it's completely melted. Let it cool until it's just slightly warm. (If you don't have a large enough heatproof glass for the entire recipe to fit in, use a small one and then transfer the melted chocolate to a large mixing bowl.)

Whip the egg whites in a mixer until soft peaks form. Then add the 113 grams (½ cup) sugar and beat until they're stiff but not dry. Set them aside.

Whip the 240 ml (1 cup) cream in a mixer, in a clean bowl, until stiff peaks form.

Fold a bit of the beaten egg whites into the melted chocolate mixture to lighten it. Then add the rest of the egg whites and all of the whipped cream and gently but thoroughly fold the mousse all together.

It will be slightly runny.

PUTTING THE CONCORDE CAKE TOGETHER:

Place a disc of cocoa meringue inside the 24 cm (9 inch) spring form pan.

Pour in about half of the chocolate mousse.

Place another disc of cocoa meringue on top of the mousse layer.

Pour almost the rest of the chocolate mousse. Make sure you leave about 4 tablespoons of mousse to finish the sides of the cake.

Place the third disc of cocoa meringue bottom side up on top of the second mousse layer.

Freeze the cake so it will be easier to take out. Remove the ring and pull the frozen cake off of the base. Spread the rest of the chocolate mousse around the sides and top of the concorde cake with a knife or long flexible spatula.

Gently and carefully press the meringue sticks onto the sides of the cake all around the outside.

Break some of the remaining cocoa meringue sticks and press them on to the top of the cake. If you find that you don't have enough meringue sticks left for the top, you can leave the top undecorated or just sift some cocoa over it.

Make sure the cake is not frozen when you serve it - either put it into the fridge the day before serving it, or take it out of the freezer with enough time for it to thaw.

CHOCOLATE PECAN CAKE

I always found non-dairy baking to be particularly challenging. This recipe made life easier for me in the bakery, but at home you should really try it sometime using only dairy ingredients. This cake has a rich, brownie-like texture and is topped with an intense chocolate-coffee glaze. And, as we always told the customers, you absolutely must eat this cake at room temperature to really have it at its best.

Makes one 24 cm (9 inch) cake
■ 24 cm (9 inch) spring form pan, lined with parchment paper for easy removal of the cake later.

CAKE:

PREHEAT THE OVEN TO 180°C (350°F).

Melt the chocolate together with the margarine in a large glass heatproof bowl in the microwave for 5 minutes at half power. Stir until it's smooth. Whisk in the pecans and flour.

Whip the egg yolks with the 134 grams (2/3 cup) of sugar in a mixer until they're pale and fluffy. Then fold them gently into the chocolate mixture.

Whip the egg whites until soft peaks form in a clean mixer bowl. Then slowly sprinkle in the 67 grams (1/3 cup) of sugar and whip them until they're stiff but not dry.

CAKE:

215 g (7½ ounces) chocolate, chopped

215 g (7½ ounces) butter-flavoured margarine

5 egg yolks

134 g (2/3 cup) sugar

140 g (5 ounces) pecans, finely ground

22 g (3 tablespoons) flour

5 egg whites

67 g (1/3 cup) sugar

La Cuisine Bakery Recipes / Cakes 91

160 g (5½ ounces) chocolate, chopped

90 ml (⅓ cup plus 1 tablespoon) non-dairy heavy whipping cream

4 g (2 teaspoons) instant espresso granules

DECORATION:

85 g (3 ounces) pecans, chopped and toasted

Fold half the egg whites into the chocolate mixture lightly but not thoroughly. Then scrape in the rest of the egg whites and fold them in gently but thoroughly.

Scrape the mixture into the pan.

Bake the cake for 40 minutes.

Let it cool for 10 minutes, then press down the top of the cake evenly with a flat cake bottom or with your fingers. Cool completely. Cut the cake around the sides with a regular kitchen knife, loosening it from the outside ring. Refrigerate it for at least one hour.

Remove the cake carefully from the pan and peel off the parchment paper. Place it upside down on a cardboard cake round or directly onto a serving plate.

GLAZE:

Melt all the ingredients together in the microwave in a small glass heatproof bowl for 5 minutes at half power; stir it until it's smooth. Cool the glaze almost to room temperature. Take a bit of the glaze and with a small knife spread it around the sides of the cake so the chopped decorative nuts will stick.

DECORATION:

Press the nuts onto the sides of the cake.

Pour the rest of the glaze onto the top of the cake, coaxing it to the edges evenly with the help of a long flexible spatula or a knife.

This cake, like all cakes made with nuts, tastes better the next day.

---

non-dairy

CHOCOLATE DACQUOISE CAKE

A dacquoise is a meringue made of nuts, and like all cakes that contain nuts, it tastes better the day after it's assembled.

The rich and robust flavours of chocolate and toasted hazelnuts will leave you wondering if this cake is really non-dairy. Layers of chocolate sponge cake, hazelnut ganache filling, hazelnut meringue, chocolate ganache topping, and chocolate glaze, make this recipe worth the extra effort required for its preparation. To lighten your workload, you can make the different parts on different days at your leisure.

Makes one 24 cm (9 inch) cake
■ 24 cm (9 inch) spring form pan, lined with parchment paper for easy removal of the cake later.

HAZELNUT GANACHE FILLING:

Put the cream, chocolate, and nougat powder in a heatproof glass bowl or measuring cup and microwave it for 5 minutes at half power. Take it out and whisk it until it's smooth. If it's still lumpy, return it to the microwave for 20 more seconds at a time at half power and then whisk it until it's smooth. Whisk in the extract (if you're using it). Let it cool and then refrigerate for 6-8 hours or overnight.

HAZELNUT GANACHE FILLING:

500 ml (2 cups) non-dairy heavy whipping cream

225 g (8 ounces) chocolate, chopped

100 g (3½ ounces) nougat powder or paste*

2 g (½ teaspoon) hazelnut or almond extract (optional)

Chocolate Ganache Topping:

Put the cream and the chocolate in a heatproof glass bowl or measuring cup and microwave it for 5 minutes at half power. Take it out and whisk it until it's smooth. If it's still lumpy, return it to the microwave for 20 more seconds at a time at half power and then whisk it until it's smooth. Let it cool and refrigerate for 6-8 hours or overnight.

Hazelnut Meringue:

Draw 2 circles with a pencil or marker on the wrong side of parchment paper on a baking sheet, using your 24 cm (9 inch) spring form pan ring as the stencil. Draw the lines inside the ring, making the circles slightly smaller than the pan. Turn the paper over ink side down so you don't get any ink on your meringues.

Preheat the oven to 165°C (325°F).

Process the hazelnuts, flour, and 134 g (2/3 cup) sugar together in a food processor. Set the mixture aside. (Processing nuts together with other dry ingredients prevents them from over-processing and becoming oily.)

Beat the egg whites in a mixer until they're almost stiff. Add the 67 g (1/3 cup) sugar slowly, and beat until they're stiff and shiny but not dry.

Add the hazelnut mixture and fold it gently but thoroughly into the beaten egg whites.

Spoon the mixture into a disposable icing bag with a small round tip and pipe in a circular motion to fill the 2 circles on your baking paper. Make sure to keep the meringue piped within the circles as they swell during baking.

Bake the meringues for 30 minutes. Let them cool.

Assembly:

Place one hazelnut meringue layer into the paper-lined spring form pan.

Beat the hazelnut ganache filling in a mixer with the paddle until it's thick and creamy.

Scrape half the filling onto the hazelnut meringue layer and smooth it with a spatula.

Place the layer of cocoa sponge cake base on top of the filling in the pan, and brush it with all of the soaking syrup. Make sure you brush all the way to the edges to moisten everything.

Scrape the remaining half of the hazelnut ganache filling onto the cocoa layer and smooth it with a spatula. Don't wash the mixer bowl, paddle, or spatula yet.

Place the remaining layer of hazelnut meringue upside down, with the flat side facing up, onto the hazelnut ganache filling. (That way the finishing of the top of the cake is smooth and more even.)

Beat the chocolate ganache topping in the same mixer bowl you used before, with the paddle, until it's thick and creamy. Set aside 4 tablespoons for the final decoration, if you're going to glaze the cake.

Scrape the chocolate ganache topping onto the top of the cake and smooth it with a spatula.

Refrigerate the chocolate dacquoise cake 6-8 hours or overnight before removing it from the pan (or freeze it for 2-3 hours).

Chocolate Ganache Topping:
250 ml (1 cup) non-dairy heavy whipping cream

113 g (4 ounces) chocolate

Hazelnut Meringue:
250 g (9 ounces) toasted hazelnuts

18 g (2 tablespoons) flour

134 g (2/3 cup) sugar

7 egg whites

67 g (1/3 cup) sugar

One 24 cm (9 inch) layer of cocoa sponge cake base (pg 149) (Bake the cocoa sponge cake base as directed, cool, then cut the cake horizontally into three equal layers. Use one here, wrap and freeze the other two.)

Assembly:
60 ml (1/4 cup) soaking syrup (pg 151) mixed with 1 tablespoon liqueur of your choice

Take the cake out of the pan. You can serve it like this, or you can glaze it as follows:

GLAZE:

Melt the chocolate and the oil together in the microwave in a small heatproof bowl for 4 minutes at half power. Take it out and stir until it's smooth. Let it get back down to a temperature where it will feel just warm if you dab a bit on your upper lip - this is a quick-temper that will allow the glaze to stay shiny on the cake.

Lay the cake on a rack and put it over a baking sheet that is lined with either a piece of baking paper or a piece of plastic wrap. That way you can collect all the extra glaze that runs off the cake, and either add it to this cake, or sieve out any loose crumbs that may have fallen in and freeze it to use another time.

Spread the 4 tablespoons of the beaten chocolate ganache topping (that you had set aside for the final decoration) with a knife around the outside of the cake, making it as smooth as you can.

Pour the glaze carefully over the top and sides of the cake, smoothing it with a long spatula. Refrigerate the cake to set the glaze, but serve the cake at room temperature.

* Nougat powder or paste is available at baking supply shops. If you can't find it, you can double the amount of hazelnut extract to 4 g (1 teaspoon).

GLAZE:

180 g (6½ ounces) chocolate

75 ml (4½ tablespoons) canola oil

NOTE: You can make the hazelnut meringue into small round circles; they make delicious cookies.

non-dairy

LINZER CAKE

This very European-style cake was added to the La Cuisine repertoire by my Swiss baker, Yohanan. This is a traditional, classic version that seems to get moister and tastier as the days go by. Make sure to taste your batch of walnuts first for freshness (a stale walnut has a horrible aftertaste) and use only the very best apricot jam you can find.

Makes one 24 cm (9 inch) cake
■ 24 cm (9 inch) spring form pan, lined with parchment paper for easy removal of the cake later.

CAKE:

PREHEAT THE OVEN TO 180°C (350°F).

Mix together the flour, cake crumbs, walnuts, cinnamon, and baking powder in a medium bowl. Set it aside.

Cream the margarine and the sugar with an electric mixer with the paddle until it's light and fluffy.

Add the 2 eggs plus the yolk slowly to the cream and sugar mixture

CAKE:

150 g (5½ ounces) butter-flavoured margarine

150 g (¾ cup) sugar

2 eggs

1 egg yolk

and beat. Scrape it down with a rubber spatula once or twice to make sure everything is well mixed.

Add the dry ingredients and mix them in just until the flour disappears.

Scrape ¾ of the mixture (you don't have to be exact here) into the pan and smooth it down with a spatula. Add the jam and smooth it down all the way to the outer edges of the cake.

Scrape the remainder of the cake mixture into a pastry bag with a plain hole tip and pipe the batter out over the jam in 4 or 5 thin strips that cross over each other, diagonally and horizontally. You should be able to still see pockets of apricot jam in between the strips of cake batter.

Bake the cake for about 35 minutes until it's golden. Check the cake after 25 minutes - if it's getting too dark, loosely cover it with foil or a silicon mat for the last 10 or so minutes.

Allow the cake to cool. Cut the cake around the outer edge with a knife to loosen it from the spring form ring, and remove the ring.

DECORATION:

Heat the 4 tablespoons of apricot jam and brush it over the top and sides of the cake - this will keep it moist and shiny.

If desired, press the finely chopped walnuts into the glazed sides of the linzer cake.

> NOTE: You can also use whole pieces of walnuts and big chunks of cake when making the main batter of the linzer, and then process the flour, cake, walnuts, cinnamon, and baking powder together in a food processor. Set these dry ingredients aside until they're called for in the recipe. Processing nuts together with other dry ingredients prevents them from over-processing and becoming oily.

75 g (½ cup) flour

225 g (8 ounces) plain cake crumbs (either La Cuisine white sponge cake base, pg 149, or crumbs from a plain store-bought sponge or pound cake)

150 g (5½ ounces) walnuts, finely ground or grated

2 g (½ teaspoon) cinnamon

8 g (2 teaspoons) baking powder

2 g (½ teaspoon) vanilla

225 g (8 ounces) apricot jam

DECORATION:

4 tablespoons apricot jam

¾ cup walnuts, finely chopped (optional, for decorating the sides)

FRUIT CHARLOTTE

Non-dairy

A moulded dessert in the French tradition, it features light ladyfingers that enclose two layers of two different fruit mousses. In the bakery, we alternated flavours, using mango, cassis (black currant), raspberry, or passion fruit in the fillings. We used imported, concentrated fruit purées such as Boiron - try to get some from a baking supply shop because regular puréed fruit won't give you a strong enough flavour in the mousse. Once unmoulded, this simple yet elegant dessert can be garnished with fresh berries, whipped cream, or a shiny glaze.

Makes one 22 cm (8 inch) cake

■ 22 cm (8 inch) spring form pan, lined with parchment paper for easy removal of the cake later.

LADYFINGERS:

4 eggs, separated

50 g (¼ cup) sugar

4 g (1 teaspoon) vanilla

60 g (⅓ cup) sugar

95 g (⅔ cup) flour

Powdered sugar (a few tablespoons)

LADYFINGERS:

This amount will make 2 ladyfinger discs and a long strip of fingers that should be enough to line the sides of the pan. Use how many you need to make the charlotte, and any remaining ladyfingers (if you have any) are great to nibble on, or can be wrapped well and stored in the freezer.

Using your spring form pan ring as a stencil, draw 2 circles with a pencil or marker on the wrong side of parchment paper. Draw the lines inside the ring, making the circles slightly smaller than the pan. Then measure the height of your pan about ¾ of the way up, and with a ruler draw a rectangle down the length of your parchment-lined pan that is as wide as that measurement. (For example, if your spring form pan is 7 cm (2¾ inches) high, draw your long rectangle 5¼ cm (2 inches) wide.) Draw 2 of these rectangles, as you'll probably have enough batter. Make sure you then turn the paper over, ink-side down, so you don't get ink on your ladyfingers.

PREHEAT THE OVEN TO 180°C (350°F).

Beat the egg yolks with 50 g (¼ cup) sugar in a mixer until they are thick and creamy.

Beat the egg whites in a clean bowl until soft peaks form. Slowly add 60 g (⅓ cup) sugar until the peaks are stiff but not dry.

Fold half of the beaten egg whites into the egg yolks with a large rubber spatula. Add the rest of the egg whites and the flour, and fold it all together gently but thoroughly.

Spoon the batter into a piping bag with a small round tip and pipe in a circular motion to fill the 2 circles on your baking paper. Make sure to keep the batter piped within the circles as they swell during baking.

Pipe short lines of mixture to form ladyfingers that almost touch each other crosswise to fill the rectangle. These short lines will become the strips of ladyfingers that go around the circumference of the finished charlotte, the height of the cake.

Sprinkle the powdered sugar generously over all the piped ladyfingers and circles with a small sieve.

Bake the ladyfingers for about 11 minutes, until golden. Cool them on a rack.

Fruit Mousse Filling:

Put the flavoured fruit purées into two separate large mixing bowls.

Whip the non-dairy whipping cream, one half at a time, with a mixer, until stiff peaks form. Add a half to each bowl of fruit purée; don't mix them yet.

Whip the egg whites, in a clean bowl, with a mixer until soft peaks form. Then slowly add the sugar and continue whipping until the peaks are stiff but not dry.

Scrape one half of the beaten egg whites into each of the bowls of fruit purée - you now have two big bowls that each contain fruit purée, whipped cream, and beaten egg whites.

In the first bowl, fold everything together gently but thoroughly with a large rubber spatula; set it aside.

Do the same with the second bowl.

Assembly:

Lay one ladyfinger circle on the bottom of spring form pan.

Now line the insides of the pan with the long strip of ladyfingers (they should be mostly attached) with the rounded, powdered top against the sides of the pan, and the flat bottom part facing in towards where the filling will be.

Brush the bottom and insides of the pastry with a little more than half the soaking syrup.

Pour in one flavour of the fruit mousse filling.

Lay down the second ladyfinger circle on top of the first filling. Brush it with the remaining syrup.

Pour in the second fruit mousse filling. Smooth the top with a spatula.

Refrigerate or freeze the charlotte until it's set, or until you need it.

If you're going to leave it in the freezer for more than a few hours, wrap it well.

Fruit Mousse Filling:

100 g (3½ ounces) pure fruit purée of your choice (in one flavour)

100 g (3½ ounces) pure fruit purée in a second flavour

200 g (7 ounces) non-dairy heavy whipping cream

3 egg whites

100 g (3½ ounces) sugar

Assembly:

120 ml (½ cup) soaking syrup (pg 151) plus 1 tablespoon liqueur of your choice (curaçao, Cointreau, or kirsch)

APPLE STRUDEL

Being the child of Holocaust survivors, I never had the privilege of having a grandmother, let alone one I could watch pulling strudel dough out on a tablecloth, dexterously nudging and stretching it out to the size of the table. But I did have the privilege of watching my Swiss baker Yohanan make strudel at La Cuisine. It really is quite easy, and provides a really lovely non-dairy dessert that will truly impress your guests and family.

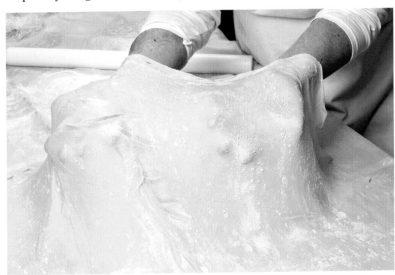

DOUGH:

375 g (2/3 cups) flour

190 ml (¾ cup plus 1 tablespoon) water

6 g (1 teaspoon) salt

1 small egg

45 ml (3 tablespoons) canola oil

10 g (1 tablespoon) vinegar

FILLING:

1½ kg (3¼ pounds) peeled, cored, and chopped apples

190 g (1 scant cup) sugar

190 g (7 ounces) La Cuisine white sponge cake base (pg 149), ground into crumbs (or crumbs that are ground from any other sponge or pound cake)

100 g (3½ ounces) ground walnuts

3 g (1 teaspoon) cinnamon

75 g (2½ ounces) raisins

DOUGH:

Mix all the ingredients together with the paddle in a mixer. Cut a large piece of plastic wrap and sprinkle it and the dough with a bit of flour. Then turn the sticky dough out onto the plastic wrap and roll it up into a ball. Let it rest at room temperature for an hour or two. When it rests, the strands of gluten in the dough relax and it will be easier to roll it out, otherwise it will fight you and keep springing back.

Make the filling while the dough is resting.

FILLING:

Mix everything together.

PREHEAT THE OVEN TO 200°C (400°F).

Either make one very large strudel from this dough, or divide it into two or three, whichever way you're most comfortable.

Sprinkle some flour on a large, clean white tablecloth. Some people prefer to roll strudel dough out on a darkly coloured cloth so that they'll know, by seeing the colour of the cloth through the dough, when they've rolled the dough thinly enough. But the disadvantage is that you run the risk of incorporating darkly coloured fuzzy bits of the cloth into your dough. If you prefer to roll it on a dark colour, make sure the tablecloth is very smooth and silky, and that it has been washed many times.

Roll the dough out in all directions with a lightly floured rolling pin until you have a large circle. Then, gently start picking up parts of the dough and stretching it out with your fingers until it's nice and thin. If you end up poking some small holes in the dough, don't worry - you can pinch them together as you're rolling it up (just be careful, you don't want a thick piece of dough in your strudel - it gets hard and not tasty when it's thick). Stretch it into a large rectangle.

Crumb Mixture:

Sprinkle the crumb mixture evenly all over the surface of the dough, to absorb the juices of the fruit.

Mound the filling evenly across the bottom width of the dough, along the longer side, across approximately the bottom quarter of it. Start rolling up the strudel by picking it up with the tablecloth and gently easing the dough up and over the fruit filling, folding in the two ends while rolling. Try not to press too much dough together at any point, even not at the ends. If you see any thick parts of dough, cut them off with a knife.

Roll the strudels onto a parchment paper-lined baking sheet. If you made one long strudel instead of three smaller ones, you will have to coil it to fit onto the baking sheet.

Brush the strudels with some canola oil (or melted butter if you're making it dairy) and bake them for about 45 minutes until they're golden.

Serve them warm or cold, sprinkled with some powdered sugar.

> **Note:** The apples can be replaced by ripe, unpeeled nectarines or plums, or a mixture of any or all of them. You can use this strudel dough and method to make savoury strudels as well. Try filling it with cooked cabbage flavoured with lots of browned onions and paprika, or with sautéed mushrooms, or with a spinach and Bulgarian (salty white) cheese filling.

Crumb Mixture:

135 g (5 ounces) breadcrumbs

3 g (1 teaspoon) canola oil

40 g (1½ ounces) sugar

dairy or non-dairy

TRIFLE

This dramatic dessert is anything but complicated to assemble. Traditionally it includes a combination of cake, creams, fruits, and liqueur that are layered in a pretty glass bowl for maximum effect. At La Cuisine, we used to sell a dairy trifle based on our delicious vanilla pastry cream, and a non-dairy trifle based on our non-dairy lemon curd. Either way, use the best, most attractive and ripe fruit in season and you're sure of a fun and delicious dessert.

INGREDIENTS:

One white sponge cake base (pg 149)

One lemon curd (pg 150) or vanilla pastry cream (pg 151)

Heavy cream, dairy or non-dairy (you will be weighing the ready lemon curd or pastry cream, and you'll need the equal amount of cream by weight)

Fresh fruit in season - any of the following or any mixture of the following: Strawberries or other berries, nectarines or peaches, kiwi, grapes, apricots, star fruit, plums, or whatever else you fancy – the amount depends on the size of the trifle bowl and how much fruit you want, the average tends to be about 3 cups of fruit

About 120 ml (½ cup) curaçao or Cointreau liqueur

About 120 ml (½ cup) pure fruit purée (such as Boiron) of your choice (optional, but it really enriches your trifle)

Makes one bowl that serves about 12
◾ Large trifle or other glass serving bowl.

Slice the sponge cake horizontally into 3 layers (you might not need to use all of it).

Weigh the lemon curd or vanilla pastry cream that you're going to use, and in another bowl weigh an equal amount of heavy cream.

Whip the heavy cream in a mixer until it has soft peaks. Fold it into the either the lemon curd or vanilla pastry cream. Set aside.

Prepare all the fruit - either dice it all or make attractive slices.

Start layering the trifle into the bowl. Put in some sponge cake, sprinkle the cake with some liqueur. Add some fruit purée (if using). Then sprinkle with some diced fruit and/or layer attractive slices of fruit against the glass bowl. Pour on some of the cream.

Continue layering the trifle until you either reach the top of the bowl or you run out of ingredients.

It's best to try to end up with the cream on top of the trifle. Otherwise you can just decorate the top with pretty fruit or extra whipped cream.

FRESH FRUIT TART

dairy or non-dairy

This striking tart was so much in demand that we offered both a dairy and a non-dairy version. Beginning with our versatile La Cuisine tart crust, the dairy tart was filled with vanilla pastry cream (made with real vanilla beans) while the non-dairy tart featured fresh lemon curd. Both versions were topped with a generous selection of fresh, seasonal fruit: strawberries, kiwi, mango, grapes (green, red, and purple - all in season), plums, nectarines, apricots, and pomegranate seeds. We preferred to arrange the fruit in rings on top of the tart, but you can really get creative here and pile up the fruit however you like.

To preserve the colour and texture of the fruit, we always brushed on a layer of shiny gel after the fruit was assembled.

Makes one 24 cm (9 inch) tart

Fill the baked and cooled tart with your chosen filling.

Arrange the fruit attractively on the top, making sure to cover all the filling.

Heat the jam or glaze and brush it over all the fruit.

INGREDIENTS:

One fully baked 24 cm (9 inch) La Cuisine tart crust, dairy or non-dairy, (pg 142)

One batch lemon curd (pg 150) or

One batch vanilla pastry cream (pg 151)

About 2 cups assorted fruit, attractively sliced

About 120 ml (½ cup) best quality apricot or peach jam, or imported glaze

dairy or non-dairy

Seasonal Baked Fruit Tart

This fabulous tart combines the two wonderful flavours of almonds and fresh fruit. The classic almond filling is called a "frangipane" cream. If you absolutely must have it non-dairy, go ahead and use margarine here, but this tart just cannot be beat made with pure butter. At least promise me that you'll try it! Also, if you make this filling non-dairy, add the freshly grated rind of a lemon - it helps mask the flavour of the margarine.

Ingredients:

One partially pre-baked 24 cm (9 inch) La Cuisine tart crust, dairy or non-dairy, (pg 142)

75 g (2½ ounces) butter or butter-flavoured margarine

100 g (3½ ounces) powdered sugar

100 g (3½ ounces) almonds - blanched or natural

2 eggs

7 g (1 tablespoon) flour

8 g (2 teaspoons) vanilla

Makes one 24 cm (9 inch) tart

PREHEAT THE OVEN TO 160°C (325°F).

Process all the ingredients except the crust together in the food processor, and scrape it into the pre-baked crust.

SEASONAL FRUIT FOR TOPPING:

Cut one of the following choices of fruit in half, remove the pits, and thinly slice.

Place the slices on the tart, fanning them out a bit, and press them lightly into the topping.

Bake the tart for 40-45 minutes until it's set and lightly golden.

GLAZE:

Warm the apricot or peach jam in a glass heatproof bowl in the microwave for a minute or two until it's melted and runny. Brush it over the top of the tart gently for a nice, shiny glaze that will moisten and protect the fruit.

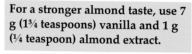

For a stronger almond taste, use 7 g (1¾ teaspoons) vanilla and 1 g (¼ teaspoon) almond extract.

SEASONAL FRUIT FOR TOPPING:

6 large purple plums

4 nectarines

3 apples

3 ripe pears

2 cups fresh apricots

1½ cups strawberries

GLAZE:

About 120 ml (½ cup) best quality apricot or peach jam

dairy or non-dairy

LEMON MERINGUE TART

A perennial favourite that never goes out of style, loved by children and adults alike. Fresh lemon juice is the secret to this winning recipe that combines fresh, tangy lemon curd with swirls of light, sweet, homemade meringue. For a real treat, if possible, skip the margarine and go for the butter!

INGREDIENTS:

One fully baked 24 cm (9 inch) La Cuisine tart crust, dairy or non-dairy, (pg 142)

One batch lemon curd (pg 150), dairy or non-dairy

MERINGUE:

6 egg whites

300 g (1½ cups) sugar

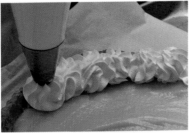

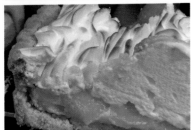

Makes one 24 cm (9 inch) tart

PREHEAT THE OVEN TO 200°C (400°F).

INGREDIENTS:

Fill the baked and cooled tart with your chosen lemon curd. Stick it in the freezer while you make the meringue - I found that there's less chance of those dreaded beads of sweat that sometimes form on lemon meringue tarts when the bottom part of the tart goes into the oven cold.

MERINGUE:

Put the whites and the sugar in the bowl of a mixer, and prepare a large whisk and an oven mitt with which to hold the bowl (the bowl will get hot).

Pour two cups of water into a small or medium saucepan (the mixer bowl must be able to fit snugly on top of it) and bring to a simmer. Place the mixer bowl on the saucepan, and whisk the egg white mixture constantly for a few minutes until it feels very warm to the touch. You will need to hold onto one side of the bowl with an oven mitt on, while whisking with your other hand so the bowl doesn't tip over.

The way you know if you've heated the egg white mixture enough is by the following test - touch the white mixture with your index finger, and rub it between your index finger and your thumb - if you do not feel any grains of sugar, it's ready and you can proceed. If it still feels a bit grainy, continue heating and whisking for a minute or two and test it again. Make sure you don't stop whisking, otherwise you might get scrambled egg whites.

Take the mixer bowl off of the saucepan, attach it to the mixer with the whisk attachment, and whip the warm whites on high speed for 10 minutes, until the bottom of the bowl feels cool.

Immediately transfer the beaten whites to a pastry bag fitted with a star tip, and pipe the meringue in billowy rosettes all over the top of the prepared tart.

Bake the tart for 4 minutes. It should be slightly, beautifully golden on the tips of the rosettes. If it's not dark enough for your liking, either return it to the oven for 1-2 minutes, or use a small kitchen torch.

Chill the tart.

---

dairy

PEAR TART

This pear tart is especially good served warm; so good, in fact, that when I make it at home I try to have it ready to pop into the oven only when we sit down to eat so it's freshly baked for dessert. I love when the browned bits from the butter get into the filling, but some of my bakers preferred to pour the filling through a sieve. Of course, try to use ripe, fragrant pears.

Don't be deceived by the simplicity of this recipe - it is one of our all-time best-selling desserts.

Makes one 28 cm (11 inch) tart

INGREDIENTS:

One partially baked 28cm (11 inch) La Cuisine dairy tart crust (pg 142)

4 large, ripe pears, sliced or chopped

PREHEAT THE OVEN TO 180°C (350°F).

INGREDIENTS:

Arrange the pear slices attractively in the partially baked crust, or just fill the crust with the slices or chunks.

FILLING:

Heat the butter in a small saucepan over high heat until the foam subsides, and the butter that's left is brown and fragrant.

Whisk together the sugar, flour, and eggs. Whisk in the browned butter.

Pour the mixture into the crust over the pear slices.

Bake the tart for about 30-35 minutes until it's golden and set.

FILLING:
230 g (1 cup plus 2 tablespoons) sugar
40 g (5 tablespoons) flour
3 eggs
170 g (6 ounces) butter

APPLE HAZELNUT TART

dairy

This is a far cry from your basic "American apple pie." Buttery, caramelized apples are sandwiched between a double hazelnut crust. Naked or *à la mode,* if you are a fan of baked apples this is the way to go.

Makes one 24 cm (9 inch) tart
- 24 cm (9 inch) tart pan with a removable bottom.

CRUST:

Mix the flour and the hazelnuts in a small bowl.

Cream the butter and sugar in a mixer with the paddle until it's fluffy. Add the egg and the vanilla and mix briefly. Add the flour and hazelnut mixture. Mix until it all comes together into a ball of dough.

Tip the dough out onto a sheet of plastic wrap. Knead the dough together a few times with your palms and wrap it up. Refrigerate the dough until it's cold, at least one hour.

PREHEAT THE OVEN TO 180°C (350°F).

Cut the dough almost in half, so that one piece is a littler bigger than the other. Roll out the larger piece on a floured surface or between two floured pieces of baking paper. Line the tart pan with the larger piece of dough. This will be the bottom half of the tart.

Partially bake the bottom crust for 15 minutes.

FILLING:

Cook the apples, butter, and sugar in a medium saucepan, for about 30 minutes, until the apples are soft and caramelized. If there is still a lot of liquid left in the pan, strain the apples. (Use the delicious liquid with another dessert or over ice cream.) Mix in the raisins, vanilla, and cinnamon.

Let cool.

Fill the partially baked tart crust with the apple mixture, packing it down with the back of a spoon.

Roll out the remaining, smaller portion of tart dough and lay it down

CRUST:
140 g (5 ounces) butter, cut in cubes
80 g (¼ cup plus 2 tablespoons) sugar
1 egg
4 g (1 teaspoon) vanilla
200 g (1½ cups) flour
50 g (2 ounces) hazelnuts, ground

FILLING:
1.1 kg (2½ pounds) peeled, cored, and chopped or thinly sliced apples
50 g (2 ounces) butter
250 g (1¼ cups) sugar
75 g (3 ounces) golden or dark raisins
6 g (1½ teaspoons) vanilla
4 g (1 teaspoon) cinnamon
1 egg, beaten

on top of the filled tart. Press the edges down to enclose the filling.

Brush the top of the tart with the beaten egg, and press in a pretty design on the dough with the tines of a fork.

Return the filled tart to the oven and bake for about 45 minutes, until it's well browned.

Let it cool and then remove the tart from the pan.

---

non-dairy

APPLE TORTE

This European version of apple pie was a staple in our non-dairy kitchen. A few times a week, we had to peel, core, and slice one or two crates of fresh apples with our old-fashioned little machine; the kind that screwed onto the table, with the peel falling off straight into the garbage bin. I don't know which way I like it better - fresh when the delicious sliced almond topping is crispy, or after a few days when it soaks in the moisture from the apples and becomes caramelly and chewy.

Makes one 24 cm (9 inch) torte in a standard pie pan

CRUST:

PREHEAT THE OVEN TO 180°C (350°F).

Cream the margarine and sugar in a mixer with a paddle, until it's light and fluffy.

Add the egg and beat.

Add the dry ingredients and mix them in.

Chill the dough in the fridge for at least one hour. Roll it out on a floured surface to a circle wider than your pie plate. Lift it onto the rolling pin and place it into the pie plate, fitting it in smoothly with your fingers. Trim any overhang with a small sharp knife.

CRUST:

113 g (4 ounces) butter-flavoured margarine

67 g (⅓ cup) sugar

1 egg

168 g (scant 1¼ cups) flour

42 g (1½ ounces) hazelnuts, ground

Pinch salt

Pinch cinnamon

APPLE FILLING:

Mix all the ingredients in a bowl and then pile them into the pie pan on top of the bottom crust.

TOPPING:

Mix all the ingredients in a bowl and pat them onto the apple filling in the crust.

Bake the apple torte for about 45 minutes. If it gets too dark at the edges after 30 minutes, cover it with foil or a silicon mat for the last 15 or so minutes.

This is a nice, strong pie. When it's thoroughly chilled you should be able to easily slip it out of the pan onto a more decorative serving plate. The best way to do it is to loosen the pie all around the pan (with your fingers if it's a disposable foil pie pan, or with a small knife if it's not) and jiggle it a bit to make sure it's not stuck. Then put a plate or a flat tray upside down over the pie, hold the top and the bottom carefully with both hands, and flip it over so that the pie is now upside down. Lift off the pie pan. Then do the same thing again with a serving platter, holding it upside down over the upside down pie, holding the top and the bottom carefully with both hands, and flipping it over again to turn it back right side up.

The edges will almost always be a little bit over-browned by the time the middle is done all the way, so sprinkle the edges with powdered sugar.

This is really great served with ice cream.

APPLE FILLING:

500 g (18 ounces) peeled, cored, and chopped or sliced apples

50 g (1½ ounces) white sponge cake base crumbs (pg 149, or store bought)

45 g (¼ cup) sugar

30 g (1 ounce) apricot jam

25 g (1 ounce) light or dark raisins

20 g (¾ ounce) breadcrumbs

1 g (¼ teaspoon) cinnamon

TOPPING:

165 g (6 ounces) sugar

85 g (3 ounces) blanched sliced almonds

3 g (¾ teaspoon) cinnamon

2 egg whites

CHOCOLATE PASSION FRUIT TART

dairy

Take a walk on the wild side with this exotic pairing of aromatic passion fruit curd and an intense chocolate custard topping. I like this tart extra deep and creamy - otherwise you can make it in a 28 cm (11 inch) tart pan.

Makes one deep 24 cm (9 inch) tart

PREHEAT THE OVEN TO 150°C (300°F).

PASSION FRUIT CREAM:

Put the sugar, passion fruit purée, and butter in a small saucepan. Bring it to a gentle boil.

Whisk the 3 eggs in a separate bowl.

When the butter is entirely melted in the saucepan, pour the mixture into the eggs while whisking (get someone to help you if you feel you're not coordinated enough), and then pour the mixture back into the saucepan.

Bring the mixture back to a simmer while whisking. When bubbles start to break the surface and the curd thickens slightly, pour it out through a sieve into a clean bowl.

Pour the curd into the fully baked tart crust. Freeze it for a few minutes while you prepare the chocolate custard.

One fully baked 24 cm (9 inch) La Cuisine dairy tart crust (pg 142), made in a deeper pan - 3½ cm (1½ inches) deep

PASSION FRUIT CREAM:

100 g (½ cup) sugar

120 ml (½ cup) imported, concentrated passion fruit purée, such as Boiron

85 g (3 ounces) butter

3 eggs

CHOCOLATE CUSTARD:

180 ml (¾ cup) heavy cream

150 g (5½ ounces) chocolate, chopped

2 eggs

1 egg yolk

40 g (1½ ounces) butter

4 g (1 teaspoon) vanilla

CHOCOLATE CUSTARD:

Bring the cream to a boil in a small saucepan. Remove from the heat. Whisk in the chocolate, eggs, egg yolk, butter, and vanilla until everything is melted and smooth.

Pour the chocolate mixture into the pan with the passion fruit curd in it, and let it stand at room temperature for 15 minutes.

Bake the tart for 30 minutes. It will still be wobbly, but it will set as it chills.

Serve this tart cold.

NOTE: As a delicious variation, you can substitute pure orange juice concentrate for the passion fruit purée.

dairy

CHOCOLATE CARAMEL TART

This was one of my absolute favourite desserts we made at La Cuisine. The delicious, cloying sweetness of the caramel, heightened by a touch of saltiness, against the slight bitterness of the chocolate ganache, tastes to me like perfection. My youngest son still requests it for every birthday! The caramel topping is a slightly different recipe than the caramel sauce that tops the cheesecake; they are not interchangeable.

Makes one 28 cm (11 inch) tart

28 cm (11 inch) fully baked La Cuisine dairy tart crust, (pg 142) cooled.

CHOCOLATE GANACHE FILLING:

270 ml (1 cup plus 2 tablespoons) heavy cream

255 g (9 ounces) chocolate, chopped

CARAMEL FILLING:

125 ml (½ cup) water

230 g (1 cup plus 2 tablespoons) sugar

125 ml (½ cup) heavy cream

100 g (3½ ounces) butter

3 g (¾ teaspoon) vanilla

Generous pinch salt

CHOCOLATE GANACHE FILLING:

Heat the cream and chocolate in a heatproof glass bowl in a microwave for 5 minutes at half power. Take it out and whisk until it's smooth. If it's still lumpy, return it to microwave for 20 more seconds at a time at half power and then whisk it until it's smooth.

Pour the ganache into the tart crust, leaving behind about 1-2 tablespoons that you'll use later to drizzle the decoration. It should fill the tart halfway.

Put the tart in the freezer for an hour while you make the caramel filling.

CARAMEL FILLING:

Pour the water into a heavy-bottomed medium saucepan and then add the sugar. Stir it occasionally with a wooden spoon over low heat until the sugar is totally dissolved.

Increase the heat to high and bring it to a boil. Keep a cup of water and a pastry brush nearby, and use it to occasionally wash down the crystals of sugar from the sides of the saucepan above the mixture, but stop doing that once you start seeing a hint of colour. Let it boil until it turns a beautiful amber colour and has a caramel smell. Don't let it get too dark or it will have a bitter taste, but neither should you stop when it's not dark enough because then it won't have a strong enough caramel taste.

If it crystallizes and collapses (you'll know what I mean if it happens), just chuck it out and start over. Don't waste the cream and the butter by adding them as well.

When the colour is just right, lower the heat and carefully add the cream - stand back a bit, it sputters and steams angrily. Stir it with a whisk over low heat until it smoothes out. Turn off the heat.

Add the butter, vanilla, and salt. Stir it until it's smooth.

If it caramelizes beautifully yet has a few crystals in it, you can usually save it by merely passing the sauce through a sieve.

Allow the caramel to cool slightly, about 15-20 minutes, then gently pour it on top of the chocolate layer in the tart.

Warm the remaining 1-2 tablespoons of chocolate ganache you left behind for a few seconds in the microwave. Then drizzle it decoratively over the caramel filling, pulling the chocolate into a nice design with a toothpick or the point of a knife.

Chill it in the fridge for at least two hours until it's set (or freeze it to set it faster if you're in a hurry to sink your teeth into it!).

This tart lasts for many, many days in the fridge, and it freezes perfectly.

White Chocolate And Raspberry Tart   dairy

Personally I'm not a big fan of white chocolate alone - I find it a bit cloying - but I love it combined with something tart, like lemon or raspberry. Here I pair it up with a berry mixture; you can also spread about one cup of lemon curd on the baked crust instead. To highlight the tartness, I also add some lemon rind into the crust.

Makes one 28 cm (11 inch) tart
▪ 28cm (11 inch) tart pan with a removable bottom.

CRUST:

Mix the flour, butter, sugar, and lemon rind in a mixer with the paddle until the mixture is crumbly.

Add the yolks, water, and vanilla, and mix until it all comes together into a ball of dough.

Tip the dough out onto a sheet of plastic wrap. Knead the dough a few times with your palms, and wrap it up. Refrigerate the dough until it's cold, at least one hour.

PREHEAT THE OVEN TO 180°C (350°F).

When you're ready to roll out the dough, whack it a few times with your rolling pin. Roll it out on a floured surface or between two sheets of baking paper. Put it in the tart pan.

CRUST:
240 g (1¾ cups) flour
150 g (5½ ounces) butter, cut in cubes
50 g (¼ cup) sugar
1 tablespoon lemon rind
2 egg yolks
¼ teaspoon vanilla
1/8 teaspoon water

Prebake the crust by covering it with a large piece of aluminum foil. Press it in well with your fingertips especially hugging the sides of the tart with the foil. Fold the extra foil down over the outside edge of the pan, pressing it tightly. This will keep the dough up against the pan without the need to fill the dough with pie weights or beans. (I like shortcuts like these, but if you want to be really professional or accurate, you of course could weigh it down with pie weights or dry beans - I'm just trying to save you the bother...)

Bake the tart crust for 15-20 minutes and then take it out of the oven. Remove the foil very carefully.

Return the tart to the oven for another 8-10 minutes until it's golden and fully baked. Allow it to cool.

RASPBERRY FILLING:

2 cups raspberries (cheaper ground frozen berries work especially well here)

67 g (1/3 cup) sugar

3 g (1 teaspoon) corn flour

Cook this mixture in a small saucepan, constantly whisking it until it thickens.

Purée it with an immersion blender (then you don't have to worry about sieving out all the little annoying seeds; if you don't have one, you'll have to pass it through a sieve).

Cool for 5-10 minutes. Spread the mixture onto the fully baked and cooled crust. Stick it in the freezer for about a half hour to set the raspberry filling.

WHITE CHOCOLATE FILLING:

170 g (6 ounces) white chocolate, chopped

170 g (6 ounces) butter, cut in cubes, softened to room temperature

60 g (½ cup) powdered sugar

3 eggs

Melt the white chocolate in a small glass heatproof bowl in the microwave for 2 minutes at half power. Stir it with a heatproof spatula or a whisk. If it's still lumpy, return it for 30-second increments at 20% power and stir it every time until it's smooth. *Be very careful melting white chocolate as it burns easily* - trust me, I speak from experience. Cool it to just barely warm, about 20 minutes.

Beat the soft butter in a mixer with the paddle until it's light. Slowly add the sugar. Add the white chocolate. Add the eggs one at a time on high speed, beating until the mixture gets fluffy after each addition.

Spread the white chocolate filling over the raspberry filling already in the crust. Smooth it with a spatula, making sure it gets to the sides of the tart crust.

Refrigerate the tart for at least 2 hours to set the filling.

This can be eaten straight out of the fridge, but it tastes better if it's been at room temperature for at least thirty minutes.

This also tastes delicious with some melted dark chocolate drizzled decoratively over the top.

PECAN TART

This tart is the real McCoy. At La Cuisine we made it only on the dairy side, because the taste and depth of flavour of browned butter just can't be beat. We sold it mostly in the 28 cm (11 inch) size, so that's the recipe I'm giving you here. Feel free to mix and match the kinds of nuts you use if you want a change from the usual - pecans mixed with macadamia nuts, hazelnuts, and pine nuts make an especially dramatic and beautiful tart.

Makes one 28 cm (11 inch) tart

PREHEAT THE OVEN TO 180°C (350°F).

INGREDIENTS:

Scatter the nuts in the partially baked crust.

Heat the butter in a small saucepan over high heat until the foam subsides and it's brown and fragrant. Whisk all the rest of the ingredients together in a large bowl, then whisk in the butter.

Pour the mixture carefully onto the nuts in the crust, making sure the nuts remain spread out evenly.

Bake the tart for 35-45 minutes. Some people like this tart more runny inside than others, so you'll have to decide how long to bake it after the first time you make it. Bake it until it's golden and only wobbles slightly.

If it gets too dark and is still too wobbly, cover it loosely with some foil or with a silicon sheet for a few more minutes until it's done.

> Variation - you can add 85 g (3 ounces) unsweetened melted chocolate to the filling before baking. Yum. Chocolate pecan tart.

One partially baked 28 cm (11 inch) La Cuisine dairy tart crust (pg 142)

INGREDIENTS:

160 g (6 ounces) pecans

28 g (1 ounce) butter

240 ml (1 cup) corn syrup

100 g (½ cup) white sugar

100 g (½ cup) brown sugar

2 eggs

2 egg yolks

QUICHE

From the time we began La Cuisine, our quiches were the most popular savoury item on our menu. A classic dish that never seems to lose its appeal, it's equally at home as an everyday main course or side dish, or as a fancy cocktail or appetizer.

Success begins with the dough, and this recipe is the same one I've been using for over thirty years, simply because it is still the best. I know it's no picnic to roll out dough by hand, but in this case it is so worth the extra effort. Chances are that you won't approach my personal record of hand-rolling over 800 mini quiches at one sitting, using only my trusted old wooden rolling pin. That little exercise earned me twelve sessions of physiotherapy to get my shoulder back in proper working order.

The variations for fillings are endless, so I have included a sample of our all-time favourites. By all means, feel free to experiment.

Yes, this recipe does tend to the fattening side of baking, but don't cut corners if you want a really amazing quiche - just eat a smaller portion.

Makes one 28 cm (11 inch) quiche

Basic Quiche Filling:

PREHEAT THE OVEN TO 180°C (350°F).

Whisk the ingredients for the filling together in a bowl. Set it aside. You could substitute milk or yogurt for the cream (although cream is better). If you use milk, one or two extra egg yolks will enrich the filling.

Put the selected filling (from below) and the basic quiche filling into the partially baked crust, and bake for about 35 minutes, until the quiche is set and golden.

Mushroom Quiche:

Sauté the mushrooms in a frying pan with the butter until the mushrooms are cooked. (They will be soft and lightly browned.) If the mushrooms release a lot of juice, pour the juice off or drain the mushrooms so you don't end up adding too much liquid to the quiche.

Scatter the cheese onto the partially baked quiche crust, add the cooked mushrooms, and then pour in the filling. Sprinkle the chopped green onions on top.

Onion Quiche:

Any tasty yellow cheese works well here, preferably a Swiss-tasting one.

Sauté the onions in a frying pan with the butter until they are soft but not browned. If the onions release a lot of juice, pour the juice off or drain the onions so you don't end up adding too much liquid to the quiche.

Scatter the cheese onto the partially baked quiche crust, add the cooked onions, and then pour in the filling.

Red Pepper Quiche:

Sauté the peppers and the garlic in a frying pan with the olive oil until the peppers are soft.

Scatter the cheese onto the partially baked quiche crust, add the cooked peppers and basil, and then pour in the filling.

Spinach Quiche:

Wash spinach well a few times in water as it's often filled with sand, and chop.

Sauté the spinach in a frying pan with the butter until the spinach is wilted.

Scatter any tasty yellow cheese onto the partially baked quiche crust, add the cooked spinach, scatter on the green onions, and then pour in the filling.

BASIC QUICHE FILLING:

240 ml (1 cup) heavy cream

3 eggs

3 g (½ teaspoon) salt

Generous pinches of pepper and nutmeg

MUSHROOM QUICHE:

350 g (12 ounces) mushrooms, cleaned and sliced

30 g (1 ounce) butter

150 g (5 ounces) shredded cheese - any tasty cheese works well here, preferably a Swiss-tasting one

Handful of chopped green onions

ONION QUICHE:

3 large onions, chopped

30 g (1 ounce) butter

150 g (5 ounces) shredded cheese

RED PEPPER QUICHE:

3 large red peppers, cleaned and chopped

4 garlic cloves, minced

2 tablespoons olive oil

2 tablespoons chopped fresh basil

150 g (5 ounces) shredded goat or other tasty cheese

SPINACH QUICHE:

350 g (12 ounces) fresh spinach,

30 g (1 ounce) butter

Handful of chopped green onions

150 g (5 ounces) shredded cheese

Swiss Chard Quiche:

One year there was a local shortage of fresh spinach, so we substituted Swiss chard, washed well a few times in water as it's often filled with sand, and chopped. It was so well-received that we added it to our line.

Sauté the Swiss chard, onions, and garlic in a frying pan with the olive oil until the vegetables are soft.

Scatter the cheese onto the partially baked quiche crust, add the cooked vegetables, and then pour in the filling. Scatter the chopped walnuts on the top.

Mediterranean Quiche:

Sauté the onion, zucchini, and eggplant in a frying pan with the olive oil until the vegetables are soft. (Alternatively toss them together, spread them on a baking sheet, and roast in the oven at 200°C (400°F) for about 30 minutes until they're soft.)

Mix together the cooked vegetables, chopped tomato, za'atar, Bulgarian cheese, and the filling all together in a large bowl. Pour the whole thing into the partially baked crust.

SWISS CHARD QUICHE:

350 g (12 ounces) fresh Swiss chard

1 large onion, chopped

2 cloves garlic, minced

2 tablespoons olive oil

30 g (1 ounce) walnuts, chopped

150 g (5 ounces) crumbled Bulgarian (salty white) cheese

MEDITERRANEAN QUICHE:

1 large onion, chopped

1 large zucchini, chopped

1 small eggplant, peeled and chopped (about 1½ cups)

2 tablespoons olive oil

1 large tomato, chopped

½ teaspoon za'atar (a Mediterranean herb)

150 g (5 ounces) crumbled Bulgarian (salty white) cheese

CHERRY TOMATO QUICHE:

2 tablespoons Dijon mustard

300 g (1½ cups) cherry tomatoes, halved

2 tablespoons chopped fresh basil (or 1 tablespoon ready-made pesto)

40 g (1½ ounces) pine nuts

150 g (5 ounces) grated kashkeval cheese (or other cheese of choice)

Cherry Tomato Quiche:

Spread the Dijon mustard on the partially baked crust with a pastry brush. Scatter on the cheese.

Arrange the halved cherry tomatoes cut side down on the cheese, and sprinkle on the chopped basil or dab on the pesto.

Pour in the filling. Sprinkle on the pine nuts.

Sweet Potato Quiche:

PREHEAT THE OVEN TO 200°C (400°F).

Toss the sweet potato slices with the olive oil, spread them out on a baking sheet, and roast in the oven for about 30 minutes, until they're soft.

Scatter the cheese on the partially baked quiche crust. Lay down the sweet potato slices and sprinkle them with the green onions and thyme.

Pour in the filling.

Smoked Salmon Quiche:

Prepare the onion quiche without the cheese, until the part where you spread the prepared onion filling onto the partially baked quiche crust.

Scatter on the chopped smoked salmon.

Pour in the filling. (Sprinkle on the chopped fresh dill if using.)

Tuna Quiche:

Prepare the mushroom quiche, with the following variation:

Instead of the handful of green onions, sauté the chopped onion in butter for 2-3 minutes. Add the mushrooms and cook until done.

Add the drained tuna.

Mix together the cooked mushrooms, onions, filling, and cheese all together in a large bowl.

Pour the whole thing into the partially baked crust.

Note: These same quiches were served in miniature form at all our catered events, both as cocktails or as part of the main course. To make these quiches, cut out 8 cm (3¼ inch) circles of rolled out quiche dough and fit them into muffin pans. Press them in well with the tips of your fingers. Fill them with your chosen filling up to the top of the crust, and bake them for 20 minutes.

One recipe for a 28 cm (11 inch) quiche will make 12 mini muffin quiches.

SWEET POTATO QUICHE:

1 kg (about 2 pounds) sweet potatoes, peeled and sliced thickly

2 tablespoons olive oil

Handful of green onions, chopped

1 teaspoon fresh thyme leaves

150 g (5 ounces) shredded cheese - any tasty yellow cheese or goat cheese

SMOKED SALMON QUICHE:

200 g (7 ounces) chopped smoked salmon

1 tablespoon fresh dill, chopped (optional)

TUNA QUICHE:

1 can tuna, drained

1 large onion, chopped

Butter, for sautéing

150 g (5 ounces) shredded cheese - any tasty yellow cheese

non-dairy

Norene Gilletz's Nutritious Carrot Cake

When I got married in 1981, everyone I knew was cooking out of the most popular book at the time for the kosher kitchen, *The Pleasures of Your Processor* by Norene Gilletz. I think it was even the first engagement gift that I received. I went through the book, cover to cover, the first few years in my own kitchen, and still use many of the wonderful recipes today.

This carrot cake was always a crowd pleaser in our bakery - simple, moist, and tasty. Some of my customers showed up like clockwork for their carrot cake, and nothing else. If you want an even healthier version, it works really well with whole-wheat flour.

This recipe has been adapted from: *The NEW Food Processor Bible: 30th Anniversary Edition*, Revised and Updated, by Norene Gilletz (Whitecap Books).*

Ingredients

3 carrots, trimmed and peeled

1 apple, peeled and cored

3 eggs

225 g (1¼ cups) sugar

240 ml (1 cup) canola oil

280 g (2 cups) flour

10 g (2 teaspoons) baking soda

4 g (1 teaspoon) baking powder

6 g (2 teaspoons) cinnamon

190 g (1 cup) raisins

One fluted tube pan sprayed with non-stick oil spray and dusted with flour

PREHEAT THE OVEN TO 180°C (350°F).

Grate the carrots and the apple and measure them together to equal 480 ml (2 cups).

Whisk together the eggs and sugar in a bowl until the mixture is light and fluffy. Whisk in the oil.

Mix together the flour, baking soda, baking powder, and cinnamon in a separate bowl. Then add it to the first bowl and mix just until the flour disappears. Add in the raisins.

Pour the batter into the pan.

Bake the cake for about 40-50 minutes, until the cake tests done (until a toothpick or skewer inserted in the centre of the cake comes out dry).

In the bakery we used to glaze this cake with a white fondant icing. (Ready-made fondant can be purchased in a baking supply store.) Simply put about 225 g (8 ounces) of white fondant in a heatproof glass bowl or cup (I always found it most comfortable to heat it in a glass measuring cup so I could pour it directly onto the cake from the spout) with a small amount of water and heat it in 30-second bursts in the microwave, stirring after each time until it's completely smooth and melted. Some fondants are stiffer than others and will require a bit more water, while some might be so runny to begin with that you shouldn't add any water at all. Use your judgement so you have a nice icing consistency. Pour it carefully onto the very top of the bundt-shaped cake, and let the fondant drip gracefully down the sides.

*Norene Gilletz is the leading author of kosher cookbooks in Canada. She is the author of nine cookbooks and divides her time between work as a food writer, recipe editor and indexer, culinary consultant, spokes-person, cooking instructor, and lecturer. Norene lives in Toronto, Canada and her motto is "Food that's good for you should taste good!"

For more information, visit her website at www.gourmania.com or email her at goodfood@gourmania.com.

Date Bread

dairy

For the first few years of catering, I don't think there was a single event at which I didn't put out a tray of this date bread. It is one of Marvin's and my favourite baked things - Marvin loves it spread with cream cheese, and I don't think it needs any embellishment other than a cup of tea or coffee. If you're going to keep it longer than 2 or 3 days you should put it in the fridge.

Makes one loaf
■ Standard loaf pan, 23 x 13 cm (9 x 5 inches), lined with baking paper.

PREHEAT THE OVEN TO 180°C (350°F).

Place the dates and the raisins in a bowl. Stir the baking soda into the boiling water and pour it over the date mixture. Let it sit while you prepare the rest.

Beat the butter and the sugar with a mixer until it's light and fluffy. Add the egg and the vanilla and beat until fluffy. Add the flour and mix it in. Then add the date mixture with all the liquid and mix on low speed. Scrape it all down with a rubber spatula and give a final stir.

Pour the mixture into the loaf pan.

Bake the date bread for 50-60 minutes until the cake tests done (until a toothpick or skewer inserted in the centre of the cake comes out with moist crumbs).

Check after 40 minutes. If it looks very dark on top and yet is still wet inside, cover the date bread loosely with some foil or a silicon mat for the last while until it tests done.

Let it sit for 10 minutes and then take it out of the pan to finish cooling.

INGREDIENTS
240 g (8½ ounces) pitted, chopped Medjool dates
120 g (4 ounces) golden raisins
240 ml (1 cup) boiling water
5 g (1 teaspoon) baking soda
113 g (4 ounces) butter
200 g (1 cup) sugar
1 egg
4 g (1 teaspoon) vanilla
190 g (1 1/3 cups) flour

Marble Cream Cake

dairy

I love a cake that can be eaten at breakfast, lunch, and dinner, and this moist, chocolate sour cream coffeecake definitely fits the bill. If you don't wrap it up well and hide it, you might find yourself nibbling at it all day long.

Makes one 24 cm (9 inch) cake
■ Fluted 24 cm (9 inch) tube pan sprayed with non-stick oil spray and dusted with flour.

PREHEAT THE OVEN TO 180°C (350°F).

Cream the butter and sugar in a mixer with the paddle until it's light and fluffy. Slowly add the egg and vanilla. Beat until it's light and fluffy, scraping down the mixture with a rubber spatula once or twice. Mix in the sour cream. Scrape it down once again. Mix the flour, baking powder, and salt in a small bowl and add it to the mixer bowl, mixing it only until the flour disappears.

INGREDIENTS
170 g (6 ounces) butter
300 g (1½ cups) sugar
1 egg
8 g (2 teaspoons) vanilla
400 ml (1 2/3 cup) sour cream
210 g (1½ cups) flour
8 g (2 teaspoons) baking powder
Pinch salt
85 g (3 ounces) chocolate, chopped
25 ml (5 teaspoons) strong coffee or espresso

Melt the chocolate with the espresso in a small heatproof glass bowl or cup in the microwave at half power for 2 minutes. Stir it until it's smooth.

Scrape half of the batter into a separate clean bowl and fold in the melted chocolate mixture.

Fill the tube pan with alternating spoonfuls of white and chocolate batter. Do it gently, being careful not to overwork the mixture. When it's all in the pan, run a knife through the batter once around the pan to make a pretty design.

Bake the cake for about 50 minutes, until it tests done (until a toothpick or skewer inserted in the centre of the cake comes out dry).

Let it cool for about 15 minutes, and then turn it out of the pan to cool completely.

dairy

ALMOND BUTTER CAKE

(financier cake)

This is a buttery, delicate tea cake full of toasted almond flavour. The best part of making it is nibbling all the crunchy bits that fall off as you're unmolding the cake...(but isn't that true of everything baked)?

Makes one standard loaf

To Prepare the Pan:

- Standard loaf pan 23 x 13 cm (9 x 5 inches)

Pour the butter into the loaf pan and brush the entire inside of the pan with it. You should have extra butter left on the bottom of the pan - that's fine as it will help ensure the release of the cake from the pan later.

Sprinkle in the sliced almonds, shake them around the inside of the pan. With your fingers, gently press down on the almonds to help them adhere to the buttered sides and bottom of the pan.

Cake:

Preheat the oven to 165°C (325°F).

Mix the ground almonds, the 185 g (heaping 1¾ cups) sugar, flour, and corn flour in a large bowl (large enough to hold all the dry ingredients, egg whites, and enough mixing room).

Whip the 6 egg whites with a mixer until soft peaks form. Slowly pour in the 100 g (½ cup) of sugar and beat until the peaks are stiff but not dry.

Fold half of the beaten egg whites into the dry mixture with the largest rubber spatula that you have - it will be difficult to fold it in; do it gently with a cutting motion, only until it's partially mixed.

Scrape in the rest of the beaten egg whites and pour in the melted butter - fold it all together gently but thoroughly.

Pour the mixture into the prepared loaf pan. Smooth the top gently.

Bake it for 35-40 minutes. Let it cool for 10 minutes.

Using a small, sharp knife gently cut around the cake and turn the cake out onto a rack. Promptly eat all the delicious bits that fall out, and cool the cake completely.

This cake, like all cakes made with nuts, tastes better the next day.

To Prepare the Pan:
40 g (1½ ounces) blanched sliced almonds
25 g (1 ounce) melted butter

Cake:
185 g (6½ ounces) blanched ground almonds
185 g (heaping 1¾ cups) sugar
85 g (scant 2/3 cup) flour
15 g (2 tablespoons) corn flour
6 egg whites
100 g (½ cup) sugar
85 g (3 ounces) melted butter

Hazelnut Marzipan Cake

non-dairy

A lovely tea cake recipe from my baker Yohanan. It's not as difficult to make as it looks. Use a top-quality marzipan that has a high percentage of almonds, and don't get the sugarless kind as there is no other sugar in this cake.

Note: This one is really worth making with butter, if you ever get the chance.

Makes one standard loaf

To Prepare the Pan:

- Standard loaf pan 23 x 13 cm (9 x 5 inches)

Grease the inside of the pan with the soft margarine. Sprinkle in the ground hazelnuts and shake them around the inside of the pan.

To Prepare the Pan:
25 g (1 ounce) hazelnuts, finely ground
A pat of soft margarine

Hazelnut Base:

3 egg whites

82 g (⅓ cup plus 1 tablespoon) sugar

75 g (2½ ounces) hazelnuts

8 g (1 tablespoon) flour

4 g (2 teaspoons) cocoa

Hazelnut Base:

Preheat the oven to 165°C (325°F).

Grind the hazelnuts, flour, and cocoa finely in the food processor. Set aside.

Beat the egg whites in a mixer with the whisk until soft peaks form. Add the sugar and beat until the peaks are stiff but not dry.

With a large rubber spatula, fold the hazelnut mixture into the beaten egg whites. Scrape the mixture into a piping bag with a plain round tip. Pipe it into the prepared loaf pan along the bottom and up the sides. Set it aside, and quickly mix the marzipan cake.

Marzipan Cake:

95 g (3¼ ounces) butter-flavoured margarine

190 g (6¾ ounces) marzipan

2 eggs

2 g (½ teaspoon) almond extract

40 g (5 tablespoons) flour

Marzipan Cake:

Beat the margarine in a mixer with the paddle until it's light and fluffy. Add the marzipan and continue beating until the mixture is smooth and fluffy. Add the eggs, scraping down the mixture once. Add the almond extract. Add the flour and beat only until the flour is incorporated.

Scrape the mixture into the hazelnut base that is lining the loaf pan. Smooth it down gently with a spatula.

Bake the cake for 45-50 minutes, until the top is golden and springs back when you touch it with your finger. Cool it on a rack for 10 minutes. Carefully loosen the cake from the edges of the pan with a knife and tip it out onto the rack to cool completely. The bottom of the cake becomes its top.

CHOCOLATE CHIP COOKIES

dairy

These are really fabulous, especially when they come out fresh from the oven as they did almost every single morning at our bakery. In fact, they were the very first thing that we brought out to the La Cuisine storefront and sold on our opening day, July 8, 1998. But bake them at your own risk - they are habit-forming, and after scarfing down one or two warm ones every day for fourteen years, I can actually point to the parts of my body on which they landed.

INGREDIENTS:

225 g (8 ounces) butter, room temperature

100 g (½ cup) white sugar

200 g (1 cup) brown sugar

2 eggs

4 g (1 teaspoon) vanilla

280 g (2 cups) flour

5 g (1 teaspoon) salt

5 g (1 teaspoon) baking soda

285 g (10 ounces) chocolate chips

Makes about 6 dozen cookies

PREHEAT THE OVEN TO 180°C (350°F).

Cream together the butter, white sugar, and brown sugar in a mixer with the paddle until it's light and fluffy.

Add the eggs and vanilla and beat well.

Stir together the flour, salt, and baking soda in a separate small bowl. Then add it to the mixer bowl and mix well.

Stir in the chocolate chips.

Shape it into small balls with two teaspoons, and place the balls on parchment paper-lined cookie sheets, about 7 cm (3 inches) apart.

Bake the cookies for 8-10 minutes, until they're slightly golden but still soft. They'll harden as they cool.

Note: In this recipe, the quality of the vanilla, the brown sugar, and the chocolate chips really makes the cookie. The vanilla was our own home-made brand (recipe pg 156), the darker heavier brown sugar gave the cookie a more caramelly taste, and the smaller-sized chocolate chips (we used a Spanish brand) gave the perfect chocolate-to-cookie ratio per bite.

At the bakery we would pipe out the dough into cookie-shaped mounds and freeze them unbaked on baking paper - piling the sheets, once frozen solid, one on top of the other, ready to pop into the oven at any given moment.

Oatmeal Raisin Cookies

Like our chocolate chip cookies, these were a daily "must" in our bakery. Fragrant and mildly spicy, these are so good when they're fresh and warm. People always have a definite opinion as to whether they like their oatmeal cookies chewy or crispy - these seem to be both, especially when they're removed from the oven before they get too hard.

Makes about 36 cookies, depending on the size

PREHEAT THE OVEN TO 180°C (350°F).

Stir the flour, baking soda, cinnamon, salt, nutmeg, and cloves together in a bowl. Set aside.

Cream together the butter and brown sugar in a mixer with the paddle until it's light and creamy.

Add the eggs and the vanilla slowly scraping down occasionally with a rubber spatula. Gradually add the mixed dry ingredients.

Add the oats and the raisins. Mix it well.

Divide the dough into three parts, and pat each part into a long log. If they're too soft to roll, refrigerate the three mounds of dough for about 15-20 minutes and then roll them.

Roll each log in plastic wrap. Chill them thoroughly in the fridge until they are cold and solid and easier to cut. You can freeze the logs at this point if you prefer.

Slice each log into cookies, about 1 cm (1/3 inch) wide and arrange them on cookie sheets.

Bake the cookies for 8-10 minutes, until they're golden but still soft - they harden as they cool.

INGREDIENTS:

210 g (1½ cups) flour

3 g (¾ teaspoon) baking soda

2 g (½ teaspoon) cinnamon

2 g (¼ teaspoon) salt

2 g (¼ teaspoon) nutmeg

2 g (¼ teaspoon) cloves

170 g (6 ounces) butter

260 g (1⅓ cups) brown sugar

2 eggs

4 g (1 teaspoon) vanilla

200 g (7 ounces) oats

160 g (6 ounces) dark raisins

ALMOND BUTTER COOKIES

The contrasting texture of a buttery, melt-in-your-mouth biscuit with a crispy, chewy almond centre makes this cookie a winner. My first partner, Meir, came back with this recipe from a trip to northern Italy hosted by one of our suppliers. To me, it was worth the trip for this little gem alone!

Makes about 40 cookies, depending on the size
■ Pastry bag with a star tip (a closed star or a French star, if you have), and a pastry bag with a plain hole tip.

Make the filling first, allowing it to cool slightly while you mix and pipe out the cookies.

ALMOND FILLING:
Heat the glucose, sugar, and butter in a small saucepan while stirring until everything is melted and smooth. Remove the pan from the heat. Break the almonds a little bit with your hands, and stir them into the glucose mixture.

COOKIE:

PREHEAT THE OVEN TO 180°C (350°F).

Mix the flour, baking powder, and salt together in a small bowl
Cream the butter and sugar in a mixer with the paddle until it's light and fluffy. Beat in the egg yolk, liqueur, and vanilla. Scrape down the sides with a rubber spatula and then beat again until smooth. Add the flour mixture to the mixer and beat just until the flour disappears. Scrape the dough into a pastry bag fitted with a 1½ cm (½ inch) star tip. Squeeze out 3½ cm (1½ inches) cookies onto the baking sheets, spacing them about 2 cm (1 inch) apart.
Keep a small dish with some water next to you. Dip the tip of your index finger into the water, and then press an indent in the centre of each cookie.

ALMOND FILLING:
60 g (2 ounces) glucose (see note pg 129)
60 g (heaping ¼ cup) sugar
60 g (2 ounces) butter
60 g (2 ounces) blanched, sliced almonds

COOKIE:
170 g (6 ounces) butter, soft
75 g (2/3 cup) powdered sugar
1 egg yolk
15 ml (1 tablespoon) curaçao liqueur (or any other clear orange liqueur)
4 g (1 teaspoon) vanilla
210 g (1½ cups) flour
2 g (½ teaspoon) baking powder
Pinch salt

Scrape the almond mixture into a piping bag with a plain hole in the tip, and squeeze small amounts of the filling into the indentations. Bake the cookies for 14 minutes, until they're golden at the edges.

dairy

Butter Pecan Cookies

(Norene Gilletz's Melting Moments)

This is another recipe from Canada's leading author of kosher cookbooks, that became a best seller at La Cuisine. These cookies really do melt in your mouth. A few mornings a week you could see our driver endlessly rolling little balls of this dough in between deliveries. We kept these unbaked in the freezer, ready to pop into the oven at a moment's notice.

This recipe has been adapted from: *The NEW Food Processor Bible: 30th Anniversary Edition*, Revised and Updated, by Norene Gilletz (Whitecap Books).*

INGREDIENTS:

170 g (6 ounces) butter

65 g (1/3 cup) brown sugar

4 g (1 teaspoon) vanilla

210 g (1½ cups) flour

100 g (3½ ounces) pecans, finely chopped

Powdered sugar

Makes about 45 cookies

PREHEAT THE OVEN TO 180°C (350°F).

Cream together the butter, brown sugar, and vanilla in a mixer. Add the flour and pecans and mix, just until the flour disappears.

Form the dough into 2½ cm (1 inch) balls and place them 2 inches apart on baking sheets.

Bake the cookies for about 20 minutes. When they cool, sprinkle them heavily with powdered sugar.

Norene Gilletz is the leading author of kosher cookbooks in Canada. She is the author of nine cookbooks and divides her time between work as a food writer, recipe editor and indexer, culinary consultant, spokesperson, cooking instructor, and lecturer. Norene lives in Toronto, Canada and her motto is "Food that's good for you should taste good!" For more information, visit her website at www.gourmania.com or email her at goodfood@gourmania.com.

Palmiers

dairy

Palmiers are buttery, flaky cookies made of puff pastry that are rolled in sugar and caramelized around the edges during baking. Their distinctive shape is meant to remind us of "palm leaves," but they are often referred to as "elephant ears." Texture and size vary according to taste - in Paris I was surprised to see huge cookies that were very dark and crunchy alongside the smaller, lighter version.

Makes about 30 cookies

▪ 2 baking sheets lined with baking paper.

Sprinkle your work surface with the sugar. Let the puff pastry sit for 10 minutes at room temperature; hit it a few times with the rolling pin to soften it a little bit. Roll it out on the sugar, into a rectangle approximately 20 x 45 cm (8 x 18 inches) and 3¼ mm (1/8 inch) thick.

Fold the two long sides into the centre, meeting in the middle. Fold the top long half of the dough down over the bottom half. Press down lightly with your hands.

PREHEAT THE OVEN TO 200°C (400°F).

Slice the strip of puff pastry with a sharp knife into slices 1 cm (½ inch) thick. Arrange the slices on the baking sheets 5 cm (2 inches) apart. (You can sprinkle the sugar that's left on the rolling surface onto the cookies, if you like them very sugary.) Let the cookies rest for 20 minutes before baking.

Bake the cookies for 10-15 minutes, or until they're golden. Eat all the little uneven ones, preferably while they're warm.

INGREDIENTS:

455 g (16 ounces) ready-to-use puff pastry dough (pg 145)

255 g (9 ounces) sugar

Alfajores Cookies

dairy

I think this is the best recipe that I've tried for these popular Argentinean caramel sandwich cookies. Even if you don't like coconut, please at least try it here - the cookies are very delicate, and simply melt in your mouth.

Makes about 20 cookie sandwiches

COOKIES:

Beat the butter with the powdered sugar in a mixer with the paddle. Add the egg yolks and brandy.

Mix together the corn flour, flour, and baking powder in a small bowl, and then beat them into the mixture.

Scrape out the dough onto the plastic wrap, pat it down into a disc, wrap it up in the plastic and refrigerate until it's chilled.

PREHEAT THE OVEN TO 120°C (250°F).

Roll the dough out to a thickness of 5 mm (a bit less than ¼ inch) and cut out 5 cm (2 inch) circles.

Arrange them on a baking sheet about 2-3 cm (1 inch) apart.

Bake them for 35-40 minutes.

Chill the baked cookies in the fridge for a few hours so they'll be easier to handle and then fill them while they're cold.

COOKIES:

125 g (4½ ounces) butter

75 g (2/3 cup) powdered sugar

3 medium egg yolks

25 ml (1 tablespoon plus 2 teaspoons) brandy

150 g (1¼ cups) corn flour

100 g (¾ cup) flour

3 g (1 scant teaspoon) baking powder

ASSEMBLY:

About 300 g (11 ounces)
purchased dulce de leche
spread

About 80 g (3 ounces)
shredded coconut, plain or
lightly toasted

ASSEMBLY:

Spread some dulce de leche on the bottom flat side of half the cookies with a small knife. Then place an undecorated cookie on top to make a "sandwich."

Spread a bit more dulce de leche around the outer edge of the sandwich, and roll the edge in the coconut.

CHOCOLATE VERSION:

Everything is the same as the recipe above, except:
Replace 100 g (¾ cup) flour with
68 g (½ cup) flour and
32 g (¼ cup) cocoa

NOTE: *Dulce de leche* is basically long-cooked, caramelised sweetened condensed milk. It is a well-known South American spread that can be bought in most good food shops. The Hebrew name for it translates as "milk jam," which is really a lovely thought. As well as a filling for alfajores cookies, it can be used to spread on crèpes or pancakes, or to fill blintzes or doughnuts. I've been known to simply eat a spoonful of it straight from the jar when there's nothing else sweet in the house to accompany my mug of tea...

non-dairy or dairy

FLORENTINE COOKIES

Florentines were one of the most popular cookies at La Cuisine throughout all the years, and we tried very hard to keep them in stock at all times, otherwise some customers became very ornery. No other cookie raised the hackles of so many people or were the object of so many differing tastes and opinions. I had customers who only wanted the dark, crispy ones, while others specially requested the pale, chewy ones - even if I had to repack boxes for them. Some customers waited with bated breath for the crisp, autumn under 18°C (65°F) days when we would start dipping half of each cookie in chocolate, some of them never accepting my explanation that we simply couldn't sell a chocolate-dipped cookie in the sweltering summer days of the Middle East. Others specially ordered them plain, without chocolate, even all winter long. As the saying goes: Different strokes for different folks. Any way you bake them or eat them, they're rich and chewy and wonderful.

Makes about 60 cookies, depending on the size

PREHEAT THE OVEN TO 180°C (350°F).

Bring the sugar, water, and butter or margarine to boil in a large, heavy-bottomed saucepan until the butter or margarine melts.

Add all the rest of the ingredients and cook, stirring constantly, until the mixture is very thick and almost dry, about 10-15 minutes.

Cool the mixture slightly, and while it's still lukewarm, either plop spoonfuls or pipe it out of piping bag with a plain hole into small plops onto baking paper-lined cookie sheets, about 5-6 cm

INGREDIENTS:

240 g (1½ cups) sugar

150 ml (½ cup plus 2
tablespoons) water

80 g (3 ounces) butter or butter-
flavoured margarine

200 g (7 ounces) mixed dark
and golden raisins

200 g (7 ounces) mixed nuts,
chopped medium

50 g (1/3 cup) flour

50 g (2 ounces) white sponge
cake base crumbs (recipe
pg 149, or store bought)

(2-2½ inches) apart.

Bake the cookies for about 12-14 minutes. You'll learn the texture and the colour you prefer of the finished product after you've made it once or twice. I'm really not kidding about people's preferences here!

NOTE: Our favourite combination was 80 g (3 ounces) almonds, 80g (3 ounces) hazelnuts, and 40 g (1½ ounces) pistachios - but you can use any combination of any nuts, including walnuts and cashews.

SABLÉ COOKIES

non-dairy or dairy

These classic French cookies were made only on the non-dairy side at La Cuisine, which is why we added the lemon rind to the dough. It masked the taste of the margarine. *Sablé* is French for "sand," a reference to the texture of this cookie. We always kept unbaked logs in the freezer, ready to slice for last minute baking. I suggest you do that in your house as well. If you use butter (and I strongly recommend you do) you may never go back to the non-dairy variation.

Makes about 70 cookies, depending on the size

Cream together the butter or margarine and the powdered sugar in a mixer with the paddle, until it's fluffy.

Beat in the egg, and add the lemon rind. Scrape down the batter once or twice with a rubber spatula.

Mix in the flour.

Divide the dough into three parts, and pat each part into a long log. If they're too soft to roll, refrigerate the three mounds of dough for about 15-20 minutes, and then roll them. Roll each log in plastic wrap. Try to roll them no thicker than 3 cm (1¼ inches). The size of your final cookie will depend on the size of your logs so don't make them too thick.

Chill the logs thoroughly in the fridge until they are cold and solid and easier to cut. You can freeze the logs at this point if you prefer.

PREHEAT THE OVEN TO 180°C (350°F).

INGREDIENTS:

320 g (11 ounces) butter or butter-flavoured margarine

160 g (1⅓ cups) powdered sugar

1 egg

2 tablespoons lemon rind (you can use less, I happen to like a lot here)

400 g (scant 3 cups) flour

Handful of sugar

Spread the sugar onto a flat pan or cookie sheet. Unwrap the logs and roll them thoroughly in the sugar. Slice each log into cookies, about 6 mm (¼ inch) thick and arrange them on cookie sheets. Place them on the cookie sheets about 5 cm (2 inches) apart.

Bake the cookies for about 11-12 minutes until they're set and slightly golden at the edges.

NOTE: Try to keep a supply of lemon rind on hand - soap a few fresh lemons and grate them. Then put the rind in a small container and keep it in the freezer. You will love having freshly grated lemon rind at hand (you can do it with oranges also) and you'll find yourself readily throwing it into all kinds of things, including doughs, sauces, and salads.

Hazelnut Jam Cookies

In the La Cuisine bake shop we only made these on the non-dairy side, but do try them with butter if you can. This cookie was extremely popular because the deep nutty taste of the hazelnuts helped mask the taste of the margarine. And be sure to use a very top quality jam for the filling.

Makes approximately 45 cookies, depending on the size

PREHEAT THE OVEN TO 180°C (350°F).

INGREDIENTS:

150 g (5½ ounces) butter-flavoured margarine

150 g (¾ cup) sugar

2 eggs

150 g (5½ ounces) hazelnuts

150 g (1 cup plus one heaping tablespoon) flour

Pinch salt

About 110 g (4 ounces) apricot or raspberry jam

Grind the hazelnuts, flour, and salt finely in a food processor.

Cream the butter-flavoured margarine and sugar in a mixer with the paddle until it's light and fluffy, scraping it down occasionally with a rubber spatula.

Gradually add the eggs while continuing to beat. Scrape it down again.

Add flour mixture and fold in.

Scrape the mixture into a pastry bag with a plain hole tip and pipe small balls onto a baking paper-lined cookie sheet, about 5-6 cm (2-2½ inches) apart.

Dip the tip of your finger occasionally into water and use it to press an indentation onto the top of each cookie.

Scrape the jam into a clean pastry bag with a plain hole tip and pipe small dabs of jam into the indentation of each cookie.

Bake the cookies for about 10-12 minutes until golden.

When you collect these to store them or serve them, try not to pile them up into even stacks, because the jam will tend to stick to the bottom of the next cookie. Try instead to pile them up in a more haphazard way, unless you prefer to indulge in a stack of tightly glued together cookies at one go.

Almond Tile Cookies

This is one of the most exquisite cookies ever - it's actually a cross between a cookie and a candy. You must use a candy thermometer to make it, but don't let that scare you off. They are very delicate and breakable, so the trick is to pack them carefully into a sturdy container or gift box. It's worth a trip to a baking supply store to pick up some glucose - there are two other recipes in this book that call for it (almond butter cookies, pg 123, and the chocolate glaze, pg 80), and it lasts forever.

Makes about 50 cookies, depending on the size

PREHEAT THE OVEN TO 180°C (350°F).

INGREDIENTS:

40 g (1½ ounces) butter

50 g (2 ounces) heavy cream

50 g (2 ounces) glucose

100 g (½ cup) sugar

100 g (3½ ounces) blanched, sliced almonds

Put the butter, cream, glucose, and sugar into a heavy bottom, medium saucepan and bring it to a boil. Hook a candy thermometer onto the saucepan and boil until it reaches exactly 116°C (240°F).

Quickly (and carefully - this mixture is hot boiling sugar, and if you've read the memoir section of this book, you'll know exactly how a burn from that feels!) add in the sliced almonds. Give it a mix with a wooden spoon or a silicone spatula, and scrape it out into a stainless steel bowl to cool down (but not until it's totally cold).

When the mixture is only slightly warm to the touch (if it's too hot, it will be too difficult to pinch, yet if it gets totally cold, it might get too hard to work with) start pinching off little bits (about half a teaspoon) of the mixture, and place the little balls 5-6 cm (2 inches) apart on cookie sheets lined with baking paper. With experience, you'll learn what size of cookie you prefer.

Bake the cookies for 7-10 minutes until they're a light golden caramel colour.

If they've run into each other, don't panic - just cut them apart with a sharp knife while they're still warm.

Let them cool completely before trying to pick them up.

You won't believe how good these are.

> **NOTE:** Glucose is very thick and sticky - it's easier to take it out if you dip your hand into water and pick up small blobs of glucose with your wet hand.

HAMANTASCHEN

non-dairy or dairy

When I was young, there were only two choices of filling and two choices of dough for these triangular-shaped Purim holiday favourites - prune or poppy seed filling, and cookie or yeast dough. Now, of course, hamantaschen ideas have burst forth with creativity, and you can find all kinds of wild choices in bakeries and coffee shops. But in the years of La Cuisine, we stuck with two. The dough is based on a recipe I saw years ago in the Jerusalem Post newspaper.

Makes about 50 hamantaschen

Prepare chosen filling (see below).

Mix the flour, sugar, baking powder, and salt in a mixer with the paddle. Add the butter or butter-flavoured margarine and blend it until the mixture forms small particles. Mix the egg, egg yolk, rind, and 1 tablespoon orange juice in a small bowl. Pour it into the mixture. Mix until it all comes together into a ball of dough. If it seems too dry add 1 more tablespoon orange juice. Tip the dough out onto a sheet of plastic wrap and knead the dough a few times with your palms. Then wrap it up. Refrigerate the dough until it's cold, at least three hours.

PREHEAT THE OVEN TO 180°C (350°F).

INGREDIENTS:

525 g (3¾ cups) flour

180 g (1½ cups) powdered sugar

6 g (1½ teaspoons) baking powder

1 g (¼ teaspoon) salt

300 g (10½ ounces) butter or butter-flavoured margarine, cut in cubes

1 egg

1 egg yolk

Grated rind of one orange (about 1 tablespoon)

1-2 tablespoons orange juice

POPPY SEED FILLING:

150 ml (scant 2/3 cup) water

150 g (5½ ounces) ground poppy seeds

125 g (2/3 cup) sugar

30 g (1 ounce) golden or dark raisins

10 g (½ ounce) butter or margarine

80 g (3 ounces) ground cake crumbs (either La Cuisine white sponge cake base (pg 149) or store-bought)

4 g (2 tablespoons) freshly grated lemon rind

1 large tart apple, peeled, cored, and grated

RAISIN-APPLE FILLING:

113 g (4 ounces) golden raisins

113 g (4 ounces) dark raisins

56 g (2 ounces) currants or dried blueberries

1 large, tart apple, peeled, cored, and grated

4 g (1 teaspoon) cinnamon

Juice and rind of one lemon

Work with half the dough at a time.

Roll the dough out on a floured surface to a thickness of about ¼ cm (1/8 inch). Cut out 7 cm (2 ¾ inch) circles. Place a scant teaspoon of filling on each circle. Close each of the cookies firmly and tightly into a triangle. Pinch them closed well, flouring your fingers if necessary, so the cookie doesn't open up during baking.

Bake the hamantaschen for 15 minutes, or until they are slightly golden at the tips.

POPPY SEED FILLING:

This version of the Hungarian classic is hard to beat, and can be used to fill danishes and tarts as well as hamantaschen. A respected Supreme Court judge regularly requested a special order of this filling instead of apples in the dairy apple hazelnut tart (pg 105).

Simmer the water, poppy seeds, sugar, raisins, and butter or margarine in a small saucepan until the mixture becomes thick and almost dry, stirring constantly, about 10 minutes. Stir in the cake crumbs, lemon rind, and grated apple. Allow to cool before using it.

RAISIN-APPLE FILLING:

This recipe was given to me by our friend Penny, who used currants back in England (we don't get them here in Jerusalem…).

(Penny sometimes adds some crushed nuts).

Grind everything together in the food processor, but leave it a bit chunky.

MUFFINS

Canadians love their muffins. How much? A whole lot. They eat two to four times more of them than anyone else. Moist and cakey, with a slightly crispy crown, muffins are the perfect comfort food with which to begin one's day.

For six years while I worked out of my home, I got up every morning at 6 a.m. to prepare two different types of muffins for a popular coffee shop in town. Marvin then delivered them while carpooling our boys to their elementary school in the Old City of Jerusalem.

Later, when we opened the La Cuisine bakery, our muffins became a featured morning treat. Initially it was something of an uphill battle to introduce this most Canadian staple to the local palate. For months we gave away more than we sold, but eventually our perseverance paid off, and our muffins were often sold out by midday.

Muffins are from the biscuit family, and require a very, very light hand when mixing in the dry ingredients. Don't worry if you still see a bit of flour and a few lumps. If you stir the batter until it's smooth and satiny, you'll end up with smaller, tougher, drier and possibly holeyer (not "holier") muffins.

I've included our trademark La Cuisine muffins, along with a selection of other tried and tested favourites.

Trademark La Cuisine Muffins

This is the famous muffin that we made just about every day at La Cuisine, changing the fruit according to the season, availability and my mood. I also made these as mini muffins for breakfast events. Most muffins should be eaten within a few hours of baking; these, however, will stay moist and yummy for two days. (That's due to the generous amounts of brown sugar and canola oil.) Because the batter itself is a bit sweet, I find that tart fruits such as blueberries, mixed berries, red or black currants, apples, cranberries and plums work best, but they also are amazing with mangoes, peaches, and apricots in season. If and when you can get your hands on fresh or frozen uncooked rhubarb,* it's a real treat in these muffins.

INGREDIENTS:

300 g (1½ cups) brown sugar

1 egg

160 ml (2/3 cups) canola oil

350 g (2½ cups) flour

240 ml (1 cup) buttermilk

5 g (1 teaspoon) baking soda

5 g (1 teaspoon) salt

1 teaspoon vanilla

1 heaping cup diced fruit (see above) or whole fruit if it's small blueberries or other berries or currants that you're using

Makes 12

■ Muffin pan lined with 12 paper muffin cups.

PREHEAT THE OVEN TO 165°C (325°F)

Put the brown sugar, egg, and oil into a large mixing bowl and stir with a wooden spoon.

Pour the buttermilk into another bowl, and add the baking soda, salt, and vanilla. Mix it well with a small spatula (or a small whisk, but you'll be using the spatula to scrape out the mixture so you can save dirtying a utensil here), making sure not to leave any lumps.

Add half the flour to the sugar and egg mixture, and mix it lightly with the wooden spoon. Don't mix too aggressively - let most of the flour still show.

Add the buttermilk mixture. (Scrape it all out of the cup with the spatula; don't leave any behind!)

Give 2 or 3 more strokes with the wooden spoon. Now add all the rest of the flour and the fruit. Toss the fruit a bit with the spoon to cover it with flour, and then carefully and delicately give a few stirs to mix everything all together. Don't be too thorough, otherwise you'll have tough little muffins. Let some flour still show. It will continue to mix as you spoon it into the pan.

Divide the mixture evenly into the 12 paper-lined muffin cups.

Bake the muffins for 25-30 minutes, until they are golden and the tops feel dry to the touch.

Take them out of the pan and cool them on a rack.

RHUBARB: The rhubarb season is very short, and here in Jerusalem it's hard to come by. Whenever I saw rhubarb, I would order a huge case of it. You should definitely avoid the leaves, since they are considered poisonous. To use rhubarb, trim both ends of the stalks by cutting into the tough end (but not cutting all the way through), and using the knife to pull the strings off from both ends. After washing the stems thoroughly, dry them and chop them into small chunks. Put them into plastic storage bags and keep them in the freezer. They are ready to use as is - just add them to muffin batter, to a cake mixture, or into compote or fruit crumble.

Banana Chocolate Chip Muffins

I heartily recommend buying bananas and letting them fully ripen almost to black just to use them in this recipe. I've even frozen ripe bananas and then used them at a later date. You can use 6 tablespoons of canola oil instead of the butter, but butter is better here.

Makes 10
- Muffin pan lined with 10 paper muffin cups.

PREHEAT THE OVEN TO 165°C (325°F).

Mix the bananas, butter, sugar, egg, and vanilla in a bowl with a wooden spoon.

Mix the flour, baking soda, baking powder, and salt in a separate, smaller bowl. Add this to the banana mixture. Add the chocolate chips. Stir delicately with the wooden spoon only enough to moisten the flour. It's okay to still see a bit of flour - don't over mix!!

Divide the mixture evenly into the 10 paper-lined muffin cups.

Bake the muffins for about 20-25 minutes until they are golden and the tops feel dry to the touch. (Be careful when you're touching the tops of these because the bits of melted chocolate are very, very hot!)

Take them out of the pan and cool them on a rack.

dairy

INGREDIENTS:

1 cup mashed very, very ripe bananas (about 3 big ones)

85 g (3 ounces) melted butter

100 g (½ cup) sugar

1 egg

4 g (1 teaspoon) vanilla

210 g (1½ cups) flour

5 g (1 teaspoon) baking soda

4 g (1 teaspoon) baking powder

5 g (1 teaspoon) salt

95 grams (3½ ounce) chocolate chips

Chocolate Muffins

Bear in mind, these muffins are not cupcakes. They have a drier crumb, but for those of us who love a chocolaty jolt with our morning cup of coffee – they are the ticket.

Makes 12
- Muffin pan lined with 12 paper muffin cups.

PREHEAT THE OVEN TO 165°C (325°F).

Mix together the hot water and espresso powder in a small bowl. Let it cool.

Whisk in the buttermilk, canola oil, eggs, and vanilla.

Mix the flour, sugar, brown sugar, cocoa powder, baking powder, baking soda, and salt in a separate large bowl with a whisk, or with your fingers, to break up any possible lumps of dry ingredients.

Add the buttermilk mixture and stir it altogether very gently with a wooden spoon until everything is barely combined, adding the chocolate chips while folding.

Divide the mixture evenly into the 12 paper-lined muffin cups.

Bake the muffins for about 20-25 minutes until the tops look just set. It's easy to over bake these because it's difficult to tell when they're a golden colour, so watch the time carefully. (Be careful when you're touching the tops of these to check them because the bits of melted chocolate are very, very hot!)

Take them out of the pan and cool them on a rack.

These are best eaten the same day. If you have any left over, wrap them well and freeze.

dairy

INGREDIENTS:

60 ml (¼ cup) hot water

5 g (1 tablespoon) instant espresso granules

120 ml (½ cup) buttermilk

120 ml (½ cup) canola oil

2 eggs

4 g (1 teaspoon) vanilla

245 g (1¾ cups) flour

100 g (½ cup) sugar

100 g (½ cup) brown sugar

20 g (3 tablespoons) cocoa powder

4 g (1 teaspoon) baking powder

5 g (1 teaspoon) baking soda

5 g (1 teaspoon) salt

190 g (7 ounces) chocolate chips

dairy

INGREDIENTS:

1 whole washed seedless orange, peel and all, cut into chunks

100 g (½ cup) sugar

1 egg

113 g (4 ounces) butter, cut into chunks

113 g (4 ounces) pitted Medjool dates, cut into chunks

125 ml (½ cup) orange juice

210 g (1½ cups) flour

5 g (1 teaspoon) baking soda

4 g (1 teaspoon) baking powder

4 g (¾ teaspoon) salt

dairy

INGREDIENTS:

60 ml (¼ cup) oil

100 g (½ cup) brown sugar

60 ml (¼ cup) honey

2 eggs

240 ml (1 cup) milk

170 g (1½ cups) bran

140 g (1 cup) flour

6 g (1½ teaspoon) baking powder

2½ g (½ teaspoon) baking soda

4 g (¾ teaspoon) salt

90 g (3 ounces) golden raisins

Orange-Date Muffins

I made these muffins once for a Tu Bishvat party (the Jewish version of Arbour Day) and once for an Israel Independence Day breakfast because they use two of Israel's most popular fruits. They were so good that I added them to the bakery's menu.

Makes 12
■ Muffin pan lined with 12 paper muffin cups..

PREHEAT THE OVEN TO 165°C (325°F).

Process orange, sugar, egg, butter, dates and juice in a food processor until almost ground but still with tiny bits.

Mix flour, baking soda, baking powder, and salt in a bowl, with a wooden spoon. Scrape out the orange mixture from the processor with a spatula into the flour mixture. (Don't leave any behind!)

Mix it together very delicately with the wooden spoon, just enough to moisten the flour. Don't over mix.

Divide the mixture evenly into the 12 paper-lined muffin cups.

Bake the muffins for about 25-30 minutes until they are golden and the tops feel dry to the touch.

Take them out of the pan and cool them on a rack.

Bran Muffins

The classic granddaddy of muffins. They are a good source of fibre, and are at their best eaten fresh, fresh. If you have any left over, just wrap them and freeze them and take them out to thaw and warm up as you need them.

Makes 12
■ Muffin pan lined with 12 paper muffin cups.

PREHEAT THE OVEN TO 165°C (325°F).

Mix the oil, brown sugar, honey and eggs in a large bowl, with a wooden spoon.

Add the milk, and then the bran.

Mix together the flour, baking powder, baking soda, and salt in a separate, smaller bowl.

Add the flour mixture and the raisins to main bowl.

Mix everything all together lightly with the wooden spoon just until the flour almost disappears. It's okay to still see traces of flour; don't over mix!!

Divide the mixture evenly into the 12 paper-lined muffin cups.

Bake the muffins for about 20-25 minutes until they are golden and the tops feel dry to the touch.

Take them out of the pan and cool them on a rack.

DANISH PASTRIES

A good Danish pastry is all about the yeast dough and this recipe is about as good as it gets. Yes, hand-rolling the rich dough is a bit of a chore, but trust me, the reward is so worth the effort. The smell of homemade Danish pastry coming from your own home oven is enough to endanger just about any diet.

I've included some of the fillings that were bestsellers in our bakery. I've written the recipe options below for half a batch of dough at a time, so you can make two different kinds of Danishes from one recipe of dough.

Makes about 25 Danishes, depending on the size
- 2 baking pans lined with baking paper

Cinnamon Danish:

Pour boiling water on the raisins in a small bowl. Set aside.

Roll out the dough on a floured surface to a large rectangle about 28 cm x 43 cm (11 x 17 inches). Spread on all the melted butter.

Mix the sugar and cinnamon in a small bowl. Sprinkle it over the butter.

Drain the raisins, dry them well, chop, and sprinkle over the cinnamon sugar.

Roll up the dough from the long end and form a long cylinder. Cut the roll into 14 slices. Lay the slices carefully on the baking pans about 5 cm (2 inches) apart. Flatten them down a little bit with your hand. Brush them with the beaten egg, and then let them rise at room temperature for about an hour.

PREHEAT THE OVEN TO **180°C (350°F)**.

Bake the Danishes for about 15 minutes until they're golden brown.
GLAZE:

Heat the jam in the microwave until it's melted, for 20 seconds at a time. Brush the glaze on all the Danishes. Drizzle on the powdered sugar mixed with water.

Cheese Danish:

Mix together the cream cheese, egg yolk, sugar, and vanilla sugar or seeds in a small bowl. Set aside.

Roll out the dough on a floured surface to a large rectangle about 28 cm x 43 cm (11 x 17 inches). Cut the dough into 12 squares. Put a tablespoon of cheese filling in the centre of each square, and fold the dough up over the cheese like an envelope - bringing each of the four points of the square into the centre. Lay the pastries carefully on the baking pans about 5 cm (2 inches) apart.

INGREDIENTS:
One batch Danish dough, pg 148, ready to roll out

INGREDIENTS:
½ batch Danish dough
100 g (3½ ounces) dark raisins
56 g (2 ounces) butter, melted
150 g (¾ cup) sugar
15 g (4 teaspoons) cinnamon
1 egg, beaten

GLAZE:
120 ml (½ cup) apricot jam
120 g (1 cup) powdered sugar mixed with 1 tablespoon water

INGREDIENTS:
½ batch Danish dough
200 g (7 ounces) 30% cream cheese
About ¼ of an egg yolk
50 g (¼ cup) sugar
5 g (big pinch) vanilla sugar, or ¼ teaspoon of the scraped out seeds of a vanilla bean
1 egg, beaten

CRUMB MIXTURE:

100 g (3½ ounces) butter

100 g (3½ ounces) sugar

200 g (scant 1½ cups) flour

CRUMB MIXTURE:

Process together to form crumbs. (It can be stored in the freezer and used as needed.)

Brush the pastries with the beaten egg, sprinkle them with some of the crumb mixture, and then let them rise at room temperature for about an hour.

PREHEAT THE OVEN TO **180°C (350°F)**.

Bake the Danishes for about 15 minutes until they're golden brown.

Apple Danish:

INGREDIENTS:

½ batch Danish dough

Apple filling from apple
   hazelnut tart, pg 105

1 egg, beaten

Roll out the dough on a floured surface to a large rectangle about 28 cm x 43 cm (11 x 17 inches). Cut the dough into 12 squares. Place 2-3 tablespoons of apple filling on one side of each square. Fold the dough in half over the filling, pressing closed the three open ends of the dough. Turn the Danish over so the seam is on the bottom, and make a little slit through the top of the dough with the tip of a sharp knife. Lay the pastries carefully on the baking pans about 5 cm (2 inches) apart. Brush them with the beaten egg, and then let them rise at room temperature for about an hour.

PREHEAT THE OVEN TO **180°C (350°F)**.

Bake the Danishes for about 15 minutes until they're golden brown. Glaze as for the Cinnamon Danishes.

Lemon Danish:

INGREDIENTS:

½ batch Danish dough

lemon curd, pg 150

1 egg, beaten

Roll out the dough on a floured surface to a large rectangle about 28 cm x 43 cm (11 x 17 inches). Cut the dough into 12 squares. Fold each of the four points of the square of dough into the centre, like an envelope. Lay the pastries carefully on the baking pans about 5 cm (2 inches) apart. Put a large tablespoon of lemon curd on the centre of each Danish. Brush the exposed dough with the beaten egg, and then let the pastries rise at room temperature for about an hour.

PREHEAT THE OVEN TO **180°C (350°F)**.

Bake the Danishes for about 15 minutes until they're golden brown. Glaze as for the Cinnamon Danishes.

Poppy Seed Danish:

INGREDIENTS:

½ batch Danish dough

1 batch poppy seed filling for
   hamantaschen, pg 130

1 egg, beaten

1 tablespoon whole poppy
   seeds

Roll out the dough on a floured surface to a large rectangle about 28 cm x 43 cm (11 x 17 inches). Cut the dough into 12 squares. Place 1 tablespoon of poppy seed filling on one side of each square. Fold the dough in half over the filling, pressing closed the three open ends of the dough. With the tip of a sharp knife, make little cuts down the sealed side of the Danish (not the open side with the pressed close seam). Stretch the Danish into a curved shaped with the slits on the outside. Lay the pastries carefully on the baking pans about 5 cm (2 inches) apart. Brush them with the beaten egg, and then let them rise at room temperature for about an hour. Sprinkle the whole poppy seeds on the Danishes.

PREHEAT THE OVEN TO 180°C (350°F).

Bake the Danishes for about 15 minutes until they're golden brown. Glaze as for the Cinnamon Danishes.

Vanilla Danish:

Roll out the dough on a floured surface to a large rectangle about 28 cm x 43 cm (11 x 17 inches). Cut the dough into 12 squares. Place 1 heaping tablespoon of vanilla pastry cream on one side of each square. Fold the dough in half over the filling, pressing closed the three open ends of the dough. Turn the Danish over so the seam is on the bottom, and make a little slit through the top of the dough with the tip of a sharp knife. Lay the pastries carefully on the baking pans about 5 cm (2 inches) apart. Brush them with beaten egg, and then let them rise at room temperature for about an hour.

INGREDIENTS:
½ batch Danish dough
1 batch vanilla pastry cream pg 151
1 egg, beaten

PREHEAT THE OVEN TO 180°C (350°F).

Bake the Danishes for about 15 minutes until they're golden brown. Glaze as for the Cinnamon Danishes.

NOTE: As a variation or perhaps for a Sabbath morning treat, try making the Danish dough into large loaf cakes instead of individual pastries. Judging by the amount we sold in our shops every Friday, you will have a lot of satisfied customers of your own.

The full recipe of Danish dough should make 5 loaves, in buttered standard 23 cm x 13 cm (9 x 5 inch) loaf pans.

Roll out the full dough into a large rectangle and cut it into 5 even rectangles.

• For a Cinnamon Danish Cake, make the Cinnamon Danishes as outlined and stand 5 Danishes up against each other in one pan.

• For a Cheese Danish Cake, lay one piece of dough onto a flat surface and with the tip of a sharp knife, make a few cuts into the 2 long sides of the rectangle. Lay the dough into the loaf pan, fill it with a few tablespoons of cheese filling, then close the dough up over the cheese filling by wrapping the cut sides of the dough over each other. Sprinkle on some of the crumb topping.

• For a delicious Apple Danish Cake, mix the apple filling with vanilla pastry cream (pg 151). Lay a piece of dough into the loaf pan, put in a few tablespoons of apple-vanilla filling, and close the dough up over the filling.

• For a Poppy Seed Danish Cake, lay a piece of dough into the loaf pan, put in few tablespoons of poppy seed filling, and close the dough up over the filling.

• Lemon filling doesn't work in a large Danish cake.

For all the loaf variations, continue as in the recipe, but after 15 minutes in the oven you should cover the loaf loosely with a silicon mat or a piece of aluminum foil and bake for another 15 minutes or so to make sure the Danish is well baked all the way through. Glaze all but the cheese as for the Cinnamon Danishes.

---

dairy

CROISSANTS

Butter. Buttery, flaky dough. That pretty much says it all. These croissants are as close as I could come to duplicating the ones I made while studying at L'Ecole Lenôtre in Paris. There, they were quite adamant about keeping the croissants a dainty size and not bombastic. Here, at La Cuisine, we compromised to a medium size. Enjoy these with jam, but I'd skip adding any butter…

Makes about 32 croissants

▪ 2 baking sheets lined with baking paper.

INGREDIENTS:

1 batch croissant dough, pg 147, ready for rolling out into croissants

1 egg, beaten

Roll out the block of croissant dough on a lightly floured surface into a large rectangle about 20 cm x 80 cm (8 x 32 inches).

Cut the dough lengthwise across the middle with a sharp knife, and then cut each strip into eight squares 10 x 10 cm (4 x 4 inches) each. Cut each square into two triangles. Stretch each triangle a little bit to even out the bottom two points of the narrow end.

Make a small cut with the tip of a sharp knife into the middle of the narrow bottom of the triangle (that allows the croissant to roll up easier with less pressure that might hold down the "puff"), and starting from that narrow bottom, roll up the croissant to the tip. Curve the two long ends downwards to form a crescent shape, and place them on the baking sheets 5 cm (2 inches) apart, with the tip side down. Brush them lightly with the beaten egg (you don't want extra egg wash to inhibit the rising power of the laminated dough) so that they don't dry out.

Now you need to let them rise slowly in a moist environment. My favourite way to do this is to turn the oven on to the lowest temperature for a few minutes with an open bowl of water on the floor of the oven. Turn off the heat and put the croissants in for 1½ - 2 hours, until they double in size and get very puffy. Take them out of the oven and let them rest at room temperature while the oven preheats. (If you can't spare your oven for this, just cover them with a towel and let them rise for two hours at room temperature.)

PREHEAT THE OVEN TO **220°C (425°F)**.

Put the croissants into the hot oven and immediately turn down the heat to 180°C (350°F). Bake the croissants for 13 minutes. Then open the oven door and stick in something to keep the door a bit ajar, and bake for another 3 minutes until the croissants are dark golden and well baked.

NOTE: If you want to freeze the croissants, immediately stick them into the freezer to flash-freeze them until they're hard. Store them in a plastic bag. When ready to use, heat them up, directly from the freezer, in a hot oven or toaster oven (never, ever in the microwave!) for about 5 minutes.

dairy

CHEESE BROWNIES

These brownies satisfy two cravings in one mouthful - cheese and chocolate. Always in demand, we had to keep both our stores stocked with them every day. They taste best at room temperature, but they should be stored in the fridge.

Makes one 33 cm x 23 cm (9 inch x 13 inch) rectangular pan

PREHEAT THE OVEN TO 180°C (350°F).

CHOCOLATE BASE:

Melt the chocolate and butter in a heatproof glass bowl or cup in the microwave at half power for 5 minutes. Stir it until it's smooth.

Beat the butter with the sugar in the bowl of a mixer with the paddle until it's fluffy. Then slowly beat in the eggs until smooth. Add the vanilla, almond extract, salt, and the melted chocolate mixture. Whisk in the flour.

Spread the batter into the pan.

CHEESE TOPPING:

Beat the cream cheese and butter in a mixer with the paddle until it's fluffy.

Beat in the sugar and the flour.

Whisk the eggs lightly and add them to the batter.

Beat in the cream and vanilla.

Carefully pour the mixture onto the chocolate base.

Bake the brownies for about 40 minutes until the brownie puffs up and turns slightly golden.

Allow them to cool and then refrigerate.

Cut the brownies into whatever size you prefer - chances are, you'll have to make more anyway…

CHOCOLATE BASE:

340 g (12 ounces) chocolate, chopped

85 g (3 ounces) butter, cubed

150 g (¾ cup) sugar

3 eggs

6 g (1½ teaspoons) vanilla

½ teaspoon almond extract

½ teaspoon salt

105 grams (¾ cup) flour

CHEESE TOPPING:

340 g (12 ounces) cream cheese

42 g (1½ ounces) butter

150 g (¾ cup) sugar

12 g (1½ tablespoons) flour

3 eggs

45 ml (3 tablespoons) heavy cream

6 g (1½ teaspoons) vanilla

non-dairy

FLOURLESS BROWNIES

Fudgy yet light, these brownies began as a Passover recipe (we substituted potato starch for the corn flour), but they were such a hit that we decided to sell them all year round. They make a great option for your gluten-free guests.

Yields one 25 x 35 cm (9 x 13 inch) pan of brownies (line the pan with baking paper)

PREHEAT OVEN TO 180°C (350°F).

Whisk the eggs and sugar in a mixer.

Whisk in the oil.

Whisk in the salt and the cocoa.

Whisk in the corn flour.

Pour the mixture into the pan.

Sprinkle on the chocolate chips.

Bake for about 35 minutes.

INGREDIENTS:

6 eggs

600 g (3 cups) sugar

360 ml (1½ cups) canola oil

¾ teaspoon salt

130 g (1 cup plus 2 tablespoons) cocoa

240 g (1½ cups) corn flour

140 g (¾ cup) chocolate chips

CHURROS

On Chanukah, here in Israel, the fried food of choice to celebrate the "holiday of oil" is doughnuts. In fact, already a month before the 25th of the Hebrew month of Kislev (which usually comes out sometime in December), the bakeries and markets start selling all different kinds of filled doughnuts, ending in a weeklong frenzy during Chanukah itself. These doughnuts are only good fresh, the fresher the better, preferably picked up from the bakeries on the way to the meal or the party where the treats will be enjoyed. The better shops usually have lines out the door. The heavy smell of deep-frying is generally so strong at this time of year that you can often find a bakery just by following your nose.

I personally can't stand the smell of frying, and I can't stand frying. I think I was the only bakery in the country that stubbornly decided from day one that I was not going to follow the crowd and I refused to make and sell doughnuts on Chanukah. People just couldn't believe it, especially my bank manager.

What I did do, though, for Chanukah parties that I catered, was make these wonderful churros on the spot, at the event. A churro is a deep-fried choux paste (cream puff pastry) tossed with cinnamon and sugar and served warm. I also made them once every holiday for my staff to enjoy, together with a cup of rich hot chocolate - the classic accompaniment. All of my staff, including those who didn't observe Chanukah, always looked forward to this annual treat.

DEEP-FRYING IN A WOK:

I much prefer using a wok for deep-frying rather than a straight-sided saucepan. The sides of the wok flare out way beyond the edges of the oil, so they tend to catch a lot more of the splattering oil, thereby saving you on a lot of the mess. The flared sides also make it much easier to reach in with your tools to flip over or scoop out your frying food, and also to sieve out the little burning bits. And the main thing is, the narrower bottom of the wok along with the super width of the top allows you more surface area ratio to fry in with a smaller amount of oil than in a straight pot.

Makes about 5 dozen churros, depending on the size

Mix 150 g (¾ cup) sugar and the cinnamon in a small bowl.

Bring the water, salt, sugar, and butter to a boil in a medium-size saucepan.

Take it off the heat and add in all the flour.

Stir the dough vigorously with a wooden spoon. Cook it for two minutes over low heat, stirring constantly in order to dry it out.

Scrape the dough into a mixer bowl, and let it cool for 5 minutes.

Turn the mixer, with the paddle, on low, adding the eggs one at a time, until the dough is the consistency of mayonnaise.

Scoop the dough into a pastry bag fitted with a 1¼ cm (½ inch) star tip.

Heat the oil in a wok until it's very hot.

Pipe strips about 10 cm (4 inches) gently into the hot oil in the wok, cutting each strip off of the tip with a knife. Don't overcrowd the wok, cook in batches. Cook the strips about 2 minutes until they're golden brown, turning them frequently.

Take them out with a skimmer and drop them into a paper towel-lined bowl.

Put them immediately into another bowl and toss with the cinnamon-sugar mixture.

Eat them as soon as possible. (I suggest following this treat with a long, brisk walk.)

INGREDIENTS:

360 ml (1½ cups) water

3 g (¾ teaspoon) salt

22 g (1½ tablespoons) sugar

170 g (6 ounces) butter

210 g (1½ cups) flour

6 eggs

1 litre (4 cups) canola oil

150 g (¾ cup) sugar

12 g (1 tablespoon) cinnamon

dairy and non-dairy

LA CUISINE TART CRUST

This was our basic, buttery tart crust that we used for all our sweet recipes: pear tarts, pecan tarts, lemon meringue and fresh fruit tarts, seasonal baked fruit tarts, and chocolate caramel tarts. And of course, we used butter-flavoured margarine to produce a non-dairy version of the tart. If you do use the margarine, try adding a teaspoon of freshly grated lemon rind to the dough - it really helps the flavour.

The recipe is rich with sugar and egg yolks so it's not quite as sensitive to being overworked as a less rich dough would be. On the other hand, it is also a bit harder to roll out than other doughs and has a tendency to crack. As long as you are aware of this tendency, you shouldn't panic if it cracks or breaks apart - merely pick the rolled out dough up on the rolling pin or with a flat bottom of a removable tart pan, strategically place the pieces into the tart pan that you are going to fill, and press the cracks together with your fingertips while lining the pan.

INGREDIENTS:

245 g (1¾ cups) flour

150 g (5½ ounces) butter, cut in cubes (or butter-flavoured margarine for a non-dairy tart)

50 g (¼ cup) sugar

2 egg yolks

¼ teaspoon water

1/8 teaspoon vanilla

This amount is more than enough to make one 28 cm (11 inch) tart, and way more than enough for a 24 cm (9 inch) tart. So if you have a nice amount of dough left, just pat the pieces of dough together gently, wrap it up in plastic wrap and freeze it for future use. Just be sure to be gentle with the leftover pieces when you reroll it, so that you don't overwork the dough.

Makes one 24-28 cm (9-11 inch) tart, preferably in a removable-bottomed tart pan

Mix the flour, butter or margarine, and sugar in a mixer with the paddle until it's crumbly.

Add the egg yolks, water, and vanilla. Mix until it all comes together into a ball of dough.

Tip the dough out onto a sheet of plastic wrap, knead the dough together a few times with your palms, and wrap it up. Refrigerate the dough until it's cold, at least one hour.

PREHEAT THE OVEN TO 180°C (350°F).

When you're ready to roll it out, whack the dough a few times with your rolling pin to soften it a little bit. Roll it out on a floured surface or between two sheets of baking paper, and then line the tart pan with the dough.

When you are ready to bake it, either partially or fully, line the top of the dough with a large piece of aluminum foil. Press it in well with your fingertips, and especially hug the sides of the tart with the foil, folding it down over the outside edge of the tin pan and pressing it tightly. This will keep the dough up against the pan without the need to fill the dough with pie weights or dry beans. (I like shortcuts like these, but if you want to be really professional or accurate, you, of course, could weigh it down with pie weights or dry beans - I'm just trying to save you the bother...)

Bake the tart for 15-20 minutes for a partially baked crust. Take it out of the oven, and remove the foil very carefully so as not to tear the dough as you lift it off.

For a fully baked crust, return the uncovered tart to the oven for another 8-10 minutes until it's golden and fully baked.

NOTE: If you were to pre-bake the raw dough in the tart pan without somehow weighing it down, it would bubble up on the bottom unevenly and fall down and shrink on the sides. That is why professional bakers line the dough with paper and weigh it down with some kind of heavy weights (either pie weights which can be bought at professional cookware shops, or regular raw dry beans).

QUICHE DOUGH

The dough is not the place to cut corners in a quiche. Pure butter and a delicate hand are the two main ingredients. I've been making this quiche dough since way before I was married, and I have yet to find a better one. All that's left to do is to go to page 112 and prepare some wonderful vegetables and cheese, and you're good to go.

The only reason they used to say "real men don't eat quiche" is that they didn't get to eat it made with this dough.

Makes one 28 cm (11 inch) quiche base, or 24 mini quiches made in muffin pans
  ■ 28 cm (11 inch) tart pan with a removable bottom.

Mix the flour and salt briefly in a mixer with the paddle. Add the cubed butter and continue mixing until tiny crumbs form. Sprinkle in 45 ml (3 tablespoons) ice water and mix everything only until the dough starts to come together into a ball. Add a few more drops if needed.

Tip the dough out onto a sheet of plastic wrap, knead the dough together a few times with your palms, and wrap it up. Refrigerate the dough until it's cold, at least one hour.

PREHEAT THE OVEN TO 180°C (350°F).

Whack the dough a few times with your rolling pin to soften it a little bit when you're ready to roll it out. Roll it out on a floured surface or between two sheets of baking paper and then line the tart pan with the dough.

Line the top of the dough with a large piece of aluminum foil. Press it in well with your fingertips, and especially hug the sides of the tart with the foil, folding it down over the outside edge of the pan and pressing it tightly. This will keep the dough up against the pan without the need to fill it with pie weights or dry beans. (I like shortcuts like these, but if you want to be really professional or accurate, you, of course, could weigh it down with pie weights or dry beans - I'm just trying to save you the bother...)

Bake the quiche dough for 15-20 minutes until it is partially baked. Take it out of the oven, and remove the foil very carefully so as not to tear the dough as you lift it off.

Now you can go and make your quiche.

INGREDIENTS:

210 g (1½ cups) flour

3 g (½ teaspoon) salt

113 g (4 ounces) cold butter, in cubes

45-60 ml (3-4 tablespoons) ice water

Puff Pastry

Iactually travelled all the way to Paris to L'Ecole Lenôtre specifically in order to learn to make proper puff pastry, which to me has always been the king of all pastries. It is a laminated dough, which means that alternating layers of butter and flour are incorporated into dough in a unique way of folding and rolling. The bits of butter remain separate in between the flour, and when they melt in the heat of the oven, the water in the butter evaporates and pushes up the dough, causing the dough to puff.

In our bakery we had not one, but two roller machines, also known as sheeters, to take the hard work out of rolling laminated doughs and to ensure that they are made evenly and perfectly for maximum "puff." This is not an easy task for the home baker, but neither is it rocket science, and with a bit of patience and a liberal dose of muscle power, you will be pleasantly surprised by the results. Even if it doesn't come out perfectly, it will still be so delicious you'll find it hard to buy ready-made.

There are two basic points to remember when making any of these laminated doughs. First of all, the butter and the dough have to always be at the right temperature. If they are too warm, the butter will mush into the dough, creating more of a tart crust. If they are too cold, the hard pieces of butter will tear through the dough while rolling, and the steam that's so important to the rise of the puff pastry will escape through the tears. Second of all, it is very important to constantly rest the dough in the fridge - it will firm up the dough, and it will allow the gluten in the dough to relax, making it easier to roll out.

Makes 1150 g (2½ pounds) dough

Mix together the melted butter, 350 g (12¼ ounces) flour, water, vinegar, and salt in a mixer with the paddle to form a dough. Scrape the dough onto a sheet of plastic wrap on a baking tray and pat it into a rectangle. Wrap it up and refrigerate it for at least one hour.

BUTTER BLOCK:

Mix together the cubed butter with the flour in a mixer with the paddle until you don't see butter anymore. Scrape this butter block onto a sheet of plastic wrap on a baking tray and pat it into a rectangle. Wrap it up and refrigerate it for at least one hour.

TO ROLL OUT THE DOUGH:

Take the dough and the butter block out of the fridge for a few minutes - ideally they should be at the same temperature when you roll them out. Whack them both a few times with the rolling pin to slightly soften them up.

On a floured surface, roll out the dough into a large rectangle that will be twice the length of the butter block. Try to keep the edges even - it's very important to keep them even throughout this whole process to ensure an even rise and puff of the finished pastry.

INGREDIENTS:

100 g (3½ ounces) butter, melted

350 g (12¼ ounces) flour

145 ml (½ cup plus 2 scant tablespoons) water

15 ml (1 tablespoon) white vinegar

12 g (2½ teaspoons) salt

BUTTER BLOCK:

400 g (14 ounces) butter, cubed

150 g (5¼ ounces) flour

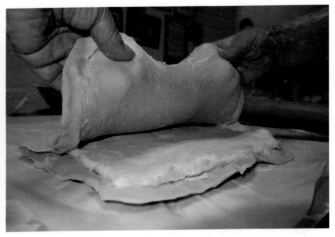

Place the butter block on one side of the dough; fold the dough up and over the butter block and press it shut. Brush off any excess flour - it can ruin your dough, interfere with the rising, and possibly cause grey streaks. Pull and adjust all the sides and corners constantly now to keep them even - some bakers prefer to keep pressing the edges up against a ruler or a straight edge of something hard. Turn the dough ¼ of the way around. Now you're going to start the actual rolling and folding.

Using all your strength and your body weight to work with you, roll the dough out, but don't press down onto the ends of the dough at any point so as not to ruin the puffing power of the edges. Keep rolling in the same direction into a rectangle about 20 x 45 cm (8 x 18 inches). Starting at the short end near you, fold the dough into three parts as if you're folding a letter into three to fit into an envelope - fold one third of the dough down, then fold the bottom third up over the first third to make a package that has three layers. This first fold is called **a single fold**.

Turn the dough sideways ¼ of the way so that the open side of the fold is on your right, and the "book spine" is on your left. Make sure the dough is positioned this way for every roll. If at any time butter starts oozing out the ends, dust that part with some flour.

Roll the dough out again into a rectangle about 20 x 45 cm (8 x 18 inches). This second fold is going to be **a double fold** - fold the dough down this time in to the middle, and fold the bottom of the dough up to meet the other part in the middle. Now close the dough by folding it in half so that you have four layers. Press two fingertips into the dough to show that you've completed two folds of the puff pastry. Place the dough in plastic wrap and refrigerate it for at least 2 hours.

Repeat **one single** and **one double** fold with the dough. Place the dough in plastic wrap and refrigerate it again, for at least 2 hours.

If at any time during your folds and rollings the dough gets too soft, or if it resists the rolling too much and keeps fighting you and bouncing back, just refrigerate it for 15 minutes or longer to chill and relax it.

The pastry is now ready to roll out and use in any recipe, or to freeze and use at a later date. It will keep up to a week in the fridge, wrapped well in plastic wrap.

Croissant Dough

dairy

This recipe follows the puff pastry recipe (pg 145) because the technique of folding layers of butter into dough to make it flaky is the same here, with the addition of yeast. I much prefer using fresh yeast, if for no other reason than its wonderful aroma.

Makes enough dough for about 32 croissants, depending on size

YEAST POOLISCH:

Dissolve yeast in the lukewarm water in a mixer bowl. Sprinkle the flour on top of the mixture. Set aside until cracks form in the dough, about 15-20 minutes.

DOUGH:

Add the flour to the yeast poolisch and stir it in a mixer with the paddle. Mix the sugar, salt, milk, and water in a small bowl. Add to the flour mixture.

Add 55 g (2 ounces) softened butter and mix in **just** to combine the ingredients.

Cover the bowl with plastic wrap and let sit at room temperature for one hour.

Punch down the dough, cover it again, and refrigerate for 2 hours.

Roll out the dough 8 mm (¼ inch) thick, in the shape of a long rectangle, 20 x 45 cm (8 x 18 inches). Spread **half the** softened butter (175 g or 6 ounces) onto the rolled out dough using your hands, then even it out with a plastic scraper.

Starting at the short end, fold the dough into three parts as if you're folding a letter into three to fit into an envelope - fold one third of the dough down, then fold the bottom third up over the first third to make a package that has three layers. This is called a **single fold**.

Turn the dough sideways ¼ of the way so that the open side of the fold is on your right, and the "book spine" is on your left. Make sure the dough is positioned this way for every roll. If at any time butter starts oozing out the ends, dust that part with some flour. You could also put it into the fridge for fifteen minutes to chill it a little.

Roll the dough out again into a rectangle about 20 x 45 cm (8 x 18 inches). Again fold the dough into three parts as if you're folding a letter into three to fit into an envelope - fold one third of the dough down, then fold the bottom third up over the first third to make a package that has three layers. **This is the second single fold.** Press two fingertips into the dough to show that you've completed two folds of the croissant dough. Place the dough in plastic wrap and refrigerate it at least two hours.

Take the dough out of the fridge and unwrap it. Roll it out again in the shape of a long rectangle, 20 x 45 cm (8 x 18 inches). Spread the second half of the softened butter (175 g or 6 ounces) onto the rolled out dough using your hands, then even it out with a plastic scraper.

Repeat two single folds, as above. You have now done two more single folds - **the third and the fourth folds.** Place the dough in plastic wrap and refrigerate it again for at least two hours, preferably overnight.

The dough is now ready to roll out to form into croissants.

YEAST POOLISCH:

20 g (¾ ounce) **fresh yeast**

100 g (3½ ounces) **lukewarm water**

75 g (heaping ½ cup) **flour**

DOUGH:

475 g (16¾ ounces) **flour**

40 g (1½ ounces) **sugar**

13 g (2½ teaspoons) **salt**

175 g (¾ cup) **milk**

20 ml (1 tablespoon plus 1 teaspoon) **water**

55 g (2 ounces) **butter, softened**

350 g (12¼ ounces) **butter, softened**

Danish Dough

The third in my series of laminated doughs, Danish dough is the richest variation with the addition of eggs and sugar. Use this dough to make the pastries in my recipe on page 135, and you're assured of a real treat. The method is basically the same as for puff pastry and croissant dough although I only use a butter block in my puff pastry. Try to make this dough when it's cool in your kitchen - it used to be a real challenge making this in our bakery in the sweltering heat of a Mediterranean summer. For the best results, keep letting the dough rest, and keep returning it to the fridge to chill.

Makes enough for about 25 Danishes, depending on the size, or 5 Danish loaves

DOUGH:

25 g (1 ounce) fresh yeast

240 ml (1 cup) lukewarm milk

50 g (¼ cup) sugar

2 eggs

500 g (3½ cups) flour

10 g (2 teaspoons) salt

BUTTER BLOCK:

340 g (12 ounces) butter, cubed

50 g (¼ cup) flour

DOUGH:

Mix the yeast, milk, and sugar in a mixer with the paddle or the dough hook. Let it sit 5 minutes until it starts to bubble. Add the rest of the ingredients and mix it to form a soft dough. Cover the bowl with plastic wrap and let it sit at room temperature for about 45 minutes. Punch it down and scrape it out onto the piece of plastic wrap, close it up, and refrigerate for two hours. Meanwhile make the butter block.

BUTTER BLOCK:

Mix together the cubed butter with the flour in a mixer with the paddle until you don't see butter anymore. Scrape this butter block onto a sheet of plastic wrap on a baking tray and pat it into a rectangle. Wrap it up and refrigerate for at least one hour, or until the dough is ready to be rolled out.

Remove the dough and butter block from the fridge, unwrap them and lay them down on a lightly floured surface. Try to have them both at approximately the same temperature and the same elasticity for ease of rolling. Whack them both a few times with the rolling pin to slightly soften them up.

Roll the dough into a large rectangle that will be twice the length of the butter block.

Place the butter block on one side of the dough, fold the dough up and over the butter block and press it shut. Turn the dough ¼ of the way around. Now you're going to start the actual rolling and folding.

Roll the dough into a rectangle about 20 x 45 cm (8 x 18 inches).

Starting at the short end, fold the dough into three parts as if you're folding a letter into three to fit into an envelope - fold one third of the dough down, then fold the bottom third up over the first third to make a package that has three layers. This **single fold is the first fold.**

Turn the dough sideways ¼ of the way so that the open side of the fold is on your right, and the "book spine" is on your left. Make sure the dough is positioned this way for every roll.

Roll the dough out again into a rectangle about 20 x 45 cm (8 x 18 inches). Fold the dough again into three parts the same way as in the

25 kilos of butter in our bakery.

first single fold. Press two fingertips into the dough to show that you've **completed two folds** of the Danish dough. Wrap the dough in plastic wrap and refrigerate it for at least 2 hours.

Repeat the first two folds with the dough, so that **by now you have rolled out and done four folds**. Refrigerate it again for two hours.

If at any time during any of your folds and rollings the dough gets too soft, or if it resists the rolling too much and keeps fighting you and bouncing back, just refrigerate it for 15 minutes or longer to chill and relax it.

The Danish dough is now ready to roll out and use, or to freeze and use at a later date. This dough doesn't keep well for more than a day or two in the fridge because of the yeast.

White Sponge Cake Base

non-dairy

This cake was used in our bakery as a base for many different recipes, and we were never without it in our freezer, in various shapes and sizes. I suggest you also bake one or two to keep on hand. We used it, among other things, as a base to hold a mousse cake or an unbaked cheesecake, as broken pieces to soak with syrup and fruit purée and layer in a trifle, or ground up to use as crumbs in strudel, apple torte, Florentine cookies, or poppy seed filling for danishes and hamantaschen. Our lovely first assistant baker Debra used to claim that this was her favourite La Cuisine cake, eaten warm out of the oven.

Makes one 24 cm (9 inch) round or square cake or two 18 cm (7 inch) cakes

■ 24 cm (9 inch) spring form pan, or two 18 cm (7 inch) rings, lined with parchment paper for easy removal of the cake later.

Whip the egg yolks and 95 g (scant ½ cup) sugar with a mixer until it's light and fluffy. Add the oil and water and whip it until it's thick.

PREHEAT THE OVEN TO 180°C (350°F).

Whip the egg whites in a clean bowl until soft peaks form. Slowly add the other 95 g (scant ½ cup) sugar, and whisk it until the peaks are stiff but not dry and lumpy.

Fold half of the egg whites into the yolks; fold it together lightly, not thoroughly.

Add the rest of the egg whites and the flour, and fold it all together gently but thoroughly while turning the bowl and scraping up from the bottom.

Pour the batter into the pan.

Bake the cake for about 35 minutes until the top is golden and feels springy to the touch.

Cool it on a wire rack.

COCOA SPONGE CAKE BASE VARIATION: This cocoa sponge cake base, as with our white sponge base, was always on hand in various shapes and sizes in our bakery freezer. It was used as a base for mousse cakes, and in a pinch could be crumbled and layered with any kind of mousse or cream in tiny mousse glasses to provide a quick, easy, delicious dessert. The ingredients and instructions are the same as for the white sponge cake base above, except for the following substitution:

Instead of 190 g (1 1/3 cups) flour, use 166 g (1 cup plus 2 tablespoons) flour mixed with 24 g (3½ tablespoons) cocoa.

INGREDIENTS:

5 eggs, separated

95 g (scant ½ cup) sugar

40 ml (3 tablespoons) oil

40 ml (3 tablespoons) water

95 g (scant ½ cup) sugar

190 g (1 1/3 cup) flour

dairy and non-dairy

LEMON CURD

Lemon curd is a wonderful filling or topping for tarts, danishes, cheesecakes, sponge cakes, and roulades. Don't even dream of using bottled lemon juice, as your curd will taste tinny and processed and will ruin your delicious homemade baked goods.

INGREDIENTS:

115 g (½ cup plus 1 tablespoon) sugar

120 ml (½ cup) freshly squeezed lemon juice

85 g (3 ounces) butter or butter-flavoured margarine

2 teaspoons grated lemon rind

3 eggs (if you want it extra rich, use 2 eggs plus 2 yolks)

Put the sugar, lemon juice, butter/margarine, and lemon rind in a small saucepan. Bring it to a gentle boil.

Whisk the 3 eggs in a separate bowl.

When the butter/margarine is entirely melted in the saucepan, pour the mixture into the eggs while whisking (get someone to help you if you feel you're not coordinated enough), and then pour the mixture back into the saucepan.

Bring the mixture back to a simmer while whisking. When bubbles start to break the surface and the curd thickens slightly, pour it out through a sieve into a clean bowl.

The lemon curd lasts 4-5 days in the fridge.

> NOTE: To make a delicious and easy lemon mousse, simply weigh the amount of lemon curd you want to use and weigh an equal amount of heavy cream. Whip the cream and fold it into the curd. *Voilá!!* Lemon mousse.

Vanilla Pastry Cream (crème pâtissière)

dairy

I f you don't have a real vanilla bean, you can add one teaspoon of your excellent quality La Cuisine homemade vanilla, or any other pure, quality vanilla extract. Pastry cream is used to fill a tart before you cover it with fresh fruit, or it can be folded with equal amounts of whipped cream to use as a mousse for a layered trifle. It's also excellent as a filling for a Danish.

Makes enough to fill one 24 cm (9 inch) tart

Pour the milk into a small saucepan. Slit the vanilla bean open with a knife and scrape all the seeds into the milk. Add the empty pod as well. Bring the milk to a boil. (If you're not using a vanilla bean, bring just the milk to a boil in a small saucepan.)

In a separate medium-size bowl whisk together the egg yolks, sugar, and corn flour.

Pour the hot milk through a strainer (if you're not using a vanilla bean, just pour the hot milk directly) into the egg yolk mixture while whisking (get someone to help if you feel you're not coordinated enough). Immediately pour the hot mixture back into the saucepan and return to the heat.

Bring the mixture to a boil while constantly whisking until it thickens.

Pour it into a bowl to cool. (If you're not using the vanilla bean, you now stir the vanilla extract into the cream.)

Smear the butter onto the surface to prevent a skin from forming on the cream. Then cover it with plastic wrap. Poke a few holes into the plastic with the tip of a sharp knife to allow the heat to escape.

It will last for 2 or 3 days in the fridge, no longer.

NOTE: If you want to make the pastry cream non-dairy, the best substitute I have found for the milk is almond milk. Skip the smear of butter at the end (or use margarine if you don't mind the taste).

INGREDIENTS:

375 ml (1½ cups) milk

5 egg yolks

113 g (½ cup plus 1 tablespoon) sugar

30 g (4 tablespoons) corn flour

Half of a good vanilla bean, or

6 g (1½ teaspoons) vanilla

Pat of butter, room temperature

Soaking Syrup

non-dairy

This is a basic "1:1" syrup that can be used to brush on any cake or cake layer to moisten and/or flavour it. It keeps for a long time in the fridge. You can also add a small amount (up to 2 tablespoons) of an extract flavouring (such as vanilla or almond) instead of the liqueur.

Makes 2 cups

Bring the water and sugar to a boil in a small saucepan, stirring occasionally to dissolve all the sugar granules. Boil for 2 minutes. After it cools, add the liqueur or flavouring.

INGREDIENTS:

240 ml (1 cup) water

200 g (1 cup) sugar

Up to 80 ml (1/3 cup) liqueur such as coffee, chocolate, framboise, or curaçao,

OR

Up to 24 g (2 tablespoons) vanilla or almond extract

FOREST FRUIT SAUCE

Here in Israel we get a lovely frozen mix of berries called "forest fruits," made up of blueberries, raspberries, red and black currants, and sour cherries. This deeply coloured, beautiful sauce was served as a topping for classic, tofu, or crumb cheesecake (pgs 75, 76, and 78) as well as the dessert called "malabi" (pg 155), or pancakes and waffles at a catered breakfast. It lasts for weeks in the fridge, or you can freeze it in containers indefinitely.

Makes 3 cups

Bring the fruit, sugar, and lemon juice to a boil in a medium saucepan. Let it simmer for 5 minutes, stirring occasionally. Stir in the corn flour sludge and bring it back to a boil. Remove the sauce from the heat and let it cool.

INGREDIENTS:

1 litre (4 cups) mixed forest fruit

200 g (1 cup) sugar

60 ml (¼ cup) freshly squeezed lemon juice

16 g (2 tablespoons) corn flour, dissolved in 1 tablespoon water

CARAMEL SAUCE

Where to begin? I guess I would first say - please read Chapter Thirteen. My caramel sauce accident was a major trauma in my life, but that didn't make it any less of a mainstay in the La Cuisine kitchen. The *raison d'étre* of this sauce was to decorate our rich and creamy cheesecakes, but it's just as good spooned over vanilla ice cream, fresh figs, bananas or other fruit, crèpes, pancakes, waffles - you get the idea. Just do me a favour when you make it - please be careful.

Makes 2 cups

Pour the water into a heavy-bottomed saucepan and then add the sugar. Stir it occasionally with a wooden spoon over low heat until the sugar is totally dissolved.

Increase the heat to high and bring it to a boil. Keep a cup of water and a pastry brush nearby, and use it to occasionally wash down the crystals of sugar from the sides of the saucepan above the mixture, but stop doing that once you start seeing a hint of colour. Let it boil until it turns a beautiful amber colour and has a caramel smell. Don't let it get too dark or it will have a bitter taste, but neither should you stop when it's not dark enough because then it won't have a strong enough caramel taste.

If it crystallizes and collapses (you'll know what I mean if it happens), just chuck it out and start over. Don't waste the cream and butter by adding them as well.

When the colour is just right, lower the heat and carefully add the cream - stand back a bit, it sputters and steams angrily. Stir it with a whisk over low heat until it smoothes out. Turn off the heat.

Add the butter and vanilla. Stir until it's smooth.

If it caramelizes beautifully yet has a few crystals in it, you can usually save it by merely passing the sauce through a sieve.

INGREDIENTS:

90 ml (a bit more than 1/3 cup) water

250 g (1¼ cups) sugar

240 ml (1 cup) heavy cream

113 g (4 ounces) butter

4 g (1 teaspoon) vanilla

Fondue

Chocolate fondue is by no means a refugee from the seventies. Ours was a well-loved feature at our catered dessert parties, adding a special fun flair to the buffet. We would arrange two fondue pots on candles, one for dark chocolate and one for white, and surround the sinful elixirs with piles of beautifully cut and whole fruits, chunks of plain sponge cake, and sometimes even marshmallows! I could never stand to watch people "double dip," so instead of the usual way to present fondue with long-stemmed forks for dipping, I put two small ladles in the pots next to a pile of plates, making it politely clear to the guests that they were to ladle the sauce over the selections on their own plates.

Makes about 420 ml (1¾ cups)

Dark Chocolate:
340 g (12 ounces) dark chocolate, chopped

240 ml (1 cup) heavy cream

White Chocolate:
340 g (12 ounces) white chocolate, chopped

160 ml (2/3 cup) heavy cream

Dark Chocolate Fondue:

Heat the cream in a small, heavy-bottomed saucepan, and stir in the dark chocolate until it melts. Keep it warm over a small candle.

White Chocolate Fondue:

Heat the cream in a small, heavy-bottomed saucepan, and stir in the white chocolate until it melts. Keep it warm over a small candle, keeping a constant eye on it since white chocolate burns very easily. And I speak from experience...

MALABI

My veteran bakers, Halil and Muhammad, taught me the joys of making malabi, a Middle Eastern milk pudding perfumed with orange flower water. We made this silky, delicate custard for catering either in large baking pans, or in individual dishes or glasses. You can replace the orange flower water with rose water, and you can decorate the malabi however you like, not only the classic way suggested below.

Serves 8
■ 1 quart (1 litre) serving dish

Whisk the corn flour together with 120 ml (½ cup) milk in a small bowl. Set it aside.

Heat the rest of the milk and the sugar together in a medium saucepan. When it comes to a boil, whisk in the corn flour slurry and continue whisking constantly for a few minutes until the mixture thickens and bubbles break the surface. Stir in the orange flower water. Pour the malabi into the serving dish and cool to room temperature. Cover it with plastic wrap and refrigerate it until serving time.

Before serving, decorate the top of the malabi with rows of forest fruit sauce, coconut, and pistachios.

INGREDIENTS:

1 litre (4 1/3 cups) milk

200 g (1 cup) sugar

65 g (½ cup) corn flour

45 ml (3 tablespoons) orange flower water

DECORATION:
Forest fruit sauce (pg 152), shredded coconut, or ground pistachios

Vanilla Extract

This is a simple and economical way to make your own fragrant vanilla essence. Once you see how easy it is to make and how wonderful the final product is, I doubt you'll ever go back to buying it. This makes a great gift if you put it and a few of the beans in an attractive bottle with a nice label. You'll find our vanilla memoirs in Chapter Nine of the Tales.

INGREDIENTS:

One litre bottle of cheap, unflavoured vodka

12 plump, juicy, good-quality vanilla beans

Makes one litre (4 1/3 cups)

Lay the beans next to each other on a cutting board. Hold them down one at a time by the stem and slice down the centre of the bean with the tip of a sharp knife, all the way to the bottom. Drop the slit bean into the vodka. Repeat with all the vanilla beans. As you get to the last few, you'll have to pour off a little bit of the displaced vodka from the bottle. (Now would be a good time to enjoy a vodka cocktail…)

Label the bottle of vanilla with the date you prepared it so you can keep track. Keep the bottle in a dark place for at least two months. After two months, it's fragrant enough to use, but it just keeps getting better and better with time.

La Cuisine Catering Recipes
A Word or Two about Our Catering...

Fresh, seasonal, eye-catching, and above all else, tasty - very tasty. That pretty much sums up the guiding philosophy of La Cuisine's catering from the day we began taking orders from our home, twenty-one years ago. To us, it made no difference if we were catering an intimate house party or a family celebration for two hundred guests – our commitment to excellence and good taste was uncompromising.

We never adhered to the "everything but the kitchen sink" approach to catering. We preferred to keep our dining simple - plenty of food on hand but not too many choices. Other caterers were known for offering ten different salads on their buffet tables, of which five featured some variation of cherry tomatoes. Not us. There is only so much room on the biggest of dinner plates.

Oh yes, and fun. Entertaining should be about fun and enjoying oneself, without stress. The Hebrew word for family celebration is *simcha,* which literally means a "happy occasion". That, I believe, says it all.

Think out of the box. For years, I used my mini quiches (pg 115) as cocktails, as an appetizer, and even as a main course. If you need to stick to a budget, be flexible; soups and cocktails alongside a show-stopping dessert table will elicit the same enthusiastic accolades as a formal salmon dinner. If you do decide to entertain in some sort of creative way, just make sure you properly invite and prepare your guests; you wouldn't want them to arrive at a 7 p.m. dessert party expecting a full dinner.

A Final Word… - You don't have to be a professional caterer to entertain family and friends, you just need the right inspiration… I hope that these recipes will help.

Vegetables And Dip

These days, a stunning centrepiece of fresh produce may seem a bit passé, but some twenty-one years ago this was considered pretty new wave catering. Inspired by Martha Stewart's landmark tome, *Entertaining*, this was my answer to the ubiquitous plain bowl of carrot and cucumber sticks that was always accompanied by onion soup mix dip. For years my buffet tables featured an assortment of wicker baskets and trays overflowing with piles of colourful, seasonal *crudités* cut in odd and uneven shapes. Purple and green cabbages together with different shaped and coloured squash were hollowed out to house my favourite dips.

When they were available, I loved to include specialty items like Belgian endives, snow peas, blanched asparagus, and broad green beans.

An elegant addition to any formal catering, *crudités* and dip can be easily scaled down for an informal cocktail party or served as an accompaniment to any bar table alongside a fine selection of fancy cheeses or some interesting crackers with spreads.

Be creative. Let your imagination run wild. Just be sure to use only the freshest and most attractive produce. And it should go without saying - never, ever double dip!!

Cucumbers - scrubbed and unpeeled, of course.

Carrots - we used to cut them on the diagonal just to be different.

Peppers - all colours. Wash and dry them, cut them in half from the stem lengthwise, clean out all the seeds and membranes, and then cut them into triangular chunks.

Small radishes - cut off the tips and any black or bruised spots, leaving on any cute leafy greens, and wash them well.

Cherry tomatoes - try and wash them whole while leaving them on the pretty branches and stems.

Fresh mushrooms - use only small white ones, and only if you're serving them the same day.

Fennel - trim them and remove the stringy, sometimes unattractive outer layers, and then cut them and the inside wedges into odd shapes.

Zucchini - yes, you can eat them raw. Yes, they're delicious.

Kohlrabi - pick the smaller ones. Peel them, cut them in half, then slice them. They don't keep well for the next day - their colour goes a bit off, and they sometimes get bitter.

Belgian endive - separate the leaves, also cut up the core into wedges.

Snow peas - tip each end, while pulling the strings off the pod. Good raw or blanched for a few seconds in boiling water and dried well.

Green beans or broad green beans - tip the stem end, cut off any blemishes, and drop them into boiling water until they turn bright green (about ½ minute). Strain them out and drop them into ice water to stop the cooking. Dry them well.

Asparagus - try to find asparagus of medium thickness, and try to get a bunch of even thickness. Cut off a generous stem end of each spear, until you reach the part where it's not tough anymore. Blanch them in boiling water for about 18 seconds, then strain them out and drop them into ice water to stop the cooking. Dry them well.

DIP: dairy

This was the standard La Cuisine dip that was used with the vegetable baskets.

The truth is, I have never measured the ingredients for this dip. It just seems to taste better that way.

Whisk all the ingredients together, let it rest for a few minutes so the sugar and salt dissolve, then whisk it again.

Check for flavours by tasting.

DIP:

Equal amounts of mayonnaise and yogurt (preferably thin, runny yogurt)

Garlic powder (it really tastes better in the dip than fresh garlic)

Salt

Pepper

Sugar

Worcestershire sauce

A handful of minced fresh chives (preferable) or dill

non-dairy

NOTE: I have played with gravlax, with some interesting results. Before marinating, I've covered the top of the salmon with a large, grated fresh beet along with the basic recipe which turns it a beautiful colour. I've also changed the flavouring to be a bit oriental, skipping the dill and adding some soy sauce, fresh grated ginger, and some ground star anise to the sugar, salt, and peppercorns. Grated orange rind also adds a nice flavour.

Gravlax

Our Swedish friend Zev taught me how to make this salmon dish, and at the same time introduced Marvin to the pleasures of Aquavit (both of which, by the way, go together wonderfully). My record for making this was 10 sides of gravlax for a *Kiddush* for one of my sons' bar mitzvahs - and even with that amount, it was all finished before the bar mitzvah boy could get any! Proof of how delicious it is...

About 15 servings

(Start this recipe 2-3 days before serving.)

Slide the salmon into a large plastic bag and place it on a baking sheet. With the bag open, sprinkle the sugar, salt, peppercorns, and dill all over the top of the salmon. Tie the plastic bag shut, and weigh down the salmon (I put a big platter on it, and weigh it down with a few big, heavy cans).

Turn the bag of salmon over each day for 2 or 3 days.

Before serving, take the salmon out of the bag and scrape everything off of it.

Serve it skin side down, and cut thin slices off of the skin.

This is great served with the honey-mustard dressing (pg 168).

non-dairy

Pickled Salmon

This recipe was given to me by one of my bakers who used to work in a large catering company. It is so easy to prepare, and it makes a great first course or cocktail.

(Prepare this recipe 5 days before serving.)

Serves about 15 as a cocktail or appetizer

Cover the fillet with a large handful of kosher salt. Wrap it tightly with plastic wrap and let it sit in the fridge for 2 days.

Rinse all of the salt off the fillet and dry it lightly with a paper towel.

Mix the rest of the ingredients in a dish large enough to hold the salmon fillet. Place the salmon fillet into the mixture, skin side up. Cover it tightly with plastic wrap and let it sit in the fridge for three days.

Take the salmon out of the fridge. Remove the skin and cut the salmon into cubes.

Herring

Growing up, I remember my house was never without some form of herring in our fridge. My parents preferred to buy the fish directly from the market, soak them to get rid of the salt, and then add oil and lots of sliced onions and cracked black pepper. This love affair with "Jewish sushi" continued in my own household, where my boys have been mavens from the time they were toddlers.

I can hardly remember catering a Sabbath morning *Kiddush* without serving some form of herring with a selection of crackers. The following two recipes were my most requested, but you can enjoy them at home without buying the fish straight from the barrel. Any kind of herring fillet will do, but I strongly recommend matjes. These recipes will last up to one week in the fridge.

Pineapple Herring:

My Aunt Judy (my mother's sister) was a phenomenal cook and a legendary hostess who shared many recipes with me. This one is from her.

Serves 10-12

Pour hot water over the sliced onion. Let it sit for 15 minutes and then drain.

Mix everything together including the drained pineapple and the 180 ml (¾ cup) of juice, and let sit for a few hours so the flavours meld together.

Herring Salad:

A long-time friend and customer, Mrs. Klitsner, shared this one with me. I'm sure you'll also enjoy it.

Serves 18-20

Pour hot water over the sliced onion. Let it sit for 15 minutes and then drain.

Mix everything together and let sit for at least a few hours so the flavours meld together.

Pineapple Herring:

3 whole herrings, filleted (6 strips of herring fillets), cut into small slices

550 g (19 ounce) can pineapple, chunks or crushed - save 180 ml (¾ cup) of the juice

2 large onions, sliced

180 ml (¾ cup) mayonnaise

30 ml (2 tablespoons) white vinegar

5 g (1 teaspoon) sugar

5 g (1 teaspoon) dry mustard

Herring Salad:

6-7 whole herrings, filleted (12-14 strips of herring fillets), cut into small slices

3 apples, peeled, cored, and cut in chunks

3 large onions, sliced

2 dill pickles, cut in chunks

240 ml (1 cup) tomato purée

240 ml (1 cup) white vinegar

150 g (¾ cup) sugar

5 g (1 teaspoon) dry mustard

non-dairy

Ingredients:

3 large onions, chopped

80 ml (1/3 cup) canola oil

550 g (19 ounce) can green peas, drained, except for 60 ml (¼ cup) liquid

2 hard-boiled eggs, peeled

80 g (2¾ ounces) walnuts

2-3 tablespoons mayonnaise

½ teaspoon salt

Black pepper to taste

Vegetarian Chopped Liver

In the early years of La Cuisine, a client asked me to make this version of vegetarian chopped liver for her wedding that I was catering. It was so good that it became a mainstay on the appetizer table, served with crackers.

Serves 8

Fry the onions in the oil in a medium saucepan until they are very, very brown.

Scrape the onions and all the oil into a processor.

Add the other ingredients including the drained peas and the 60 ml (¼ cup) of liquid from the peas and blend.

---

non-dairy

Ingredients:

60 ml (¼ cup) olive oil

1 large onion, chopped

6 cloves garlic, chopped

3 large red peppers, cleaned and cubed

550 g (19 ounce) can chickpeas, drained, except for 60 ml (¼ cup) liquid

1 tablespoon lemon juice

½ teaspoon salt

¼ teaspoon pepper

Pinch hot chili flakes

2 tablespoons fresh basil or coriander

Red Pepper Hummus

We almost always had this delicious spread on hand as an appetizer with crackers, next to the bar, alongside vegetarian chopped liver. You can also use it as a first course with some Belgian endive leaves or other vegetables.

Serves 8

Fry the onions and garlic in the olive oil in a medium saucepan until they're very brown. Scrape them into a processor bowl. Try to leave some of the olive oil behind in the saucepan. Add the cubed red peppers to the pan, adding a bit more olive oil if necessary, and sauté until they're soft. Scrape the peppers and the oil into the processor. Add all the other ingredients (with the 60 ml (¼ cup) liquid from the chickpeas) and process until smooth or almost smooth, however you prefer.

SOUPS

Our soups were usually served as part of our buffet table as a cocktail, which meant that they were ladled into small cups and enjoyed by the guests as they mingled about. You can also enjoy them while you are sitting at a table and eating them from a bowl.

PUMPKIN SOUP   non-dairy

Not only is our dear friend Ellen a conscientious proofreader, but she is also an accomplished cook in her own right. As far as I'm concerned, there can never be enough variations of a comforting orange soup.

Serves 8-10

Sauté the onions in the olive oil in a large soup pot until they're soft, about 10 minutes. Add all the rest of the ingredients (except for the garnish) and bring to a boil. Simmer until the vegetables are soft, about 20 more minutes.

Purée the soup with an immersion blender. Taste it to adjust the seasoning.

Garnish each portion with pine nuts and chopped fresh parsley, if desired.

PUMPKIN:

2 large onions, chopped

60 ml (4 tablespoons) olive oil

600 g (21 ounces) fresh pumpkin, peeled and cubed

300 g (10 ounces) sweet potatoes, peeled and thinly sliced

300 g (10 ounces) carrots, peeled and thinly sliced

2 large potatoes, peeled and thinly sliced

2 litres (8½ cups) stock

2 tablespoons sugar

Grated rind of one orange

Salt and pepper to taste

GARNISH:

Pine nuts, (optional)

Fresh parsley, chopped

MUSHROOM BARLEY SOUP   dairy or non-dairy

This is a very warming, hearty soup, best served on a cold winter day or evening. It can be made even more hearty by the use of a rich, meaty stock. I sometimes leave it in the crock pot to serve it on Sabbath lunch.

Serves 8-10

Simmer the pearl barley in 480 ml (2 cups) water in a large soup pot for about 25 minutes. Keep an eye on it so it doesn't burn if the water gets entirely absorbed. Add a bit more water, if necessary.

Add all the rest of the ingredients and bring it to a boil. Simmer until everything is soft, about 20 minutes. Taste it to adjust the seasoning.

MUSHROOM BARLEY:

160 g (6 ounces) pearl barley, rinsed well

480 ml (2 cups) water

500 g (1¼ pounds) mushrooms, cleaned and chopped

2 large onions, chopped

5 garlic cloves, chopped

2 litres (8½ cups) water

80 ml (1/3 cup) soy sauce

60 ml (¼ cup) dry red wine

60 ml (4 tablespoons) butter or olive oil

Salt and pepper to taste

CREAM OF LETTUCE SOUP:

60 g (2 ounces) butter

2 onions, chopped

1 head of romaine lettuce,
  washed well and chopped

3 stalks celery, washed well
  and chopped

2 large potatoes, peeled and
  thinly sliced

1 litre (4 1/3 cups) stock

240 ml (1 cup) heavy cream

Salt and pepper to taste

GARNISH:

Fresh parsley, chopped
  (optional)

Shredded lettuce (optional)

Fresh chives (optional)

GAZPACHO:

1 litre (4 1/3 cups) tomato juice

1 English cucumber, or 4-5
  smaller cucumbers, chopped

1 green pepper, chopped

1 onion, chopped

2 cloves garlic, chopped

3 tablespoons red wine vinegar

2 tablespoons olive oil

Worcestershire sauce to taste

Tabasco sauce to taste

Salt and pepper to taste

CREAM OF LETTUCE SOUP

Don't let the name put you off - this pretty, pale green soup works well both hot and cold. A catering customer once asked us to call it "cream of spring greens" for her wedding. You can call it whatever you wish, just try it.

Serves 6

Sauté the onions, lettuce, and celery in the butter in a large soup pot until everything is soft, about 10 minutes, add the potatoes, stock, some salt and pepper, and bring it to a boil. Simmer until the vegetables are soft, about 20 minutes.

Purée the soup with an immersion blender.

Add the cream and taste it to adjust the seasoning.

If you're serving it cold, let it cool to room temperature and then refrigerate it.

Garnish each portion with chopped fresh parsley, lettuce, or chives, if desired.

GAZPACHO

This traditional tomato-based vegetable soup is Spanish in origin and is served cold. No matter how many versions I've tried over the years, I always go back to this one that I first had in the home of my friend Naomi when we were young (see Chapter One in Tales section).

Serves 8-10

Blend everything together, leaving it as chunky as you like. Taste to adjust the seasonings.

> NOTE: It's nice to serve gazpacho with a few small bowls of garnishes on the table - croutons, sour cream, and chunks of cucumbers and green peppers. This is one of the very few recipes in which I like green peppers.

CHICKPEA TOMATO SALAD

dairy

What's known here in the Mediterranean as "Bulgarian cheese" is a salty white pressed Balkan-style cheese made from cow's, sheep's, or goat's milk. It is less salty, a little more delicate in taste, and less crumbly than feta. I use it in quiches, salads, and vegetable strudels. Try it served with cubed watermelon and a sprinkling of fresh mint and lemon juice. Better yet, try it while lounging on the beach the way it's enjoyed here!

One thing I learned since moving to this part of the world is to use fresh fruits and vegetables only when they're in season. There are very few imported ones in Israel, and it was sometimes difficult to explain to catering clients why certain salads were unavailable at different times of the year. Since I will not use tomatoes in the winter, I substitute cherry tomatoes that grow all year-round.

Serves 8

Mix everything together. You can serve this on a bed of lettuce, if you like.

INGREDIENTS:

550 g (19 ounce) can chickpeas, drained

3 fresh tomatoes, cubed, or 270 g (1 cup) cherry tomatoes, halved

85 g (3 ounces) Bulgarian cheese

120 ml (½ cup) green onions, chopped

80 ml (1/3 cup) fresh parsley, chopped

45 ml (3 tablespoons) olive oil

30 ml (2 tablespoons) balsamic vinegar

Black pepper to taste

ORIENTAL SALAD WITH RICE NOODLES

My Aunt Judy, who was my mom's sister from Czechoslovakia, was a terrific cook and entertainer. She made many Hungarian-style dishes. What I most loved was that her love of good food led her to find recipes from all sorts of surprisingly different cuisines. I thought it was hysterical when she excitedly taught me to deep fry rice noodles in a wok and turn them into this Oriental salad.

RICE NOODLES:

1 litre (4 cups) canola oil

200 g (7 ounces) dried rice noodle vermicelli

SALAD:

½ litre (2 cups) bean sprouts

2 carrots, peeled and julienned

2 seedless cucumbers, washed and julienned

1 kohlrabi, julienned

240 ml (1 cup) snowpeas, julienned

1 large red pepper julienned

1 large green pepper, julienned

240 ml (1 cup) mushrooms, cleaned and sliced

240 ml (1 cup) sliced canned baby corn

One tablespoon white sesame seeds

One tablespoon black sesame seeds

DRESSING:

90 ml (6 tablespoons) corn or golden syrup

90 ml (6 tablespoons) white vinegar

90 ml (6 tablespoons) canola oil

75 g (6 tablespoons) brown sugar

45 ml (3 tablespoons) soy sauce

15 ml (1 tablespoon) red wine vinegar

1 teaspoon dark sesame oil

½ teaspoon dry mustard

Few drops Tabasco sauce, to taste

Serves 12

RICE NOODLES:
Large wok
Baking sheet, lined with paper towels
Wire skimmer

HEAT OIL IN THE WOK UNTIL IT'S ALMOST SMOKING.

Cut the rice noodles with a heavy chef's knife, on a large cutting board, into manageable lengths of about 8 cm (3 inches).

Carefully throw a small handful of noodles into the hot oil, making sure they are all submerged in the oil. They will immediately puff up into crunchy white noodles. Strain the noodles out right away with the wire skimmer, and place them on the paper towel-lined baking sheet. Skim out any noodles that got left behind in the oil so that they don't burn. Repeat the process until all the noodles are done, making sure to let the oil get hot enough each time between the batches.

Keep the fried rice noodles in an open plastic bag until they're needed. They last for days.

SALAD:

Toss the vegetables together in a mixing bowl, pile them in the middle of a large platter, surround the mound with the fried rice noodles, drizzle everything with some of the dressing, and sprinkle the sesame seeds over everything.

DRESSING: **Makes about 420 ml (1¾ cups)**

Whisk everything together.

GREEN SALAD WITH SOY DRESSING

non-dairy

This salad is good with or without the greens, as described in Chapter Six of the Tales.

Serves 8

SALAD:

Toss all the salad ingredients in a big salad bowl, with enough dressing to coat the greens and sprouts.

SOY DRESSING:

Makes 600 ml (2½ cups)

Whisk together everything but the oil.
Whisk in the oil.

SALAD:

2 litres (8 cups) torn lettuce or mixed baby greens

½ litre (2 cups) bean sprouts

240 ml (1 cup) canned baby corn, sliced

4 green onions, washed and chopped

50 g (2 ounces) sliced almonds, lightly toasted

SOY DRESSING:

120 ml (½ cup) cider vinegar

80 ml (1/3 cup) soy sauce

12 g (3 teaspoons) dry mustard

3 g (1½ teaspoons) pepper

8 ml (1½ teaspoons) Dijon mustard

5 g (1 teaspoon) salt

5 g (1 teaspoon) garlic powder

360 ml (1½ cups) canola oil

Pasta Salad With Honey Mustard Dressing

This amount of dressing is perfect for one 500 g (17 ounce) bag of uncooked pasta once it's cooked and mixed with vegetables. But don't limit yourself to only pasta salad - it's great with any kind of green salad, and goes especially well served alongside gravlax (pg 160).

Serves 10-12

PASTA:

PASTA:

500g (17 ounce) bag of uncooked pasta (corkscrews are especially nice here)

1 purple onion, sliced thinly

1 large red pepper, cleaned and julienned

1 large green pepper, cleaned and julienned

1 large yellow or orange pepper, cleaned and julienned

½ purple cabbage, cleaned and shredded

180 ml (¾ cup) black olives, pitted and sliced

Handful fresh parsley, washed and chopped

Boil the pasta in a large pot of salted water according to the package directions. Drain and allow to cool.

Mix everything together with the dressing in a large serving bowl.

DRESSING:

DRESSING:

45 ml (3 tablespoons) cider vinegar

45 ml (3 tablespoons) honey

180 ml (¾ cup) mayonnaise

15 ml (1 tablespoon) Dijon mustard

2 g (½ teaspoon) garlic powder

2 g (½ teaspoon) pepper

Pinch salt

180 ml (¾ cup) canola oil

Makes about 1½ cups

Heat the vinegar and honey in a small heatproof bowl in the microwave for 10-second increments until the honey is entirely dissolved. Allow the mixture to cool.

Whisk in everything else but the oil.

Whisk in the oil.

The dressing can last up to a week in the fridge.

Green Salad With Apple Juice Dressing

non-dairy

This sweet but tangy dressing is so easy and quick to prepare. I found that it goes great with any green salad that features fresh fruit. I used the local apple juice concentrate that we all watered down to give our kids to drink when they were little.

SALAD:

Toss the salad ingredients in a big bowl with enough dressing to coat the greens.

APPLE JUICE DRESSING:

Makes 660 ml (2¾ cups)

Whisk together everything but the oil.
Whisk in the oil.

SALAD:

Mixed greens

Sliced fruit such as ripe nectarines, peaches, apples, pears, or plums

Toasted pecans

APPLE JUICE DRESSING:

240 ml (1 cup) unsweetened, pure apple juice concentrate (usually found in health food stores)

125 ml (½ cup) cider vinegar

20 ml (4 teaspoons) freshly squeezed lemon juice

10 g (2 teaspoons) salt

6 g (1½ teaspoons) pepper

360 ml (1½ cups) canola oil

Couscous Salad With Roasted Vegetables

non-dairy

Roasted vegetables were a mainstay of our kitchen. Whatever was not used in our quiche production made its way into our various salads and pastas. Instant couscous turns a Middle Eastern staple into a quick and easy salad. I love using whole-wheat couscous, but regular works just as well.

Serves 8

Chop vegetables (or else chop two large onions, two red peppers, one zucchini, two sweet potatoes, one small eggplant, a few garlic cloves, or any variation of these amounts of vegetables, toss them with a bit of olive oil and kosher salt, and roast in the oven for about 30-40 minutes)

Bring the water, 30 ml (2 tablespoons) olive oil, and 5g (1 teaspoon) salt to a boil in a small saucepan. Add the couscous and stir with a fork. Take the couscous off the heat, cover it, and let it sit for five minutes. Fluff it up with a fork, put the cover back on, and let it sit for five more minutes. Fluff it again and turn it out into a medium salad bowl. Let it cool completely.

Add everything else to the couscous, stir, and taste to adjust the seasoning.

NOTE: Adding a batch of savoury tofu (pg 181) turns this salad into a complete main course meal.

INGREDIENTS:

350 g (12 ounces) instant whole-wheat couscous

500 ml (2½ cups) water

30 ml (2 tablespoons) olive oil

5 g (1 teaspoon) salt

600 ml (2½ cups) assorted roasted vegetables

180 ml (¾ cup) green olives, pitted and sliced

45 ml (3 tablespoons) capers, drained

100 g (3½ ounces) golden or dark raisins

100 g (3½ ounces) pine nuts

Large handful fresh parsley or coriander, chopped

60 ml (¼ cup) olive oil

45 ml (3 tablespoons) red wine vinegar

Salt and pepper to taste

non-dairy

INGREDIENTS:

2 cans tuna, drained

450 ml (2 cups) cored and
chopped green apples

225 ml (1 cup) chopped celery

113 ml (½ cup) chopped green
onions

113 ml (½ cup) sliced or
slivered blanched almonds

113 ml (½ cup) light or dark
raisins

113 ml (½ cup) mayonnaise

56 ml (¼ cup) apricot jam

1 tablespoon Dijon mustard

1 heaping teaspoon curry
powder

INGREDIENTS:

350 ml (1½ cups) long-grain
white rice

600 ml (2 ⅓ cups) water

1 teaspoon salt

1 teaspoon canola oil

120 ml (½ cup) mayonnaise

60 ml (¼ cup) apricot jam

4 tablespoons pickle juice

3 tablespoons fresh lemon
juice

4 teaspoons curry powder

1 teaspoon salt

½ teaspoon pepper

1 large apple, chopped

1 tomato, chopped

1 seedless cucumber, chopped

1 red or green pepper, chopped

1 medium onion, chopped

2 large pickles, chopped

60 ml (¼ cup) raisins

CURRIED TUNA SALAD

This is not the tuna salad your mom used to pack for your school lunches. It works equally well as a filling for sandwiches, or as a salad on its own. To jazz it up I often surrounded the tuna with a curried rice salad (see below).

Serves 8
Mix together and serve.

Curried tuna surrounded by curried rice.

CURRIED RICE SALAD
non-dairy

This delicious salad recipe is from my cousin Shula. It came without amounts, and I never used to measure exactly when I catered with it - it was the "taste and add, taste and add" method. So even when you follow the measurements, be sure to taste and add, taste and add, until you get it to the flavour balance that pleases you.

Serves 8

Bring the rice to a boil in a covered saucepan with the water, salt, and oil, then turn it down to simmer for fifteen mintes. Take off the lid and leave it on low for five more minutes.

Let it cool, and fluff it up with a fork.

Mix everything together, and taste for seasonings. Feel free to adjust all the amounts.

This is nice served around the curried tuna salad (see above).

Best Tabouli Ever

non-dairy

I'll bet you didn't even know there was a "best tabouli ever!" Thanks to our friend David Teitel of Toronto for this recipe, oh so many years ago...

Serves 8

Bring the water, tomato juice, and salt to a boil in a small saucepan. Turn off the heat and add the bulgur. Give it a stir and put the lid on. After about five minutes, give it another stir. Leave it for about ten more minutes and meanwhile make the marinade.

Marinade:

Mix the marinade ingredients in a small bowl.

Turn the bulgur out into a large bowl and add the marinade. It will look like too much liquid, but don't worry, it will get soaked in. Stir occasionally until it totally cools.

Then add the rest of the ingredients.

The following are optional: diced cucumbers, peppers, radishes, kohlrabi, olives, or sundried tomatoes. For a dairy version, you can add crumbled Bulgarian (salty white) cheese.

You can either stir everything in together, or make attractive piles around the edge of the bulgur.

Ingredients:
250 g (9 ounces) bulgur

240 ml (1 cup) water

240 ml (1 cup) tomato juice

Pinch of salt

Marinade:
2½ teaspoons crushed garlic

60 ml (¼ cup) freshly squeezed lemon juice

75 ml (1/3 cup) olive oil

1 teaspoon cumin

Lots of black pepper

Rest of Ingredients:
2 cups chopped fresh parsley

½ cup chopped green onion

2 diced tomatoes

Pomegranate Mango Salad

non-dairy

This easy to prepare salad features two of my favourite fruits. Hopefully, wherever you live, both mangoes and pomegranates are in season at the same time, as they are here.

Serves 6 - 8

Mix together all the ingredients.

This pretty salad can be served alone, on a bed of greens, on the base of Belgian endive leaves, as a relish on broiled fish fillets or chicken breasts, or as a spoonful on the edge of a plate to decorate anything else.

The finely minced hot green pepper is optional, but really perfect here to cut the sweetness and tartness of everything.

Ingredients:
190 ml (¾ cup) pomegranate seeds

450 ml (2 cups) diced mango

110 ml (½ cup) chopped green onions

56 ml (¼ cup) chopped fresh coriander

1 tablespoon olive oil

3 tablespoons freshly squeezed lemon juice

1 teaspoon hot green pepper, finely minced (optional)

2 garlic cloves, minced

Salt and pepper to taste

non-dairy

Quinoa And Fruit Salad

I fell in love with quinoa as soon as it became available in this neck of the woods. Not so all my catering customers - many of them made a face when I suggested quinoa salad for a party, but they were easily won over as soon as they tasted this one. You can vary the fruits with the season. Be sure to try it with strawberries, kiwi, mango, nectarines, fresh apricots, or pineapple.

Serves 10

SALAD:

Cook the quinoa in 3 cups of boiling, salted water for 15 minutes, until you can see the ring clearly on each grain. Drain it if necessary. Allow the quinoa to cool completely. Add the fruits and onions, and toss gently with all of the dressing.

DRESSING:

Put all the ingredients into a processor and blend until it's smooth.

SALAD:

250 g (9 ounces) quinoa, rinsed well

240 ml. (1 cup) dried cranberries, raisins, currants, or dried blueberries

480 ml (2 cups) seeded grapes, halved

120 ml (½ cup) pomegranate seeds

3 green onions, chopped

DRESSING:

75 ml (1/3 cup) olive oil

30 ml (2 tablespoons) mayonnaise

25 ml (1½ tablespoons) lemon juice

2 cloves garlic

2 teaspoons curry powder

½ teaspoon salt

2 heaping tablespoons fresh coriander, chopped

Wild Rice Pilaf

dairy or non-dairy

Once considered an exotic food item, nutty wild rice started appearing on our shelves here from North America about the time we started catering from home. Thereafter, it became a regular side dish on La Cuisine's menu. In spite of its price tag, I preferred serving it straight, rather than stretching it by mixing it with white rice as many other caterers did. I like the richness of the butter in this pilaf, but you can certainly use olive oil for a non-dairy meal.

Serves 6-8

Bring the wild rice, water, and the 5 g (1 teaspoon) salt to a boil in a medium saucepan. Lower the heat and simmer for about 50 minutes or until the grains have split open and are soft but still chewy. Drain the rice and put aside in a bowl.

Sauté the onion, pepper, zucchini, and celery in the butter or olive oil until they're soft. You can use the same saucepan or a frying pan, if you prefer.

Add the sautéed vegetables to the rice and mix together. Add the fresh parsley, salt and pepper, and stir. Serve warm.

INGREDIENTS:
240 ml (1 cup) raw wild rice, rinsed
1 litre (4 cups) water
5 g (1 teaspoon) salt
1 large onion, chopped
1 large red pepper, cleaned and chopped
1 large zucchini, cleaned and chopped
2 stalks celery, cleaned and chopped
60 g (2 ounces) butter or olive oil
Handful fresh parsley, chopped
Salt and pepper to taste

Roasted Vegetables

There are probably more "best roasted vegetables" recipes than there are types of vegetables. We prepared so many variations for our quiches and our catered events that I can confidently say that "best" or "not best," this recipe will not disappoint your family or your guests.

Preparing roasted vegetables is actually very simple: the two things to keep in mind are how each type of vegetable is going to look, and how long each type is going to take to cook properly. At La Cuisine we seasoned them very simply: a sprinkling of olive oil, kosher salt, cracked black pepper, and sprigs of fresh rosemary and thyme. That's it.

For maximum effect, roast groups of vegetables with similar cooking times together.

Have a thin sharp knife handy to prick the vegetables to check when they're ready - when the knife slides in easily, they're soft enough to eat.

The vegetables we liked to roast:

Potatoes - peeled and cut into triangular chunks, roast about 45-60 minutes

Sweet potatoes - peeled and cut into oblong chunks, roast about 30-40 minutes

Carrots - peeled, cut in half lengthwise and then into 5 cm (2 inch) chunks, roast about 40 minutes

Peppers - red, yellow, and orange (I don't like green ones…), cut in half, cleaned, and then cut into large irregular shards, roast about 30 minutes until the edges turn a bit black

Zucchini - cleaned and tipped, cut in half lengthwise and then into 5 cm (2 inch) chunks, roast about 40 minutes

Beets - peeled and quartered, roast about 45 minutes, depending on the size

Mushrooms - cleaned and left whole, roast about 25 minutes

Garlic - we like the whole head - peel off all the extra papery skin, and cut a bit of the top of the head off, exposing the cloves, roast about 50 minutes

Asparagus - cut off the tough bottoms of the stalks, roast about 20 minutes

Fennel - cut off the bottom and the top of the fennel bulbs and wash well, cut in four, roast about 30 minutes

Purple onion - peeled and quartered, roast about 40 minutes

Toss each type of vegetable separately in a bowl with some olive oil, kosher salt, and coarse black pepper. Pile them onto a baking dish or pan, according to roasting times. Place a few sprigs of fresh rosemary and thyme on top and roast.

Serve warm on a decorative platter.

If you want to serve the roasted vegetables cold or at room temperature as antipasti, sprinkle them with a bit of balsamic vinegar and add some minced fresh garlic.

SALMON

Judging by the ready availability of fresh and frozen salmon in Israel these days, one might be tempted to think that it has become a staple of the Israeli diet. This definitely was not always the case. Years ago when we began catering from our home, salmon was considered a rare treat, only available from a few select distributors and retailers and only frozen - definitely not fresh. Marvin and I would drive halfway across the city to Jerusalem's wholesale market to *schlep* home cartons of our precious Norwegian catch. The first destination for our 5-6 kg (11-13 pound) salmon was usually our spanking clean, disinfected bathtub, where they were left undisturbed to thaw at a nice, leisurely pace.

The timing of cooking salmon is a very personal thing - in my mind, the worst sin of all is overcooking it. My recipes call for the salmon to be perfectly cooked on the outside, and slightly undercooked on the inside part of the belly - which is how I adore it. However, if the thought of slightly undercooked salmon makes you squeamish, leave it in the oven for 10-15 minutes longer. And then you'll know your preference for next time.

For years my whole poached salmon was a featured mainstay at our catering buffets. Eventually, when frozen fillets became available, I was able to expand my repertoire to include the following recipes.

WHOLE OVEN POACHED SALMON:

non-dairy

PREHEAT THE OVEN TO 190°C (375°F).

Tear off a double layer of the heaviest, widest aluminum foil you can find in a length that is a bit more than double the length of the salmon. Lay down the two layers of foil, one on top of the other, across a baking sheet that will fit into your oven. Even if the fish is longer than the width of your oven, don't worry - you'll be making it fit. Lay the salmon down in the middle. Place half of the chopped vegetables and the parsley inside the fish's stomach, and the other half all over the top. Sprinkle on all the spices. Fold the two long sides of foil together over the top of the fish, and then roll up and seal the foil along the sides, leaving one spot open to pour in the wine. Pour the wine in carefully, slowly at first to make sure you sealed all the foil shut so that no wine spills out, and then seal it all up. Place the foil package of fish gently on an angle on the baking sheet, so that it will enter your oven with the longest angle possible.

Put the pan with the fish carefully into the oven - don't let the foil tear along the sides of the oven, ease it in gently. You might have to carefully bend the tail part up and hold it while you shut the oven door against it.

Bake the fish for 55 minutes.

When you take the fish out of the oven, open the foil package just a little bit on the top for the steam to escape and let it cool to room temperature. Then close it back up, leaving the salmon to sit in all the juices with all the vegetables and spices, and refrigerate it overnight.

The next day, open up the package over the sink, pouring off all the juices, and carefully pull off all the excess spices, the vegetables, and all the outer skin of the fish. Slide it onto a serving platter, and decorate it with sprouts, lettuce, lemon slices, or fresh herbs.

Mix all the sauce ingredients. Serve the salmon with the sauce.

INGREDIENTS:

1 whole 5-6 kg (11-13 pound) salmon, gutted and cleaned (if it was frozen, make sure it is completely thawed)

1 large onion, chopped

1 large carrot, chopped

2 stalks celery, chopped

1 bunch parsley

3 tablespoons kosher salt

2 tablespoons whole black peppercorns

About 1 tablespoon garlic powder

About 1 teaspoon dried thyme

8 bay leaves

1 bottle semi-dry white wine (I used Carmel Hock)

SAUCE FOR SALMON: dairy

Dip for vegetables (pg 159)

3-4 grated, unpeeled cucumbers

1 small grated onion

2 tablespoons red wine vinegar

2 tablespoons chopped, fresh dill

2 tablespoons chopped, fresh parsley

non-dairy

Salmon Fillet with Sun-dried Tomatoes:

Serves 10-12

INGREDIENTS:

1 filleted side of salmon, about 1.8 kg (4 pounds) with the skin removed

120 g (4 ounces) moist, sun-dried tomatoes

2 cups boiling water

Handful fresh parsley

6 garlic cloves

4 tablespoons olive oil

Salt and pepper to taste

Cover the sun-dried tomatoes with boiling water and let sit for 20 minutes. Drain them.

In a food processor, blend the tomatoes, parsley, garlic cloves, olive oil, and some salt and pepper to make a tomato paste.

Spread the tomato paste on the bottom and on the top of the fillet and place it in a large ovenproof dish. Marinate it for at least one hour at room temperature.

PREHEAT THE OVEN TO 220°C (430°F).

Roast the salmon in the oven for 15 minutes.

Salmon Fillet Teriyaki:

Serves 10-12

Mix the soy sauce, the water, the lemon juice, the sugar, and the garlic. Pour it onto the salmon. Let it marinate for at least one hour.

PREHEAT THE BROILER OF THE OVEN TO THE HIGHEST TEMPERATURE.

Broil for about 10 minutes, or to your taste.

Salmon Fillet with Mustard and Rosemary:

Serves 10-12

PREHEAT THE OVEN TO 220°C (430°F).

Put the sliced onions in an ovenproof dish large enough to hold the salmon fillet. Sprinkle on some of the minced rosemary, a bit of olive oil, and a little bit of salt and pepper.

Roast the onions in the hot oven for 15 minutes and then place the dish on a work area.

Carefully place the salmon fillet on top of the onions. Spread it with the mustard, and sprinkle on the rest of the rosemary, some salt, and some pepper. Drizzle on a little bit of olive oil.

Roast the salmon in the oven for about 15 minutes.

non-dairy

INGREDIENTS:
1 filleted side of salmon, about 1.8 kg (4 pounds) with the skin removed

5 tablespoons soy sauce

2 tablespoons water

2 tablespoons freshly squeezed lemon juice

1 tablespoon sugar

3 garlic cloves, minced

non-dairy

INGREDIENTS:
1 filleted side of salmon, about 1.8 kg (4 pounds) with the skin   removed

3 large onions, quartered and sliced

2 tablespoons minced fresh rosemary

1/3 cup dijon mustard

Kosher salt to taste

Coarsely crushed black pepper to taste

Olive oil for sprinkling

SALMON FILLET IN PUFF PASTRY:

Serves 10-12

PREHEAT THE OVEN TO **220°C (430°F)**.

Cut the salmon into 150 g (5½ ounce) portions - they don't have to be perfectly cut or even.

Roll out the puff pastry to a thickness of 2 mm (1/8 inch). Place the salmon portions on the puff pastry, leaving enough pastry around each piece so you can wrap them up. Cut the pastry into sections with the tip of a sharp knife. Sprinkle some salt and pepper on the salmon. Brush some beaten egg on the pastry around the edges of the salmon. This will serve as glue to hold the packages together.

INGREDIENTS:

1 filleted side of salmon, about 1.8 kg (4 pounds), with the skin removed

1 kg (2 pounds) puff pastry (pg 145, or store-bought)

Salt and pepper to taste

1 egg, beaten

NOTE: These salmon pastries could be served with the tomato cream sauce (pg 183), or with any sauce or sautéed vegetable of your choice.

Fold up the dough around each piece, and place them seam side down on a baking sheet. Brush the top of each with some beaten egg (don't let the egg drip down the sides, it could inhibit the puff pastry from rising to its fullest). Cut one or two slits on the top.

Bake for 15 minutes.

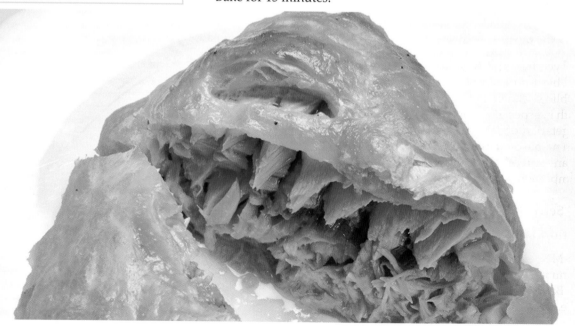

Vegetarian Cholent

non-dairy

As a vegetarian for over seventeen years, I was determined to somehow find a suitable substitute for my family's cravings for chicken soup and for cholent (a slow-cooked meat stew that is traditionally left on the heat overnight and eaten for Sabbath lunch). The soup proved to be an easier challenge, but after many experiments I settled on this cholent recipe which is pretty darn close to the real thing, minus the *flanken* (short ribs), of course. In the bakery we often prepared this dish for over two hundred. I've slightly modified the quantities for home preparation!

Serves 10-12 for lunch, 30 for *Kiddush*
- One standard 6-8 litre (6-8 quart) electric slow cooker or crock-pot

Soak the beans overnight. Pour them with their soaking liquid into the crock-pot, add everything else, and cover with water almost to the top of the vegetables.

Start the crock-pot on high and cook for two hours. Lower to the lowest heat setting for about 24 hours. Adjust the seasoning before serving.

To have this for a Sabbath lunch or *Kiddush*, soak the beans on Thursday evening, add them with everything else to a crock-pot/slow cooker Friday morning. Leave it on low heat until serving time the following day.

INGREDIENTS:

600 g (21 ounces) mixed beans - kidney, black, white, chickpeas

300 g (10 ounces) pearl barley

3 large onions, peeled and chopped

5 large potatoes, peeled and chopped

3 sweet potatoes, peeled and chopped

2 large carrots, peeled and chopped

2 large zucchini, cleaned and chopped

5 cloves garlic, minced

120 ml (½ cup) silan (also known as date honey)

260 g (9 ounce) tomato paste

Salt and pepper to taste

Savoury Tofu

non-dairy

Even though I was vegetarian for seventeen years, I was never a big tofu lover (I know it's not politically correct to admit this publicly...). A friend gave me this tofu recipe, and I just fell in love with it, especially when it gets really nice and crispy. I used it for our vegetarian offerings in our coffee shop and at catered events. You can nibble on it as it is, serve it with a stir-fry on top of rice, or add it to any sort of salad. Even the kids used to eat it this way. I often got compliments for it, even from people who don't usually like tofu.

Serves 8

PREHEAT THE OVEN TO 180°C (350°F).

Mix everything together gently and marinate for at least 20 minutes.

Bake the tofu for about 20 minutes, or until it gets as crispy as you like.

INGREDIENTS:

300 g (11 ounces) tofu, cut into cubes

60 ml (¼ cup) soy sauce

1 teaspoon freshly grated ginger

2 cloves garlic, chopped

2 teaspoons honey

1 teaspoon dark oriental sesame oil

SAVOURY BREAD PUDDING

I'm a pushover for a good bread pudding- either sweet or savoury. Our dear friend Celia really couldn't stand cooking anymore after she retired, but she gave me this recipe and said that I would love it. She was so right. It originally said "cheddar cheese," but I ended up experimenting with all kinds of wonderful cheeses. I'm sure you'll enjoy it with your favourite.

INGREDIENTS:

14 slices of any kind of bread that you like, cut into cubes

113 g (4 ounces) butter, melted

350 g (12 ounces) grated cheese - cheddar, kashkeval, or Swiss

5 eggs

720 ml (3 cups) milk

¾ teaspoon salt

¾ teaspoon paprika

¼ teaspoon pepper

Serves 12
- 23 x 33 cm (9 x 13 inch) baking dish

(Start this recipe one day before serving)

Toss the bread cubes with the melted butter. Pour half the bread cubes into the baking dish. Sprinkle on half the cheese. Add the rest of the bread cubes. Sprinkle on the rest of the cheese.
Whisk the eggs and milk with the salt, paprika, and pepper. Pour the mixture over the bread and cheese.
Let it sit overnight in the fridge.
Remove the uncooked bread pudding from the fridge.

PREHEAT OVEN TO **180°C (350°F)**.

Bake the bread pudding for 45 minutes, until it's golden and puffed up.

SOUFFLÉ ROLL WITH CREAMED SPINACH

An elegant way to entertain with eggs. The spiral slices of this roll are very pretty served warm either as a main course or side dish with a sauce on the side. Try it with different fillings and sauces, such as mushroom, zucchini, or pumpkin. The roll is also good filled with salmon mousse or tuna salad and served cold.

SPINACH FILLING:

500 g (18 ounces) frozen spinach, thawed and squeezed dry

240 ml (1 cup) heavy cream

5 g (1 teaspoon) salt

1 g (¼ teaspoon) pepper

1 g (¼ teaspoon) nutmeg

5 green onions, cleaned and chopped

Serves 8, makes one roll

- 28 x 38 cm (11 x 15 inch) baking pan lined with baking paper, plus an extra sheet of baking paper

SPINACH FILLING:

Mix all the filling ingredients together and set aside.

Soufflé Roll:

Preheat the oven to 190°C (375°F).

Melt the butter in a medium saucepan. Whisk in the flour and cook for a few minutes until it just starts to turn golden. Whisk in the hot milk and stir it until it thickens and bubbles break the surface. Take it off the heat, and whisk a little bit of the hot mixture into the egg yolks, and then whisk in the rest. Add the salt, pepper, and nutmeg, and let cool for about 15 minutes.

Whip the egg whites in the mixer with the whisk until the peaks are stiff but not dry. Fold some of the beaten egg whites into the egg yolk mixture and then fold in the rest, gently but thoroughly.

Pour the mixture into the baking pan. Smooth it gently, preferably with a long metal spatula.

Bake the soufflé for about 20 minutes until it's golden.

Take the soufflé out of the oven and let it cool.

Turn the soufflé over onto a sheet of baking paper. Carefully peel off the paper that is now on top. The soufflé should now be upside down.

Spread the spinach filling on the soufflé. Using the baking paper as a guide, roll the soufflé up and roll it back onto the baking pan, ready for warming up.

Before serving, cover the spinach-filled soufflé roll loosely with the removed baking paper so it doesn't dry out in the oven and warm for a few minutes on low temperature.

Serve warm slices with tomato cream sauce.

Tomato Cream Sauce:

Heat the cream, tomatoes, tomato paste, sugar, garlic powder, salt, and pepper together in a small saucepan until it simmers. Add the basil. Serve warm.

Soufflé Roll:

6 eggs, separated (put the whites in a mixer bowl and the yolks in a separate large mixing bowl)
56 g (2 ounces) butter
47 g (1/3 cup) flour
360 ml (1½ cups) hot milk
5 g (1 teaspoon) salt
1 g (¼ teaspoon) pepper
1 g (¼ teaspoon) nutmeg

Tomato Cream Sauce:

400 g (14 ounce) can crushed tomatoes
260 g (9 ounce) can tomato paste
240 ml (1 cup) heavy cream
30 g (2 tablespoons) sugar
5 g (1 teaspoon) garlic powder
5 g (1 teaspoon) salt
2 g (½ teaspoon) pepper
Handful fresh basil, chopped